# Affirming
## LGBTQ+ Students in Higher Education

# PERSPECTIVES ON SEXUAL ORIENTATION AND GENDER DIVERSITY
Maria Lucia Miville, Series Editor

*Affirmative Counseling and Psychological Practice With Transgender and Gender Nonconforming Clients*
   Edited by Anneliese A. Singh and lore m. dickey

*Affirming LGBTQ+ Students in Higher Education*
   Edited by David P. Rivera, Roberto L. Abreu, and Kirsten A. Gonzalez

*The Gender Affirmative Model: An Interdisciplinary Approach to Supporting Transgender and Gender Expansive Children*
   Edited by Colt Keo-Meier and Diane Ehrensaft

*HIV+ Sex: The Psychological and Interpersonal Dynamics of HIV-Seropositive Gay and Bisexual Men's Relationships*
   Edited by Perry N. Halkitis, Cynthia A. Gómez, and Richard J. Wolitski

*Lesbian and Gay Parents and Their Children: Research on the Family Life Cycle*
   Abbie E. Goldberg

*LGBTQ Mental Health: International Perspectives and Experiences*
   Edited by Nadine Nakamura and Carmen H. Logie

*Supporting Gender Identity and Sexual Orientation Diversity in K-12 Schools*
   Edited by Megan C. Lytle and Richard A. Sprott

*Teaching LGBTQ Psychology: Queering Innovative Pedagogy and Practice*
   Edited by Theodore R. Burnes and Jeanne L. Stanley

*That's So Gay! Microaggressions and the Lesbian, Gay, Bisexual, and Transgender Community*
   Kevin L. Nadal

# Affirming
## LGBTQ+ Students in Higher Education

*Edited by*
David P. Rivera, Roberto L. Abreu, Kirsten A. Gonzalez

AMERICAN PSYCHOLOGICAL ASSOCIATION

Copyright © 2022 by the American Psychological Association. All rights reserved. Except as permitted under the United States Copyright Act of 1976, no part of this publication may be reproduced or distributed in any form or by any means, including, but not limited to, the process of scanning and digitization, or stored in a database or retrieval system, without the prior written permission of the publisher.

The opinions and statements published are the responsibility of the authors, and such opinions and statements do not necessarily represent the policies of the American Psychological Association.

Published by
American Psychological Association
750 First Street, NE
Washington, DC 20002
https://www.apa.org

Order Department
https://www.apa.org/pubs/books
order@apa.org

In the U.K., Europe, Africa, and the Middle East, copies may be ordered from Eurospan
https://www.eurospanbookstore.com/apa
info@eurospangroup.com

Typeset in Meridien and Ortodoxa by Circle Graphics, Inc., Reisterstown, MD

Printer: Gasch Printing, Odenton, MD
Cover Designer: Gwen J. Grafft, Minneapolis, MN

**Library of Congress Cataloging-in-Publication Data**

Names: Rivera, David P., editor. | Abreu, Roberto L., editor. | Gonzalez, Kirsten A., editor.
Title: Affirming LGBTQ+ students in higher education / edited by David P. Rivera, Roberto L. Abreu, Kirsten A. Gonzalez.
Description: Washington, DC : American Psychological Association, 2022. | Series: Perspectives on sexual orientation and gender diversity | Includes bibliographical references and index.
Identifiers: LCCN 2021044400 (print) | LCCN 2021044401 (ebook) | ISBN 9781433833083 (paperback) | ISBN 9781433833335 (ebook)
Subjects: LCSH: Sexual minority college students--Counseling of--United States. | Sexual minority college students--Services for--United States. | Sexual minority college students--Psychology. | Counseling in higher education--United States. | BISAC: PSYCHOLOGY / Human Sexuality (see also SOCIAL SCIENCE / Human Sexuality) | PSYCHOLOGY / Education & Training
Classification: LCC LC2574.6 .A44 2022 (print) | LCC LC2574.6 (ebook) | DDC 378.1/982660973--dc23/eng/20211012
LC record available at https://lccn.loc.gov/2021044400
LC ebook record available at https://lccn.loc.gov/2021044401

https://doi.org/10.1037/0000281-000

*Printed in the United States of America*

10 9 8 7 6 5 4 3 2

*This book is dedicated to the many LGBTQ+ student activists who,
in spite of systemic and interpersonal oppressions, persist
and are leading us towards liberation.*

# CONTENTS

Contributors     ix

**Introduction: A Call to Action for Affirming All LGBTQ+ Students in Higher Education**     3
Kirsten A. Gonzalez, Saumya Arora, Roberto L. Abreu, and David P. Rivera

## I. CONTEXTS     15

### 1. Institutionalizing LGBTQ+ Student Support     17
Anneliese Singh

### 2. Exploring the Complexities of Black Sexual and Gender Minorities on Historically Black Colleges and Universities     33
Angela D. Ferguson

### 3. Planning and Building New Foundations: Developing Proposals for Creating LGBTQI+ Resources at Community Colleges     53
Emalinda L. McSpadden, Leilani Massey, and Ines I. Almarante

### 4. LGBTQ Students in Nonaffirming Religious Institutions     71
Theresa Stueland Kay and Joshua R. Wolff

### 5. One Model, Multiple Locations: The Salisbury University *Safe Spaces* Program     87
Diane S. Illig, Michèle M. Schlehofer, and Tara Taylor

## II. STUDENT POPULATIONS — 99

6. **Recommendations and Advocacy Strategies for Meeting the Needs of Transgender and Nonbinary Students** — 101
   Luke R. Allen and lore m. dickey

7. **Supporting LGBTQ+ College Students Living With Disabilities** — 123
   Franco Dispenza, Merideth Ray, and Jamian S. Coleman

8. **Creating Safe Spaces for Lesbian, Gay, Bisexual, Transgender, and Queer (LGBTQ+) Student-Athletes** — 141
   Taylor M. McCavanagh and Michael C. Cadaret

9. **Navigating New Terrain: Sexual and Gender Diverse College Students Who Are the First in Their Families to Attend College** — 161
   Alison Cerezo and Amaranta Ramirez

10. **Supporting Rural LGBTQ+ Communities in Higher Education** — 173
    Joel D. Goodrich and Michael James McClellan

11. **Supporting LGBTQ International Students in Higher Education** — 189
    Nadine Nakamura, Jan E. Estrellado, and Saeromi Kim

12. **Resisting Colonization in Higher Education and Empowering LGBTQ+ Students: Mobilizing Toward Liberation** — 203
    Roberto L. Abreu, Saumya Arora, Kirsten A. Gonzalez, and David P. Rivera

Index — 211
About the Editors — 223

# CONTRIBUTORS

**Roberto L. Abreu, PhD,** (he/him/él) Assistant Professor of Counseling Psychology and Director of Collective Healing and Empowering VoicEs through Research and Engagement (¡Chévere!), Department of Psychology, University of Florida, Gainesville

**Luke R. Allen, PhD,** (he/him) Counseling & Psychological Services, University of Nevada, Las Vegas

**Ines I. Almarante,** (she/her) Undergraduate student in Psychology, Hunter College, City University of New York

**Saumya Arora, BS,** (she/her) Doctoral student in Counseling Psychology, University of Tennessee, Knoxville

**Michael C. Cadaret, PhD,** (he/him) Assistant Professor of Graduate Psychology, School of Health Sciences, Chatham University, Pittsburgh, PA

**Alison Cerezo, PhD,** (she/they) Assistant Professor, Department of Counseling, Clinical & School Psychology, University of California, Santa Barbara

**Jamian S. Coleman, MS,** (he/him) Doctoral candidate in Counselor Education and Practice, Georgia State University, Atlanta

**lore m. dickey, PhD, ABPP,** (he/him) Solution Masters, PLLC, Flagstaff, AZ

**Franco Dispenza, PhD, CRC,** (he/him) Associate Professor of Counseling and Psychology, Georgia State University, Atlanta

**Jan E. Estrellado, PhD,** (all pronouns) Assistant Professor, PsyD Program, California School of Professional Psychology, Alliant International University, San Diego

**Angela D. Ferguson, PhD,** (she/her) Associate Professor of Counseling Psychology, Howard University, Washington, DC

**Kirsten A. Gonzalez, PhD,** (she/her) Assistant Professor of Counseling Psychology and Director of the Research on Social Intersections at Tennessee (ReSIsT) Lab, Department of Psychology, University of Tennessee, Knoxville

**Joel D. Goodrich, PsyD,** (he/him) Staff Psychologist, University of Kentucky Counseling Center, Lexington

**Diane S. Illig, PhD,** (she/her) Associate Professor and Chair of Sociology, Salisbury University, Salisbury, MD

**Theresa Stueland Kay, PhD,** (she/they) Licensed Clinical Psychologist and Professor, Department of Psychological Science, Weber State University, Ogden, UT

**Saeromi Kim, PhD,** (she/they) Assistant Clinical Director of Counseling and Psychological Services, University of California, Los Angeles

**Leilani Massey,** (she/her) Undergraduate student in Psychology, Bronx Community College, City University of New York

**Taylor M. McCavanagh, PsyD,** (they/them) Postdoctoral Fellow, Counseling Center, Georgia State University, Atlanta

**Michael James McClellan, PhD,** (he/him) Assistant Professor, Psychology Department, Eastern Kentucky University, Richmond

**Emalinda L. McSpadden, PhD,** (all pronouns) Associate Professor of Psychology and Faculty Director of the LGBTQI+ Resource Room, Bronx Community College, City University of New York

**Nadine Nakamura, PhD,** (she/her) Professor, PsyD Program, California School of Professional Psychology, Alliant International University, San Diego

**Merideth Ray, EdS,** (she/her) Doctoral candidate in Counselor Education and Practice, Georgia State University, and Associate Director, Office of Undergraduate Education, Emory University, Atlanta

**Amaranta Ramirez, BA,** (she/her) Doctoral student in the Department of Counseling, Clinical & School Psychology, University of California, Santa Barbara

**David P. Rivera, PhD,** (he/him) Associate Professor of Counselor Education, Queens College–City University of New York, Flushing

**Michèle M. Schlehofer, PhD,** (she/her) Professor and Chair of Psychology, Salisbury University, Salisbury, MD

**Anneliese Singh, PhD,** (she/they) Associate Provost for Faculty Development and Diversity/Chief Diversity Officer, Tulane University, New Orleans, LA

**Tara Taylor, MA,** (she/her) Managing Director, ADR Vantage Inc., Washington, DC

**Joshua R. Wolff, PhD,** (he/him) Adjunct Professor, Department of Psychology, Adler University, Chicago, IL

# Affirming
## LGBTQ+ Students in Higher Education

# Introduction

## *A Call to Action for Affirming All LGBTQ+ Students in Higher Education*

Kirsten A. Gonzalez, Saumya Arora, Roberto L. Abreu, and David P. Rivera

We want to begin by acknowledging our intention for this book in centering the experiences of lesbian, gay, bisexual, transgender, and queer (LGBTQ+) Black, Indigenous, and other People of Color (BIPOC), and other marginalized student communities, in the narrative about supporting LGBTQ+ students in higher education. As queer and ally Latinx psychologists and academics, we (the editors) saw a need to broaden discussions in institutional settings about how we attend to LGBTQ+ students while considering the interlocking systems of oppression that operate to silence and exclude LGBTQ+ BIPOC students from higher education scholarship and college campus discussions. In 2021, LGBTQ+ college students are struggling in the midst of two pandemics, the COVID-19 pandemic and the systemic racism, violence, and murders of Black people at the hands of police officers in the United States. Colleges and universities are also grappling with precisely how to challenge systemic racism on their campuses while managing the stress of navigating a public health pandemic in residential university and college settings. Taken together, these pandemics suggest that, now more than ever, colleges and universities need more direction, guidance, and support as they navigate questions of how best to support all college students, but particularly those who are marginalized including LGBTQ+ BIPOC students.

The aim of this book is to provide university faculty, staff, administrators, and students with more information on LGBTQ+ college students, who have been typically neglected or ignored in discussions about the wellness and needs of LGBTQ+ college students. We first provide a brief overview of the theories

---

https://doi.org/10.1037/0000281-001
*Affirming LGBTQ+ Students in Higher Education,* D. P. Rivera, R. L. Abreu, and K. A. Gonzalez (Editors)
Copyright © 2022 by the American Psychological Association. All rights reserved.

guiding this book, including minority stress, intersectionality, and critical race theories. Then we review the literature on LGBTQ+ college student experiences. Finally, we provide an overview of this book.

We believe that this book will serve as an essential resource for college and university administrators, faculty, staff, and students, and will allow key university figures to be more affirming and supportive of their LGBTQ+ students. This book will also be useful for researchers, student affairs professionals, professionals implementing diversity, equity, and inclusion (DEI) initiatives, college leaders, and cross-collaborative teams who do strategic planning for higher education institutions. Colleges and universities often focus on institutional outcomes (i.e., persistence, retention, and graduation) as well as student outcomes (i.e., student development, student engagement, academics, and health; see Blimling, 2014; Rankin et al., 2019; Wagner et al., 2018; Wilson & Rygg, 2013) when considering student success and well-being. Scholarship suggests that LGBTQ+ college students are more likely to experience harassment and discrimination, feel less comfortable with the overall campus climate of their institution, be more fearful for their physical safety and more likely to consider dropping out when compared with their heterosexual and cisgender peers (Rankin et al., 2010). Given these findings, we believe an important contribution of this book is concrete recommendations for how institutions of higher education can optimize LGBTQ+ student wellness, thereby improving student outcomes. All chapters in this book provide recommendations for how institutions can implement LGBTQ+ specific changes to enhance positive LGBTQ+ student outcomes to support institutional strategic DEI efforts.

## THEORETICAL FRAMEWORKS

We begin with an overview of the theories guiding this book, including minority stress, intersectionality, and critical race theories. These theories can be used to understand the experiences of LGBTQ+ BIPOC college students who experience identity-based marginalization in society.

### Minority Stress

LGBTQ+ college students experience disproportionate amounts of identity-based stress when compared with their heterosexual and cisgender peers. This minority stress (Brooks, 1981; Meyer, 1995, 2003) includes both *distal* (e.g., harassment, discrimination, victimization) and *proximal* stressors (e.g., rumination, hypervigilance) and contributes to decreased physical wellness and increased mental health struggles for LGBTQ+ people. Specific to college students, LGBTQ+ college students experience and witness heterosexist harassment (distal stressor; see Woodford & Kulick, 2015) and internalized heterosexism and cissexism (proximal stressor; see Bissonette & Szymanski, 2019), among other minority stressors. Scholarship suggests that LGBTQ+ people experienced heightened minority stress during the presidential administration of

Donald Trump (Brown & Keller, 2018; Gonzalez, Pulice-Farrow, & Galupo, 2018; Gonzalez, Ramirez, & Galupo, 2018; Riggle et al., 2018; Veldhuis et al., 2018a, 2018b). Research suggests that LGBTQ+ individuals reported increased anxiety, depression, identity-based rumination, and hypervigilance after Donald Trump was elected as president of the United States (see Brown & Keller, 2018; Gonzalez, Pulice-Farrow, & Galupo, 2018; Gonzalez, Ramirez, & Galupo, 2018; Riggle et al., 2018; Veldhuis et al., 2018a, 2018b). LGBTQ+ college students in particular face unique challenges and identity-based stress when considering the college and university environment. This stress negatively impacts a sense of belonging for them and can interfere with their academic success, interpersonal functioning, and overall wellness (Vaccaro & Mena, 2011; Woodford et al., 2014).

**Intersectionality and Critical Race Theory**

Kimberlé Crenshaw, a critical race legal scholar, first coined the term "intersectionality" in 1989 when discussing the unique experiences of Black women, who were often ignored in discussions of gender and racial discrimination in the context of antidiscrimination law (see Crenshaw, 1989; Lewis et al., 2017). Intersectionality, rooted in Black feminist thought (see Cole, 2009; Collins, 1990), suggests that multiple interlocking systems of oppression exist, and that these systems negatively impact the wellness of oppressed people. Intersectionality theory suggests that racism, classism, heterosexism, sexism, and cissexism work in conjunction to stigmatize marginalized community members with multiple marginalized identities (Collins, 2015; Combahee River Collective, 1977/1995; Crenshaw, 1991). Intersectionality theory asserts that scholars must use a multiaxis approach for understanding marginalized community members' experiences, because power structures in society (i.e., patriarchy, heterosexism, sexism, cissexism, and racism) operate simultaneously to perpetuate structural inequalities (see Crenshaw, 1989). We use intersectionality theory to situate our understanding of how power systems position LGBTQ+ students within social institutions like colleges and universities (see de Vries, 2015; Hines, 2010).

Critical race theory (CRT) emerged from the fields of law and legal studies, sociology, women's studies, history, and ethnic studies (Solórzano et al., 2000). Common elements of CRT include the importance of: (a) centering race and racism in discussions of systemic oppression, (b) challenging dominant (White) ideas and systems, (c) committing to social justice, (d) centering experiential knowledge, and (e) using interdisciplinary knowledge to explore race and racism (Solórzano et al., 2000). More directly applied as a conceptual lens for psychological science, a critical race psychology (Salter & Adams, 2013) draws on CRT tenets and offers the following empirically supported focal areas: (a) racism is a systemic societal problem, (b) individualistic ideologies reproduce racial inequalities, (c) interest convergence is needed to address systemic inequality, (d) the importance of disinvesting from White narratives and realities that perpetuate racial dominance, and (e) using counter-storytelling to challenge societal biases (see also Delgado & Stefanic, 2000; Ladson-Billings & Tate, 1995). We use intersectionality theory and CRT as frameworks to understand the experiences of LGBTQ+ college students who hold intersecting marginalized identities and experience marginalization within these interlocking systems of oppression. We pay special attention to LGBTQ+ BIPOC students and other LGBTQ+ student groups with intersecting identities so that we are centering a discussion of power in our analysis of wellness support for LGBTQ+ students in higher education.

## RESEARCH ON LGBTQ+ COLLEGE STUDENTS

When examining the experiences of LGBTQ+ college students, research has focused on a variety of topics, including intimate partner violence (Jacobson et al., 2015), health (Hood et al., 2019; Woodford et al., 2015), career development (Schmidt et al., 2011; Schneider & Dimito, 2010), and more. However, few studies utilize an intersectional approach in addressing how the experiences of LGBTQ+ college students are shaped by the other identities they hold, such as racial identity or ability status. Similarly, there is a lack of research on assessing institutional support or the influence of context, such as LGBTQ+ students at community colleges, LGBTQ+ students at historically Black colleges and universities (HBCUs), LGBTQ+ students in rural areas, and LGBTQ+ students at religious institutions, among others.

In general, the organizational structures and systems of colleges and universities lack an intersectionality framework. Diversity offices on college campuses often center a single identity, whether that be race, ethnicity, sexuality, or gender. LGBTQ+ centers on campus often focus on sexual orientation and gender identity without full consideration of race and ethnicity. Multicultural offices often center race and ethnicity while neglecting sexual orientation and gender identity. Student-run groups and organizations tend to be the same in this regard. Failing to acknowledge how interlocking systems of oppression impact the college experience can create difficulty for students needing support across their various identities. A salient example occurs in the classroom where intersectionality is seldom acknowledged, even in courses centered on human experiences and society. The lack of a comprehensive support system can create a campus climate that is alienating and invalidating for LGBTQ+ college students. Needless to say, LGBTQ+ college students who hold multiple marginalized identities are largely invisible on college and university campuses and often neglected in the psychological scholarship as well.

The microaggressions by students or professors that LGBTQ+ students encounter in classrooms are another important facet of their experiences on campus. Microaggressions can be experienced in terms of one's intersecting identities (Lewis & Neville, 2015; Nadal et al., 2014), which is why it is crucial for researchers to use a holistic view when analyzing the needs of all LGBTQ+ students. For example, microaggressions might be amplified in rural college settings, where there may be a lack of a critical presence of LGBTQ+ people and experiences as compared with urban or suburban settings. Without the intervention of administrators and diversity office staff on campus, LGBTQ+ college students might continuously experience microaggressions that eventually discourage them from attending class and achieving academic success. Currently, the need for most LGBTQ+ college students to advocate for themselves reveals staggering deficiencies in the support systems that are supposed to be designed to facilitate student success.

**Research on LGBTQ+ BIPOC Students**

At the intersection of race, sexuality, and gender identity, LGBTQ+ BIPOC are subject to the interlocking systems of racism, heterosexism, sexism, and cissexism. Over the past few years, research has shown that LGBTQ+ BIPOC generally experience high levels of psychological distress and depression, both of which lead to poorer mental health outcomes (Sutter et al., 2018; Velez et al., 2017). Thus, it is important to consider how the experiences of LGBTQ+ BIPOC students are shaped by the support systems, or lack thereof, within their college institutions. At predominantly White universities (PWIs), self-identified queer and transgender BIPOC students have reported feelings of exhaustion and frustration, as well as higher rates of depression as a result of their efforts to succeed academically while trying to advocate for themselves (Kulick et al., 2017; Vaccaro & Mena, 2011). These findings suggest that, in their attempts to create space and support for themselves on campus, LGBTQ+ BIPOC students experience negative symptoms of mental health. There is a need for more research to explore the resources available to LGBTQ+ BIPOC students, as well as the factors that contribute to continued activism. This research could inform the development of necessary interventions to support the psychological well-being of LGBTQ+ BIPOC students on college campuses. At HBCUs, where campus culture can often be defined by conservative values, Christianity, Black pride, and celebrations of traditional femininity and masculinity, Black LGBTQ+ students may find comfort in these emphasized values while also experiencing exclusion (Lenning, 2017). Thus, in a context like this, there is a need for pro-LGBTQ+ spaces and resources.

**Research on Transgender or Nonbinary College Students**

While many institutions have developed policies and created spaces for White, cisgender, and able-bodied LGBQ students, transgender and nonbinary students often face both individual and institutional discrimination on college campuses. There is considerable debate around making restrooms all-gender, and this is one of the many ways in which transgender and nonbinary students experience systemic discrimination on campus. The lack of access to this basic resource can cause great distress for this population, and even has the potential to trigger feelings of gender dysphoria for transgender and nonbinary students if they are forced to use a bathroom that does not align with their gender identity. Another prevalent issue that invalidates the experience of transgender and nonbinary students occurs when the institution's records system does not allow for accessible, seamless, and consistent procedures for name changes. The lack of appropriate name change procedures can cause severe discomfort, for example, when a professor calls out a student by their deadname, or if a student ID lists the deadname, and the student is denied access to campus resources. Furthermore, there may be professors, staff, and peers who refuse to use the correct pronouns for members of this group, even when they have been exposed to education about gender diversity. In addition to these campus-wide issues, institutions often do not have appropriate policies aimed at supporting the inclusion of transgender and nonbinary college athletes that would help buffer against discrimination they may experience in the locker room (Lucas-Carr & Krane, 2011; Singh et al., 2013)—if they are even allowed to participate in sports aligned with their gender identity. Some transgender and gender nonbinary students are excluded from participating in sports aligned with their gender identity, and are only allowed to engage in sports aligned with their assigned sex at birth. For these reasons, it is critical for research to highlight the distressing experiences of this group on college campuses and develop possible interventions to support their well-being.

**Institutional Support of LGBTQ+ Students**

Institutional policies and resources that affirm LGBTQ+ college students serve as effective, proactive interventions in fostering more positive experiences for these students (Woodford et al., 2018). Specifically, antidiscrimination policies that are inclusive of both gender identity and sexual orientation can help reduce rates of cissexist and heterosexist discrimination. The inclusion of gender identity is essential because it protects students under the trans umbrella, as well as students with gender expressions that defy social norms (Woodford et al., 2018). This can inform the nature of professional development training for staff, faculty, and students on campus, specifically in terms of the need to make a distinction between sexual orientation and gender identity. Additionally, while many institutions offer training on LGBTQ+ issues on campus, little has been done to evaluate their efficacy. By determining the long-term effectiveness of these trainings across various departments, researchers can help encourage college administrators to develop policies that require faculty and staff to attend such trainings. If colleges focus on institutionalizing support for LGBTQ+ students in this way, they can help create an affirming atmosphere that may decrease this group's drop-out rates (see Windmeyer, 2016).

**LGBTQ+ College Students: Gaps in the Literature**

In the interdisciplinary literature, there is a paucity of research on LGBTQ+ students when considering specific college and university contexts and settings. Specifically, little is known about institutionalizing LGBTQ+ student support, LGBTQ+ college students who attend HBCUs, LGBTQ+ students who attend community colleges, and LGBTQ+ college students who attend religious institutions. Additionally, a dearth of literature exists on specific LGBTQ+ college student populations within higher education institutions including transgender college students, LGBTQ+ students with disabilities, LGBTQ+ student–athletes, LGBTQ+ students who are first generation or first in their families to attend college, rural LGBTQ+ students, and LGBTQ+ students who are also international students. Given this gap in the literature, the aim of this book is to include several context chapters and several population chapters where we discuss specific LGBTQ+ populations who often get neglected and ignored in the literature on LGBTQ+ students in higher education. These chapters can be used to help university administrators, faculty, staff, and students create more affirming and supportive spaces in higher education settings.

## OVERVIEW OF THE BOOK

This book is separated into two content areas. In the first five chapters, the authors focus on higher education contexts to situate LGBTQ+ student experiences in the context in which they occur. The subsequent six chapters focus on the lived experiences of specific LGBTQ+ student populations when considering multiple aspects of their intersecting identities. Each chapter includes (a) an introduction to the topic; (b) an overview of the research and theoretical frameworks related to the topic; (c) practices, strategies, and interventions related to the topic; and (d) a conclusion. All chapters include discussion questions to promote further thought and a list or table of mental health resources that readers can use to guide their interventions to better support LGBTQ+ students.

In Chapter 1, Singh details methods for institutionalizing support for LGBTQ+ students on college and university campuses. Specifically, Singh provides concrete directions that university administrators can take to assess their campus climate for LGBTQ+ students, develop programs and initiatives to support LGBTQ+ students, and enhance partnerships across campus to improve the wellness services of LGBTQ+ students on campus. In Chapter 2, Ferguson provides an overview of LGBTQ+ college students at HBCUs and details how the campus climate of HBCUs can either be supportive or unsupportive. Ferguson discusses the HBCU context and how multiple forms of oppression negatively impact LGBTQ+ students at HBCUs. Ferguson provides practical strategies administrators at HBCUs can take to improve the climate for LGBTQ+ students. Chapter 3 details the experiences of LGBTQ+ community college students. McSpadden et al. provide recommendations for how faculty and staff who work at community colleges can be more affirming and supportive of LGBTQ+ students by creating resource centers. In Chapter 4, Kay and Wolff detail how LGBTQ+ students navigate life in the context of nonaffirming religious institutions. Kay and Wolff discuss how policies enacted by nonaffirming religious institutions negatively impact the campus climate for LGBTQ+ students and provide recommendations for how nonaffirming religious institutions can better support their

LGBTQ+ students. Chapter 5 details how Salisbury University's Safe Spaces program is being used to address macro- and meso-level interventions to improve the climate and safety of LGBTQ+ students on campus. Illig et al. detail how the Safe Spaces program is being used to change institutional structures. Recommendations for implementing a similar program at other universities and institutions are discussed.

Chapter 6 details specific recommendations and strategies for university administrators to engage in advocacy work to support and meet the needs of transgender college students. Allen and dickey provide an overview of transgender students' needs on college and university campuses and detail specific recommendations for how university administrators can engage in advocacy work to support transgender and nonbinary college students. Chapter 7 explores the experiences of LGBTQ+ college students with disabilities. Dispenza et al. provide administrators in higher education with strategies and interventions that they can use to create a more welcoming and inclusive climate for LGBTQ+ students with disabilities. In Chapter 8, McCavanagh and Cadaret detail the experiences of LGB college student–athletes. McCavanagh and Cadaret explore the coming-out negotiations of LGB athletes and provide strategies for athletic departments as they work to create more inclusive athletic spaces for LGB college athletes. Chapter 9 explores the experiences of LGBTQ+ students who are the first in their family to attend college. Cerezo and Ramirez provide concrete strategies that university administrators can use to advocate for more support of first-generation LGBTQ+ college students. In Chapter 10, Goodrich and McClellan discuss some of the challenges that LGBTQ+ students in rural college and university settings face. Goodrich and McClellan explore how educational and mental health staff can help bolster resilience and connect LGBTQ+ students with resources while attending universities or colleges in rural areas. Chapter 11 details the experiences of LGBTQ+ international students who attend institutions of higher education in the United States. Nakamura et al. explore the challenges faced by LGBTQ+ international students and provide recommendations for how college campuses can challenge the invisibility of LGBTQ+ international students and work to create a more affirming and welcoming campus climate.

Finally, in Chapter 12, we (the editors) summarize the findings from this book and provide practical strategies and recommendations for interventions to address the needs of LGBTQ+ students at the individual, interpersonal, institutional, and societal levels. We discuss future research and advocacy efforts to better support the needs of LGBTQ+ students in higher education.

We note that Chapter 5 and Chapter 8 differ from the other chapters in the book in that they are narrower in scope. Specifically, these chapters offer two case studies of safe space trainings. Chapter 5 details Salisbury University's Safe Spaces program and how the university is using the program to enhance LGBTQ+ student wellness, whereas Chapter 8 focuses on evaluating a safe space training with athletic coaches. Safe space trainings represent an early step for many schools that wish to institutionalize their support for LGBTQ+ students. Although some research has explored how safe space programs impact positive outcomes for LGBTQ+ youth (see Black et al., 2012), research on implementation of safe space trainings in institutions of higher education is farther along than research on its outcomes.

## A NOTE ON TERMINOLOGY

We know that a diverse range of definitions exist for sexual and gender identities and that people define sexual and gender identities differently. Although we (the editors) use the LGBTQ+ acronym in our introduction and conclusion, we elected not to require that our authors use a single unified umbrella term across all chapters. Instead, we encouraged the authors to use acronyms and terminology that best captured their population of focus. Thus, some chapters use the LGBTQ+ acronym, while others use different terminology and acronyms to best reflect their population of focus.

## CONCLUSION

We hope that this book serves as a call to action for more higher education scholarship on practical interventions that universities and colleges can take to better support LGBTQ+ students on campus and buffer against the negative impact of minority stress. We believe that this book is a starting point and a first step for addressing this call to action. We hope that readers find helpful resources, information, and practical strategies that institutions of higher education can use to better support LGBTQ+ students and create more affirming and inclusive campus climates.

## REFERENCES

Bissonette, D., & Szymanski, D. M. (2019). Minority stress and LGBQ college students' depression: Roles of peer group and involvement. *Psychology of Sexual Orientation and Gender Diversity*, 6(3), 308–317. https://doi.org/10.1037/sgd0000332

Black, W. W., Fedewa, A. L., & Gonzalez, K. A. (2012). Effects of "safe school" programs and policies on the social climate for sexual-minority youth: A review of the literature. *Journal of LGBT Youth*, 9(4), 321–339. https://doi.org/10.1080/19361653.2012.714343

Blimling, G. S. (2014). *Student learning in college residence halls: What works, what doesn't and why*. Jossey-Bass.

Brooks, V. R. (1981). *Minority stress and lesbian women*. Lexington Books.

Brown, C., & Keller, C. J. (2018). The 2016 presidential election outcome: Fears, tension, and resiliency of GLBTQ communities. *Journal of GLBT Family Studies*, 14(1–2), 101–129. https://doi.org/10.1080/1550428X.2017.1420847

Cole, E. R. (2009). Intersectionality and research in psychology. *American Psychologist*, 64(3), 170–180. https://doi.org/10.1037/a0014564

Collins, P. H. (1990). *Black feminist thought: Knowledge, consciousness, and the politics of empowerment*. Routledge.

Collins, P. H. (2015). Intersectionality's definitional dilemmas. *Annual Review of Sociology*, 41(1), 1–20. https://doi.org/10.1146/annurev-soc-073014-112142

Combahee River Collective. (1995). A Black feminist statement. In B. Guy-Sheftall (Ed.), *Words of fire: An anthology of African American feminist thought* (pp. 232–240). New Press. (Original work published 1977)

Crenshaw, K. W. (1989). Demarginalizing the intersection of race and sex: A Black feminist critique of antidiscrimination doctrine, feminist theory and antiracist politics. *University of Chicago Legal Forum, 1989*(1), 139–167. https://chicagounbound.uchicago.edu/uclf/vol1989/iss1/8/

Crenshaw, K. W. (1991). Mapping the margins: Intersectionality, identity politics, and violence against women of color. *Stanford Law Review, 43*(6), 1241–1299. https://doi.org/10.2307/1229039

Delgado, R., & Stefanic, J. (2000). Introduction. In R. Delgado & J. Stefanic (Eds.), *Critical race theory: The cutting edge* (2nd ed., pp. xv–xix). Temple University Press.

de Vries, K. M. (2015). Transgender people of color at the center: Conceptualizing a new intersectional model. *Ethnicities, 15*(1), 3–27. https://doi.org/10.1177/1468796814547058

Gonzalez, K. A., Pulice-Farrow, L., & Galupo, M. P. (2018). "My aunt unfriended me": Narratives of GLBTQ family relationships post 2016 presidential election. *Journal of GLBT Family Studies, 14*(1–2), 61–84. https://doi.org/10.1080/1550428X.2017.1420845

Gonzalez, K. A., Ramirez, J. L., & Galupo, M. P. (2018). Increase in GLBTQ minority stress following the 2016 US presidential election. *Journal of GLBT Family Studies, 14*(1–2), 130–151. https://doi.org/10.1080/1550428X.2017.1420849

Hines, S. (2010). Sexing gender; gendering sex: Towards an intersectional analysis of transgender. In Y. Taylor, S. Hines, & M. E. Casey (Eds.), *Theorizing intersectionality and sexuality* (pp. 140–162). Springer. https://doi.org/10.1057/9780230304093_8

Hood, L., Sherrell, D., Pfeffer, C. A., & Mann, E. S. (2019). LGBTQ college students' experiences with university health services: An exploratory study. *Journal of Homosexuality, 66*(6), 797–814. https://doi.org/10.1080/00918369.2018.1484234

Jacobson, L., Daire, A. P., & Abel, E. M. (2015). Intimate partner violence: Implications for counseling self-identified LGBTQ college students engaged in same-sex relationships. *Journal of LGBT Issues in Counseling, 9*(2), 118–135. https://doi.org/10.1080/15538605.2015.1029203

Kulick, A., Wernick, L. J., Woodford, M. R., & Renn, K. (2017). Heterosexism, depression, and campus engagement among LGBTQ college students: Intersectional differences and opportunities for healing. *Journal of Homosexuality, 64*(8), 1125–1141. https://doi.org/10.1080/00918369.2016.1242333

Ladson-Billings, G., & Tate, W. F. (1995). Toward a critical race theory of education. *Teachers College Record, 97*(1), 47–68.

Lenning, E. (2017). Unapologetically queer in unapologetically Black spaces: Creating an inclusive HBCU campus. *Humboldt Journal of Social Relations, 1*(39), 283–293. https://digitalcommons.humboldt.edu/hjsr/vol1/iss39/24/

Lewis, J. A., & Neville, H. A. (2015). Construction and initial validation of the Gendered Racial Microaggressions Scale for Black women. *Journal of Counseling Psychology, 62*(2), 289–302. https://doi.org/10.1037/cou0000062

Lewis, J. A., Williams, M. G., Peppers, E. J., & Gadson, C. A. (2017). Applying intersectionality to explore the relations between gendered racism and health among Black women. *Journal of Counseling Psychology, 64*(5), 475–486. https://doi.org/10.1037/cou0000231

Lucas-Carr, C. B., & Krane, V. (2011). What is the T in LGBT? Supporting transgender athletes through sport psychology. *The Sport Psychologist, 25*(4), 532–548. https://doi.org/10.1123/tsp.25.4.532

Meyer, I. H. (1995). Minority stress and mental health in gay men. *Journal of Health and Social Behavior, 36*(1), 38–56. https://doi.org/10.2307/2137286

Meyer, I. H. (2003). Prejudice, social stress, and mental health in lesbian, gay, and bisexual populations: Conceptual issues and research evidence. *Psychological Bulletin, 129*(5), 674–697. https://doi.org/10.1037/0033-2909.129.5.674

Nadal, K. L., Griffin, K. E., Wong, Y., Hamit, S., & Rasmus, M. (2014). The impact of racial microaggressions on mental health: Counseling implications for clients of color. *Journal of Counseling and Development, 92*(1), 57–66. https://doi.org/10.1002/j.1556-6676.2014.00130.x

Rankin, S., Garvey, J. C., & Duran, A. (2019). A retrospective of LGBT issues on US college campuses: 1990–2020. *International Sociology, 34*(4), 435–454. https://doi.org/10.1177/0268580919851429

Rankin, S., Weber, G., Blumenfeld, W., & Frazer, S. (2010). *2010 state of higher education for lesbian, gay, bisexual, & transgender people*. Campus Pride. https://www.campuspride.org/wp-content/uploads/campuspride2010lgbtreportssummary.pdf

Riggle, E. D. B., Rostosky, S. S., Drabble, L., Veldhuis, C. B., & Hughes, T. L. (2018). Sexual minority women's and gender-diverse individuals' hope and empowerment responses to the 2016 presidential election. *Journal of GLBT Family Studies, 14*(1–2), 152–173. https://doi.org/10.1080/1550428X.2017.1420853

Salter, P., & Adams, G. (2013). Toward a critical race psychology. *Social and Personality Psychology Compass, 7*(11), 781–793. https://doi.org/10.1111/spc3.12068

Schmidt, C. K., Miles, J. R., & Welsh, A. C. (2011). Perceived discrimination and social support: The influences on career development and college adjustment of LGBT college students. *Journal of Career Development, 38*(4), 293–309. https://doi.org/10.1177/0894845310372615

Schneider, M. S., & Dimito, A. (2010). Factors influencing the career and academic choices of lesbian, gay, bisexual, and transgender people. *Journal of Homosexuality, 57*(10), 1355–1369. https://doi.org/10.1080/00918369.2010.517080

Singh, A. A., Meng, S., & Hansen, A. (2013). "It's already hard enough being a student": Developing affirming college environments for trans youth. *Journal of LGBT Youth, 10*(3), 208–223. https://doi.org/10.1080/19361653.2013.800770

Solórzano, D., Ceja, M., & Yosso, T. (2000). Critical race theory, racial microaggressions, and campus racial climate: The experiences of African American college students. *The Journal of Negro Education, 69*(1/2), 60–73. https://www.jstor.org/stable/2696265

Sutter, M., Perrin, P. B., & Trujillo, M. A. (2018). Understanding the association between discrimination and depression among sexual minority people of color: Evidence for diminishing returns of socioeconomic advantage. *Journal of Clinical Psychology, 74*(6), 940–952. https://doi.org/10.1002/jclp.22558

Vaccaro, A., & Mena, J. A. (2011). It's not burnout, it's more: Queer college activists of color and mental health. *Journal of Gay & Lesbian Mental Health, 15*(4), 339–367. https://doi.org/10.1080/19359705.2011.600656

Veldhuis, C. B., Drabble, L., Riggle, E. D. B., Wootton, A. R., & Hughes, T. L. (2018a). "I fear for my safety, but want to show bravery for others": Violence and discrimination concerns among transgender and gender-nonconforming individuals after the 2016 presidential election. *Violence and Gender, 5*(1), 26–36. https://doi.org/10.1089/vio.2017.0032

Veldhuis, C. B., Drabble, L., Riggle, E. D. B., Wootton, A. R., & Hughes, T. L. (2018b). "We won't go back into the closet now without one hell of a fight": Effects of the 2016 presidential election on sexual minority women's and gender minorities' stigma-related concerns. *Sexuality Research & Social Policy, 15*, 12–24. https://doi.org/10.1007/s13178-017-0305-x

Velez, B. L., Watson, L. B., Cox, R., Jr., & Flores, M. J. (2017). Minority stress and racial or ethnic minority status: A test of the greater risk perspective. *Psychology of Sexual Orientation and Gender Diversity, 4*(3), 257–271. https://doi.org/10.1037/sgd0000226

Wagner, R., Marine, S., & Nicolazzo, Z. (2018). Better than most: Trans* perspectives on gender-inclusive housing. *The Journal of College and University Student Housing, 45*(1), 26–43. https://eric.ed.gov/?id=EJ1199440

Wilson, M. E., & Rygg, M. J. (2013). Campus housing and student development. In N. W. Dunkel & J. A. Baumann (Eds.), *Campus housing management: Vol. 2. Residence life and education* (pp. 2–23).

Windmeyer, S. (2016, April 15). *The path forward: LGBT retention and academic success.* Insight Into Diversity. https://www.insightintodiversity.com/the-path-forward-lgbt-retention-and-academic-success/

Woodford, M. R., Han, Y., Craig, S., Lim, C., & Matney, M. M. (2014). Discrimination and mental health among sexual minority college students: The type and form of discrimination does matter. *Journal of Gay & Lesbian Mental Health, 18*(2), 142–163. https://doi.org/10.1080/19359705.2013.833882

Woodford, M. R., & Kulick, A. (2015). Academic and social integration on campus among sexual minority students: The impacts of psychological and experiential campus climate. *American Journal of Community Psychology, 55*(1–2), 13–24. https://doi.org/10.1007/s10464-014-9683-x

Woodford, M. R., Kulick, A., & Atteberry, B. (2015). Protective factors, campus climate, and health outcomes among sexual minority college students. *Journal of Diversity in Higher Education, 8*(2), 73–87. https://doi.org/10.1037/a0038552

Woodford, M. R., Kulick, A., Garvey, J. C., Sinco, B. R., & Hong, J. S. (2018). LGBTQ policies and resources on campus and the experiences and psychological well-being of sexual minority college students: Advancing research on structural inclusion. *Psychology of Sexual Orientation and Gender Diversity, 5*(4), 445–456. https://doi.org/10.1037/sgd0000289

# I

# CONTEXTS

# 1

# Institutionalizing LGBTQ+ Student Support

Anneliese Singh

**KEY KNOWLEDGE AREAS**

- Administrators must think strategically about the organizational structure of LGBTQ+ support resources to ensure that there is effective collaboration around resources for LGBTQ+ students, so these resources are not campus silos that further present challenges for LGBTQ+ students to find mentorship, support, and collaborations.

- An institutional approach to LGBTQ+ student support should be grounded in knowledge of the overall history of student organizing—especially Black student organizing and the origins of EDI campus initiatives—and also ensure equity metrics and outcome data are guiding affirmative approaches to supporting LGBTQ+ students across diverse identities (e.g., race/ethnicity, gender, social class, disability, citizenship status).

- A Top 10 list of institutionalized LGBTQ+ support strategies is provided to frame institutional commitment to important areas of LGBTQ+ awareness–knowledge–skills–action necessary for administrators, faculty, staff, and students to have, as well as to inform strategic planning and resource assignment to ensure ongoing support for LGBTQ+ students.

This chapter explores the institutional university issues that contribute to minority stress for LGBTQ+ students, as well as the practices, strategies, and interventions that higher education professionals should investigate or

https://doi.org/10.1037/0000281-002
*Affirming LGBTQ+ Students in Higher Education*, D. P. Rivera, R. L. Abreu, and K. A. Gonzalez (Editors)
Copyright © 2022 by the American Psychological Association. All rights reserved.

implement institutionalizing support for LGBTQ+ students. We examine the history we know about these support systems, as well as the her-story and t-story (trans-story) that have been occluded from history books in LGBTQ+ higher education. Along the way, we draw from research and theoretical frameworks that can assist us in advancing LGBTQ+ student support for the generations to come.

## HISTORICAL, HER-STORICAL, AND T-STORICAL NARRATIVES OF STUDENT SUPPORT SYSTEMS

Despite plentiful evidence that institutions of higher education are hostile to LGBTQ+ students (Rankin et al., 2010), these students are still self-identifying at higher rates each year on campuses. This chapter lays out important research and theoretical frameworks with regard to understanding the LGBTQ+ stressors students face—from the minority stress model (Meyer, 1995, 2003, 2010, 2015) and intersectionality (Bowleg, 2008; Crenshaw, 1989; Truth, 1863) to queer theory and critical race theory (Bell, 1980). The minority stress model helps us name the discrete, real, persistent, and ongoing microaggressions that LGBTQ+ students experience, as well as their resulting harms (Mathies et al., 2019). Intersectionality theory, the gift of generations of Black feminists and womanists, reminds us that as we examine the history of any institution, we must relentlessly and intentionally identify the interlocking oppressions experienced by LGBTQ+ students as they are centered in the experience of racism (or as Wilkerson, 2020, preferred to say, the caste system in the land we now call the United States). Queer theory helps us remember that the hetero-cissexist gaze of dominance is always positioned on LGBTQ+ identities, experiences, and communities as "deviant" or "against the norm" of cis–het values and dominance. Critical race theory scholars remind us that as we explore LGBTQ+ student support efforts, it is not *if* racism exists but, instead, *how* it exists within these higher education initiatives. In doing so, critical race theory scholars plainly say that racism is a system that has very real consequences for BIPOC (Black, Indigenous, People of Color) students who are LGBTQ+ and that issues of racism are only addressed when there is white interest convergence (i.e., when white people deem an issue of racism as important and real, impacting their lives, hearts, and minds in some way).

Therefore, as we seek to understand how advocates have strived to institutionalize LGBTQ+ student support efforts, we must also understand the history of student activism and organizing—and specifically the history of Black student organizing. Knowing the research on LGBTQ+ resilience to minority stress is helpful in grasping the extent to which we still need to pursue LGBTQ+ student institutionalization efforts in higher education.

### Black Organizing Within and Outside of Higher Education

The current terms we use to describe equity, diversity, and inclusion (EDI)—and its many permutations (e.g., "diversity and inclusion," "diversity, equity, and inclusion," "equity and justice") within which LGBTQ+ student advocacy in higher education rests—came about due to the persistent organizing efforts of Black student movements in higher education, which included different models of approaches that have evolved over time. Williams and Wade-Golden (2013) categorized three periods of EDI work: "affirmative action and equity" (1950s–1970s), "multicultural and inclusion diversity" (1960s–1970s), and the "learning, diversity, and research" of the 1990–2000s. It is important to note that the current terms include words such as "antiracist" and "intersectionality."

These movements originated in the work of Black student activists, who have been heavily influential throughout their evolution. For instance, the affirmative action and equity period was a response within higher education to the Civil Rights Movement, where Black student activists and their racial allies and coconspirators demanded legal access (ultimately based on federal mandates) to institutions of higher education (Williams & Wade-Golden, 2013). As these Black students gained access to higher education, and the resulting higher education EDI efforts (e.g., affirmative action) were institutionalized, the idea of racial "diversity" was quickly realized as not sufficient to ensure the full participation of Black students and other students on the margins (mostly related to race/ethnicity). The multicultural and inclusion diversity period came about as many Black activist organizations (e.g., the Black Power movement), along with disability rights movements and LGBTQ+ rights movements, issued demands for recognition of their existence and unique student needs in higher education (Renn, 2010). During this time, many LGBTQ+ centers, women's centers, religious centers (expanding beyond a Judeo–Christian focus), multicultural/intercultural/cultural centers emerged to respond to and serve these student support needs. In the learning, diversity, and research period, EDI work shifted to position diversity as a source of strength in higher education (Williams & Wade-Golden, 2013). Bodies of literature suggest a diversity of student groups on campus promote excellence in higher education in academic and career development, preparing all students for the future world.

Although Williams and Wade-Golden (2013) noted the crucial role that Black student activists played throughout these three periods, it is the important street protests and community organizing work of Black and Brown trans women (e.g., Marsha P. Johnson, Sylvia Rivera) that began at Stonewall in the late 1960s and 1970s that have led to demands for intersectional approaches to gender, sexuality, and race within LGBTQ+ freedom movements (Baumann, 2019; Duberman, 1993). There are also civil rights activists, organizers, and icons that those working to support LGBTQ+ communities on campus should be aware of—such as Bayard Rustin, a gay Black man who was the architect of the March on Washington during which Dr. Martin Luther King, Jr. gave his powerful "I Have a Dream" speech. As these LGBTQ+ movements were gaining in resistance and popularity, another group of Black feminist and womanist intersectional scholars (e.g., Audre Lorde, Alice Walker, bell hooks, Patricia Hill Collins) were writing from within and outside of the academy about the interlocking oppressions of racism, sexism, and other oppressions, such as antilesbian bias. Their writings were often taken up in women's studies and ethnic studies courses, which fueled on-campus intersectional material demands for more affirmation and support of women's centers, LGBTQ+ centers, and cultural centers within higher education. Today, we are seeing the return to a racial reckoning ("antiracism" first coined by Angela Davis) in higher education that goes beyond access, affirmation, and material support. Universities are being asked to acknowledge that current policies and practices are based in their history of anti-Blackness; built on the Indigenous land we now call the United States of America for white, cisgender, straight, middle-to-upper class able-bodied men, whose citizenship was based on their assigned race and gender.

In many ways, therefore, the current EDI leadership positions (e.g., "chief diversity officer," "LGBT resource center director") and other initiatives (e.g., recruitment and retention of students from historically marginalized backgrounds) we see in higher education today are rooted in the histories, her-stories, and t-stories of Black freedom movements. Why is this so important to recognize? In the context of ongoing attacks against EDI issues from the conservative right, campuses will continue to scramble for sufficient resources to adequately fund deep, intersectional campus policies, procedures, and practices. This is mostly because we still have not grappled with the root of all campus EDI initiatives—that as Black students and all other students on the margins have fought for access and support on campus, they are continuously viewed and defined as "diverse" from the "norm" of homogeneously white het–cis students. This creates an "oppression Olympics" of sorts (also coined by Angela Davis), that then is used to further divide "diverse" groups on campus. As long as EDI is viewed as an "enhancement" and as an "added competency," as opposed to the definition of excellence and true community practices, then LGBTQ+ initiatives in higher education will continue to have an uphill battle within institutions.

### LGBTQ+ Resilience to Minority Stress

LGBTQ+ resilience is a crucial aspect of any LGBTQ+ initiative on campus, especially in the institutionalization of these initiatives. However, it is important to note that this focus on resilience is not a focus on the origins of everyday resilience studies that examined hardiness and individual characteristics only, which were born out of white and Western approaches (Singh et al., 2011; Singh & McKleroy, 2011; Singh et al., 2013, 2014). Rather, in this chapter, we use the definition that Singh et al., 2014 referred to: the resilience that LGBTQ+ communities have developed and/or will develop in K–12 and higher education learning environments as they navigate anti-LGBTQ+ and other intersectional oppressions. LGBTQ+ resilience can be thought of as having that buffering effect, specifically the resilience that LGBTQ+ communities develop to navigate anti-LGBTQ bias and systemic oppression (Singh et al., 2011). The research on the minority stress model has burgeoned in numerous ways after Meyer (1995, 2003, 2010, 2015) published his original model. The Institute of Medicine (2011) report, *The Health of Lesbian, Gay, Bisexual, and Transgender*

*People: Building a Foundation for Better Understanding*, identified minority stress as one of four critical theoretical frameworks to use in research, and many professional associations related to student affairs and higher education (e.g., ASHE, NASPA) have supported the expansion of the understanding of LGBTQ+ student minority stress through their journals and conference gatherings. In the minority stress model, individual (e.g., coping) and community (e.g., social support from family and family of "choice") moderators are noted that can buffer the impacts of LGBTQ+ minority stress.

The literature on LGBTQ+ resilience has evolved along the same lines as the research on LGBTQ+ minority stress. Scholars have noted that because the extent of LGBTQ+ minority stress is so well-known, we need to have strengths-based approaches that move us away from deficit approaches (Colpitts & Gahagan, 2016; Singh & McKleroy, 2011). This scholarly focus on LGBTQ+ resilience has also explored developmental implications, such as the importance of resilience for LGBTQ+ youth (Grossman et al., 2011; Singh et al., 2014) and LGBTQ+ resilience for elders that can lead to better quality of life outcomes across the lifespan (Fredriksen-Goldsen et al., 2013). Higher education is a time when LGBTQ+ students have an opportunity to explore their gender, sexual, and affectional identities in ways they may not have had due to a lack of information and support for clueing in to being LGBTQ+. Therefore, a theoretical framework of LGBTQ+ resilience helps us balance attention to minority stress with embedding LGBTQ+ strengths-based practices, strategies, and interventions into higher education institutions. As such, the remainder of the chapter, while noting the institutional issues that contribute to minority stress for LGBTQ+ students, focuses primarily on resilience-based, systemic initiatives and strategies from a systemic level that address these issues.

## TEN LGBTQ+ PRACTICES, STRATEGIES, AND INTERVENTIONS IN HIGHER EDUCATION

As discussed earlier, the numbers of LGBTQ+ students who are self-identifying their gender and sexual/affectional identities prior to attending higher education is increasing (Rankin et al., 2010), and there continue to be LGBTQ+ students who will come to identify, explore, and affirm their LGBTQ+ identity for the first time in higher education (Mundy, 2018). Therefore, a wide variety of institutional supports are needed to affirm and support LGBTQ+ students, and 10 critical practices, strategies, and interventions are noted here. It is important to note that, in each of these, attention should be given to the key areas of awareness, knowledge, skills, and actions necessary for campus leaders to have (that must be obtained through professional development) that will directly inform strategic planning and resource assignment to ensure ongoing support for LGBTQ+ students. Having clear equity indicators and outcome data within each of the following 10 strategies is also critical to make real, sustained institutional change.

## 1. Funding the Missions of LGBTQ+ Resource Centers at Adequate Levels

LGBTQ+ students come to campuses with higher expectations for services and advocates, and this positions LGBTQ+ resource centers at the leading edge of innovation as they strive to meet the support needs of LGBTQ+ students who have experienced a multitude of interlocking privileges and oppressions (Kortegast et al., 2021; Mundy, 2018). As the identified advocates for LGBTQ+ students on campus, these centers use a broad array of strategies to create affirming environments for them. Now that campuses are collecting more data about LGBTQ+ students on campus before they get to campus (e.g., demographic surveys) and while they are there (e.g., campus climate surveys), these centers are resourced with more information than ever before about LGBTQ+ student demographics on campus (Pitcher et al., 2018). LGBTQ+ resource centers also engage in focus groups with their constituents to find ways to more effectively serve, for example, their LGBTQ+ BIPOC community, people living with disabilities, first-generation college students, international students, students without documentation status, and many other intersections.

LGBTQ+ resource centers tend to be the drivers of campus-wide education programs promoting LGBTQ+ education (e.g., Safe Space or Safe Zone programs; Self & Hudson, 2015). These programs typically provide an LGBTQ+ history, her-story, and t-story of its particular campus followed by an affirming-LGBTQ+ vocabulary, information on LGBTQ+ microaggressions, and specific advocacy and support needs on campus (see Chapter 5 of this volume for a detailed analysis of Safe Space programs; Linley & Nguyen, 2015). Although some question the utility of these programs to shift campus climates to pro-LGBTQ+ environments (Woodford et al., 2014), and this is a legitimate critique, it is also important to note that these programs are typically not mandated programs, along with many other EDI foundational professional development programs in higher education. This lack of a campus mandate makes possible the enduring hetero-cissexism found on campuses. LGBTQ+ resource centers with few professional staff and inadequate budgets are expected to support the needs of LGBTQ+ students, and also engage in campus-wide LGBTQ+ education, which drains time and resources from doing direct LGBTQ+ student support programming and initiatives. Given the high rates of mental health challenges (e.g., depression, anxiety, suicidality, substance abuse) related to anti-LGBTQ+ societal and campus stressors, consistently addressing mental, physical, and sexual health, safety, and wellness is a primary role of the LGBTQ+ resource center (Mundy, 2018). It is clear that LGBTQI+ resource centers often have multiple and competing objectives that include direct student support, wellness and safety oversight, and professional development. Adequate funding and resourcing will ensure that these objectives are met without compromise.

## 2. Embedding Counseling Services Into LGBTQ+ Resource Centers

One way of addressing the broad mission of LGBTQ+ resource centers that are often understaffed and underresourced in other ways (e.g., alumni support, senior admin support) is to have counseling services on-site in order to increase attention to the minority stressors for LGBTQ+ students that are common on- and off-campus (e.g., rejection by family and/or friends, identity exploration, dating, and sex). For instance, universities such as the University of California, Los Angeles and University of California, Davis, among many others, use this model (termed "community-based counseling" at Rutgers University), in which counseling staff provide consistent, weekly services in campus cultural centers. It is imperative that these counseling services be provided by people who have strong foundations in multicultural and social justice competencies related to LGBTQ+ people and who are well-versed in how to support LGBTQ+ resilience amidst intersecting identities and interlocking oppressions (American Psychological Association, 2015; Association for Lesbian, Gay, Bisexual, and Transgender Issues in Counseling, 2009; Ratts et al., 2016). Campus leaders should gather and track data relative to LGBTQ+ student mental health—from outcome and satisfaction data about access and usage of counseling services and support groups to LGBTQ+ professional development (that is intersectional) obtained by staff.

### 3. Developing LGBTQ+ Affirming Policies

At the very least, institutions of higher education should have strong nondiscrimination policies that are inclusive of gender identity, gender expression, and sexual/affectional identity. Pitcher et al. (2018) reminded us that LGBTQ+ resource centers are beacons of support for LGBTQ+ student development, however, LGBTQ+ inclusive nondiscrimination policies are important foundations to support gender-affirming residence hall policies and also provide guardrails for students experiencing LGBTQ+ discrimination on campus.

Beyond adequate nondiscrimination policies, LGBTQ+ affirming policies should be generated, implemented, and applied broadly across campus. For instance, gender-inclusive housing and campus recreation center policies that are affirming of LGBTQ+ students are crucial, especially as trans and nonbinary students navigate their gender identities on campus. In addition, policies that require single-stall bathrooms in each new campus building, but also a reenvisioning of current buildings where single-stall bathrooms may not have been installed, signal to the LGBTQ+ students that their lives are important *and* provide safer crucial spaces for daily functional needs. Policies regarding name and pronoun use in the registrar's office and campus information systems also serve as a key indicator of LGBTQ+ student support on campus and signal to faculty the importance of staying current with LGBTQ+ knowledge relevant to the student experience. Ultimately, a systematic review of campus policies and procedures (i.e., equity audits) that might contain anti-LGBTQ+ bias is important in identifying where LGBTQ+ affirming policies need to be instituted (e.g., appropriate attire policies; Mobley & Johnson, 2019). To develop these policies, activities such as benchmarking against peer and aspirant institutions can be helpful to determine equity indicators and outcome data; however, many times the leaders in LGBTQ+ student support services may not be in this peer and aspirant group, so it is important to benchmark with the top university leaders.

## 4. Implementing Regular Campus Climate Surveys

Campus climate surveys help institutions of higher education understand attitudes towards LGBTQ+ students, the experiences they have on campus, and the impact of LGBTQ+ policies instituted to support them (Rankin et al., 2010; Renn, 2010). These surveys can help identify the resources needed to support LGBTQ+ students and also generate important dialogues about LGBTQ+ communities on campus that might not be occurring (Renn, 2010). Because LGBTQ+ language continues to evolve on campuses (Pitcher et al., 2018), these climate surveys must have a range of terms that are affirming to LGBTQ+ students concerning gender and sexual/affectional identity (Marine & Nicolazzo, 2014). The same is true of other identity categories (e.g., race/ethnicity, disability). Giving students the opportunity to self-identify with their own terms, rather than giving limited options, promotes self-determination and yields more meaningful data.

These surveys can be developed in-house or with outside consultancy (and if the latter, concerns of anonymity must be addressed, such as having data on an outside server). Regardless, a campus-wide campaign to encourage completion rates of at least 30% is very important. Campus climate surveys should be held at regular intervals (e.g., every 2–3 years), and results should be communicated widely across campus about the strengths and challenges LGBTQ+ students experience on campus, with specific follow-up actions to respond to the concerns identified—especially as they relate to academic outcomes (Hurtado et al., 2008). For instance, Woodford and Kulick (2015) noted the important relationship between mental health and a heterosexist campus climate. They found that openly identifying as LGBTQ+ was positively associated with campus acceptance, but that their experiences of LGBTQ+ harassment were positively associated with a decline in academic engagement and lower GPAs. Being able to track these trends over time allows campuses to more immediately and proactively support the academic and career success of LGBTQ+ students.

## 5. Supporting LGBTQ+ Student Leadership

LGBTQ+ students often find their "homes" in LGBTQ+ resource centers, but these homes should not become cul-de-sacs for their student experience as it relates to social engagement and leadership. LGBTQ+ students should feel broadly affirmed across all of the campus contexts; however, LGBTQ+ resource centers are places where LGBTQ+ students step into leadership roles within their community, and there are opportunities to uplift their leadership across campus. For instance, Harper and Baxter (2020) suggested a queer advisory council that advises senior administrators on a range of issues—from on-campus classroom experiences to LGBTQ+ experiences off-campus and in cocurricular environments. A council such as this can elevate the importance of LGBTQ+ student leadership and provide them with possibility models of mentorship along the way from senior administrators, and also sends a clear message to campus leaders at multiple levels within the institution that developing LGBTQ+ affirming environments is a priority. To set appropriate benchmarks for creating equitable environments for LGBTQ+ student leaders, data and equity indicators on general student leader support should be gathered and compared.

## 6. Creating Comprehensive, Campus-Wide, Intersectional EDI Professional Development

One of the present gaps in higher education is the lack of formalized, comprehensive, campus-wide EDI professional development. The killing of George Floyd, a Black man, by a white police officer on May 25, 2020, led to renewed public protests against anti-Black racism, and police violence toward BIPOC communities strengthened the Black Lives Matter movement, which in turn elevated these same calls for racial justice and antiracism training on campus. These calls have escalated the debate about mandated trainings on EDI. In thinking about the origin story of EDI movements on campus—where Black student activists developed pathway after pathway into higher education—it has become clearer than ever that holistic campus approaches to EDI education, training, and professional development are needed. Such trainings should center on the impacts of racism and anti-Black racism and should also note the important intersections of oppression and privilege for campus community members along lines of gender, sexual/affectional identity, disability, class, documentation status, first-generation status, and many more. As with other strategies in this Top 10 list, an initial activity is to benchmark internally and externally to assess where the campus is in overall EDI professional development and to wrestle with issues of how and when to mandate this training in a way that produces real changes in the levels of EDI professional development for all faculty, students, staff, and administrators.

## 7. Developing Comprehensive, Campus-Wide EDI Strategic Planning

Strategic planning is a common activity in institutions of higher education. Strategic plans often include attention to the core missions of a university: teaching, research, and service. EDI, however, is central to each of these core missions in higher education. For instance, how can we achieve "excellence" in higher education if we are not enacting EDI-informed approaches throughout all of the campus functions and activities? Affirmations of campus policies, practices, and interventions for LGBTQ+ students are fully included in the definition of strong EDI strategic planning processes.

These are the important questions that the National Association of Diversity Officers in Higher Education (NADOHE) has taken up, and that are embedded in the recently revised NADOHE Standards 2.0 (Worthington et al., 2020). Therefore, EDI should not be an "add-on" or viewed as an enhancement, but rather EDI strategic planning should be instituted to ensure that institutions of higher education are truly places of "inclusive excellence" (Williams & Wade-Golden, 2013). The NADOHE Standards advocate that "elements of equity, diversity, and inclusion are embedded as imperatives in the institutional mission, vision, and strategic plan" (Standard 2; Worthington et al., 2020, p. 2) as well as the importance of "planning, catalyzing, facilitating, and evaluation processes of institutional and organizational change" (Standard 3; Worthington et al., 2020, p. 2). Within both of these standards, EDI strategic plans are encouraged to be closely aligned to the "type, size, mission, and goals" of the campus (p. 8), and that "strategic plans should be updated periodically to reflect advancements, accomplishments, gaps, deficits, developmental progressions, and the continuously evolving nature of the institution and the profession of diversity in higher education" (p. 8). For instance, a research-intensive or teaching-intensive university may have very different EDI strategic goals, which will also influence the best ways to support LGBTQ+ students on campus. Geographic settings (e.g., rural, urban) relative to the type, size, mission, and goals of a campus can also influence EDI strategic planning. Regardless of the type, size, mission, and goals of a campus, and regardless of the overall campus budgets, specific resources should be set aside to define EDI, strategically plan for and assess EDI, and then implement these EDI strategic plans. These strategic plans, as well as equity scorecards, should reflect the perception of LGBTQ+ students as important and valued members of the campus community (Bensimon, 2004).

## 8. Recruiting and Retaining LGBTQ+ Students, Faculty, and Staff

EDI strategic plans can help identify and set specific equity indicators for recruiting and retaining LGBTQ+ students, faculty, and staff. To set recruitment and retention goals across groups, institutions should compare their current numbers of LGBTQ+ students, faculty, and staff with those of peer, aspirant, and/or other universities. If a particular campus does not have its own data, it can benchmark LGBTQ+ student, faculty, and staff recruitment and retention programs at peer institutions.

Research on LGBTQ+ student, faculty, and staff recruitment and retention remains sparse, but the use of practices with other historically marginalized groups could be helpful here. For instance, senior-level endorsement and funding of EDI and LGBTQ+ priorities sends a critical message of support to the larger campus. In addition, for faculty, dual-career hiring practices could be implemented that support spousal or partner hires, and campus supports and organizations for LGBTQ+ faculty can be highlighted (Fowler & DePauw, 2005). LGBTQ+ students can use the Campus Pride Index (n.d.) in their search for "LGBTQ-friendly" campuses, and senior-level administrators can track the evolution of their LGBTQ+ programs through this index, as well as use their score (a range from a low of 1 to a high of 5) in communications and marketing materials. Because staff often have the least amount of power in institutions of higher education, it is also important to have affirming hiring practices that intentionally use LGBTQ+ affirming language on paperwork (e.g., health benefits, campus directory) that also allows for a person's identified name and pronouns to be used and affirms the families that LGBTQ+ communities have.

Often, demographic data in recruitment and retention of faculty, staff, and students vary in terms of quality and length of time gathered. Therefore, a key activity in this area is to set a time range (e.g., 5 years, 10 years) to look back at to begin setting equity indicators based on any outcome data available. More recently, universities have increased their data collection of LGBTQ+ identities for students, but this lags behind for faculty and staff. These lags range from outright neglect in collecting this data to important concerns about how LGBTQ+ faculty and staff would experience this data collection. Having strong LGBTQ+ faculty and staff affinity groups that are affirming to those who have other multiple and intersecting identities of race/ethnicity, social class, first-generation, international, and more is a critical way to build LGBTQ+ faculty and staff community, identify resource and advocacy needs, and address recruitment and retention issues.

## 9. Strengthening Expectations for Faculty in Creating Affirming Teaching and Learning Environments for LGBTQ+ Students

Faculty have critical roles in developing teaching and learning environments that are affirming of LGBTQ+ students; however, few specific expectations have been outlined in this regard at the time of faculty hiring or faculty orientation. Despite this lack of expectations, LGBTQ+ faculty have historically been the strongest advocates for policy change relating to LGBTQ+ students (Messinger, 2011). Until clear expectations—and a whole-campus approach—for ensuring faculty have basic foundations in EDI, teaching and learning environments will continue to be inconsistent in the extent to which they are affirming for LGBTQ+ students. Research on LGBTQ+ pedagogy has largely taken place in the helping professions (e.g., social work, psychology, counseling; Burnes, 2017; Woodford et al., 2014), and LGBTQ+ content is taught in disciplines such as gender studies and sociology.

Although the research base on the attitudes that faculty have toward LGBTQ+ students and communities is nascent, and LGBTQ+ content is often taught in silos of particular disciplines, it is important to note the significant power that faculty have in institutions of higher education. Therefore, when they demonstrate their commitment to LGBTQ+ inclusive pedagogical practices, they set the tone for the classroom environment and can also serve as critical LGBTQ+ student advocates. Faculty should be held accountable for LGBTQ+ inclusive pedagogy by reviewing their syllabi for LGBTQ+ authors and content and also noting where they can integrate LGBTQ+ history, her-story, and t-story throughout their teaching (Harper & Baxter, 2020). Ideally, these LGBTQ+ teaching and learning initiatives would be embedded in an overall strategic planning process, and therefore it is crucial to collect data on how many faculty and staff have professional development in building affirmative LGBTQ+ environments, to set and increase target equity indicators, and to collect ongoing outcome data about the effectiveness of this LGBTQ+ professional development.

## 10. Communicating Campus Affirmation of LGBTQ+ Students From the Senior Administrator Level

Ultimately, senior-level administrators in higher education can send the most consistent and cohesive messages about LGBTQ students. University presidents, provosts, and human resources leaders, as well as leaders of campus facilities and vice-presidents of research, faculty, and service, can model for their units what it means to create LGBTQ+ affirming campus environments. From getting Safe Zone–trained and supporting their LGBTQ+ resource centers to recognizing Coming Out Day and International Pronouns Day, there are many public ways these senior-level administrators can express their support. In addition, as they welcome students, faculty, and staff to campus through orientation events, and as they make broad statements of commitment to EDI, they can speak explicitly about the value LGBTQ+ students bring to campus and about the importance of supporting the campus's LGBTQ+ community of students, faculty, and staff. To communicate effectively about the existing LGBTQ+ community on campus and advocacy needs, senior leaders should make LGBTQ+ outcome data, benchmarking data, and equity indicator targets data key features of their campus communications.

## CONCLUSION

Institutions of higher education can support their LGBTQ+ students in a multitude of ways, and these opportunities come at every level of the university. A whole-campus approach is required to do so effectively, and support for LGBTQ+ students should not reside solely in LGBTQ+ centers or siloed in particular disciplines. Because of the high rates of microaggressions toward LGBTQ+ people in society—which are multiplied for LGBTQ+ students who hold additional minoritized identities—campuses that strive to be safer and more affirming communities where LGBTQ+ students can thrive academically and socially are ones that can achieve a real, lived definition of inclusive excellence.

## DISCUSSION QUESTIONS

1. How has the history of Black student organizing efforts led to the establishment of LGBTQ+ resource centers and other cultural centers in higher education? What does this history look like at your own institution?

2. What are the challenges of having LGBTQ+ centers responsible for LGBTQ+ student support *and* campus-wide LGBTQ+ education? What do these challenges looks like at your own institution?

3. What are examples of policies and procedures that your institution could initiate to support intersectional whole-campus approaches to supporting LGBTQ+ students?

4. What are the strategic imperatives that upper administration can deploy to center the needs of these students?

5. What professional development do faculty, staff, students, and administrators need to be able to support affirming LGBTQ+ teaching and learning environments?

6. How are LGBTQ+ students, faculty, and staff reflected in your institution's strategic plan? Is there an EDI-specific strategic plan at your institution, and if so, how might intersectional approaches to LGBTQ+ support be addressed?

## RESOURCES

1. **Campus Pride Index** (https://www.campusprideindex.org)—a listing of registered 2-year and 4-year college campuses, with ratings of LGBTQI+ inclusivity, services, clubs, etc.

2. **Campus Pride** (https://www.campuspride.org)—a resource for students and groups wishing to foster safer college campuses for LGBTQI+ students.

3. **Consortium of Higher Education Lesbian Gay Bisexual Transgender Resource Professionals** (https://www.lgbtcampus.org)—includes resources and information on running resource spaces and creating LGBTQI+ programming.

4. **Council for the Advancement of Standards in Higher Education** (https://www.naspa.org/images/uploads/main/Lesbian,_Gay,_Bisexual,_Transgender_Programs_and_Services_SAG.pdf)—standards in higher education that guide best practices for administrators supporting EDI, LGBTQ+, and other issues on campuses.

5. **LGBTQ+ Scholars of Color** (https://lgbtqsoc.wordpress.com)—a community of LGBTQ+ BIPOC faculty, post-docs, and graduate students.

6. **National Association of Diversity Officers in Higher Education** *Standards of Professional Practice for Chief Diversity Officers in Higher Education 2.0* (https://nadohe.memberclicks.net/assets/2020SPPI/_NADOHE%20SPP2.0_200131_FinalFormatted.pdf)—a list of comprehensive equity, diversity, and inclusion (EDI) standards that guide overarching EDI work on campus.

7. **NASPA Queer People of Color in Higher Education** (https://www.naspa.org/course/queer-people-of-color-in-higher-education)—a resource for LGBTQ+ BIPOC higher education professionals.

8. **UCLA LGBTQ Campus Resource Center** (https://lgbtq.ucla.edu)—an exemplar of LGBTQ+ counseling support.

9. **Equity in Mental Health Framework** (https://equityinmentalhealth.org)—a list of 10 recommendations for supporting the mental health support and programs for BIPOC students.

10. **Trevor Project** (https://www.thetrevorproject.org)—a 24/7 hotline for LGBTQ+ young people experiencing crisis, suicidality, or general support (866-488-7386).

**REFERENCES**

American Psychological Association. (2015). Psychological practice guidelines with transgender and gender nonconforming clients. *American Psychologist, 70*(9), 832–864. https://doi.org/10.1037/a0039906

Association for Lesbian, Gay, Bisexual, and Transgender Issues in Counseling. (2009). *Competencies for counseling transgender clients.* https://www.counseling.org/docs/default-source/competencies/algbtic_competencies.pdf?sfvrsn=d8d3732f_12

Baumann, J. (2019). *Love and resistance: Out of the closet into the Stonewall era.* W. W. Norton.

Bell, D. A., Jr. (1980). Brown v. Board of Education and the interest–convergency dilemma. *Harvard Law Review, 93*(3), 518–533. https://doi.org/10.2307/1340546

Bensimon, E. M. (2004). The diversity scorecard: A learning approach to institutional change. *Change, 6*(1), 44–52. https://doi.org/10.1080/00091380409605083

Bowleg, L. (2008). When Black + lesbian + woman ≠ Black lesbian woman: The methodological challenges of qualitative and quantitative intersectionality research. *Sex Roles, 59,* 312–325. https://doi.org/10.1007/s11199-008-9400-z

Burnes, T. R. (2017). *Teaching LGBTQ psychology: Queering innovative pedagogy and practice.* American Psychological Association.

Campus Pride Index. (n.d.). *Welcome to the Campus Pride Index.* https://www.campuspride index.org/

Colpitts, E., & Gahagan, J. (2016). The utility of resilience as a conceptual framework for understanding and measuring LGBTQ health. *International Journal for Equity in Health, 15,* 60. https://doi.org/10.1186/s12939-016-0349-1

Crenshaw, K. W. (1989). Demarginalizing the intersection of race and sex: A Black feminist critique of antidiscrimination doctrine, feminist theory, and antiracist politics. *University of Chicago Legal Forum, 1989*(1), 139–167. https://chicagounbound.uchicago.edu/cgi/viewcontent.cgi?article=1052&context=uclf

Duberman, M. (1993). *Stonewall: The definitive story of the LGBTQ rights uprising that changed America.* PlumCircle.

Fowler, S. B., & DePauw, K. P. (2005). Dual-career queer couple hiring in southwest Virginia: Or, the contract that was not one. *Journal of Lesbian Studies, 9*(4), 73–88. https://doi.org/10.1300/J155v09n04_06

Fredriksen-Goldsen, K. I., Emlet, C. A., Kim, H. J., Muraco, A., Erosheva, E. A., Goldsen, J., & Hoy-Ellis, C. P. (2013). The physical and mental health of lesbian, gay male, and bisexual (LGB) older adults: The role of key health indicators and risk and protective factors. *The Gerontologist, 53*(4), 664–675. https://doi.org/10.1093/geront/gns123

Grossman, A. H., D'Augelli, A. R., & Frank, J. A. (2011). Aspects of psychological resilience among transgender youth. *Journal of LGBT Youth, 8*(2), 103–115. https://doi.org/10.1080/19361653.2011.541347

Harper, S. R., & Baxter, K. S. (2020). Engaging queer students. In S. J. Quaye, S. R. Harper, & S. L. Pendakur (Eds.), *Student engagement in higher education: Theoretical perspectives and practical approaches for diverse populations* (3rd ed., pp. 161–178). Routledge.

Hurtado, S., Griffin, K. A., Arellano, L., & Guellar, M. (2008). Assessing the value of climate assessments. *Journal of Diversity in Higher Education, 1*(4), 204–221. https://doi.org/10.1037/a0014009

Institute of Medicine. (2011, March). *The health of lesbian, gay, bisexual, and transgender people: Building a foundation for better understanding.* https://www.nap.edu/resource/13128/LGBT-Health-2011-Report-Brief.pdf

Kortegast, C. A., Jaekel, K. S., & Nicolazzo, Z. (2021). Thirty years of LGBTQ prepublication knowledge production in higher education research: A critical summative content analysis of ASHE conference sessions. *Journal of Homosexuality, 68*(10), 1639–1663. https://doi.org/10.1080/00918369.2019.1702351

Linley, J., & Nguyen, D. (2015). LGBTQ experiences in curricular contexts. In D.-L. Stewart, K. A. Renn, & G. B. Brazelton (Eds.), *Gender and sexual diversity in US higher education: Contexts and opportunities for LGBTQ college students* (pp. 41–53). Jossey-Bass.

Marine, S. B., & Nicolazzo, Z. (2014). Names that matter: Exploring the tensions of campus LGBTQ centers and trans* inclusion. *Journal of Diversity in Higher Education, 7*(4), 265–281. https://doi.org/10.1037/a0037990

Mathies, N., Coleman, T., McKie, R. M., Woodford, M. R., Courtice, E. L., Travers, R., & Renn, K. A. (2019). Hearing "that's so gay" and "no homo" on academic outcomes for LGBQ+ college students. *Journal of LGBT Youth, 16*(3), 255–277. https://doi.org/10.1080/19361653.2019.1571981

Messinger, L. (2011). A qualitative analysis of faculty advocacy on LGBT issues on campus. *Journal of Homosexuality, 58*(9), 1281–1305. https://doi.org/10.1080/00918369.2011.605740

Meyer, I. H. (1995). Minority stress and mental health in gay men. *Journal of Health and Social Behavior, 36*(1), 38–56. https://doi.org/10.2307/2137286

Meyer, I. H. (2003). Prejudice, social stress, and mental health in lesbian, gay, and bisexual populations: Conceptual issues and research evidence. *Psychological Bulletin, 129*(5), 674–697. https://doi.org/10.1037/0033-2909.129.5.674

Meyer, I. H. (2010). Identity, stress, and resilience in lesbians, gay men, and bisexuals of color. *The Counseling Psychologist, 38*(3), 442–454. https://doi.org/10.1177/0011000009351601

Meyer, I. H. (2015). Resilience in the study of minority stress and health of sexual and gender minorities. *Psychology of Sexual Orientation and Gender Diversity, 2*(3), 209. https://doi.org/10.1037/sgd0000132

Mobley, S. D., Jr., & Johnson, J. M. (2019). "No pumps allowed": The "problem" with gender expression and the Morehouse College "appropriate attire policy." *Journal of Homosexuality, 66*(7), 867–895. https://doi.org/10.1080/00918369.2018.1486063

Mundy, D. E. (2018). Identity, visibility & measurement: How university LGBTQ centers engage and advocate for today's LGBTQ Student. *Journal of Public Interest Communications, 2*(2). https://doi.org/10.32473/jpic.v2.i2.p239

Pitcher, E. N., Camacho, T. P., Renn, K. A., & Woodford, M. R. (2018). Affirming policies, programs, and supportive services: Using an organizational perspective to understand LGBTQ+ student success. *Journal of Diversity in Higher Education, 11*(2), 117–132. https://doi.org/10.1037/dhe0000048

Rankin, S., Weber, G., Blumenfeld, W., & Frazer, S. (2010). *2010 State of higher education for lesbian, gay, bisexual and transgender people*. Campus Pride. https://www.campuspride.org/wp-content/uploads/campuspride2010lgbtreportssummary.pdf

Ratts, M., Singh, A. A., Nasser-McMillan, S., Butler, S. K., & McCullough, J. R. (2016). Multicultural and social justice competencies: Guidelines for the counseling profession. *Journal of Multicultural Counseling and Development, 44*(1), 28–48. https://doi.org/10.1002/jmcd.12035

Renn, K. A. (2010). LGBT and queer research in higher education: The state and status of the field. *Educational Researcher, 39*(2), 132–141. https://doi.org/10.3102/0013189X10362579

Self, J. M., & Hudson, K. D. (2015). Dangerous waters and brave space: A critical feminist inquiry of campus LGBTQ Centers. *Journal of Gay & Lesbian Social Services, 27*(2), 216–245. https://doi.org/10.1080/10538720.2015.1021985

Singh, A. A., Hays, D. G., & Watson, L. (2011). Strength in the face of adversity: Resilience strategies of transgender individuals. *Journal of Counseling & Development, 89*(1), 20–27. https://doi.org/10.1002/j.1556-6678.2011.tb00057.x

Singh, A. A., & McKleroy, V. S. (2011). "Just getting out of bed is a revolutionary act": The resilience of transgender people of color who have survived traumatic life events. *Traumatology, 17*(2), 34–44. https://doi.org/10.1177/1534765610369261

Singh, A. A., Meng, S., & Hansen, A. (2013). "It's already hard enough being a student": Developing affirming college environments for trans youth. *Journal of LGBT Youth, 10*(3), 208–223. https://doi.org/10.1080/19361653.2013.800770

Singh, A. A., Meng, S., & Hansen, A. (2014). "I am my own gender": Resilience strategies of trans youth. *Journal of Counseling & Development, 92*(2), 208–218.

Truth, S. (1863). *Ain't I a woman*. https://www.thesojournertruthproject.com

Wilkerson, I. (2020). *Caste: The origins of our discontents*. Penguin Random House.

Williams, D., & Wade-Golden, K. C. (2013). *The chief diversity officer: Strategy, structure, and change management*. Stylus.

Woodford, M. R., Kolb, C. L., Durocher-Radeka, G., & Javier, G. (2014). Lesbian, gay, bisexual, and transgender ally training programs on campus: Current variations and future directions. *Journal of College Student Development, 55*(3), 317–322. https://doi.org/10.1353/csd.2014.0022

Woodford, M. R., & Kulick, A. (2015). Academic and social integration on campus among sexual minority students: The impacts of psychological and experiential campus climate. *American Journal of Community Psychology, 55*(1–2), 13–24. https://doi.org/10.1007/s10464-014-9683-x

Worthington, R. L., Stanley, C. A., & Smith, D. G. (2020, March). *Standards of professional practice for chief diversity officers in higher education 2.0*. National Association of Diversity Officers in Higher Education. https://nadohe.memberclicks.net/assets/2020SPPI/__NADOHE%20SPP2.0_200131_FinalFormatted.pdf

# 2

# Exploring the Complexities of Black Sexual and Gender Minorities on Historically Black Colleges and Universities

Angela D. Ferguson

### KEY KNOWLEDGE AREAS

- *Historical significance of HBCUs.* Upon their arrival to the United States, laws were enacted that denied education to Black people, barring them from learning to read and write. Historically Black Colleges and Universities (HBCUs) were established as early as 1865; their primary mission was, and still is, educating Black Americans.

- *Marginalization and fragmentation.* Black sexual and gender minority (SGM) students attending HBCUs can experience a sense of "intersectional invisibility"; consequently, they may feel marginalized within and outside of their constituent social groups. They can also feel fragmented by experiencing an "either–or" or "both–all" conflict.

- *Campus climate issues and barriers.* Forms of discrimination (e.g., sexism, heterosexism, genderism, homophobia, transphobia) may exist on university campuses in a variety of ways. Institutional practices, policies, and structures, as well as faculty, staff, and students, may directly or indirectly perpetuate a hostile, unwelcoming environment toward Black SGM students.

- *Campus support and interventions.* The campus environment is especially important in helping Black SGM students feel a sense of inclusion, acceptance, comfort, and overall safety in their day-to-day lives. Campuses that

https://doi.org/10.1037/0000281-003
*Affirming LGBTQ+ Students in Higher Education*, D. P. Rivera, R. L. Abreu, and K. A. Gonzalez (Editors)
Copyright © 2022 by the American Psychological Association. All rights reserved.

make strong administrative, faculty, and student pronouncements of their support of Black SGM students show that solidarity and advocacy exist for them on campus.

Research focused on college students, their selection process, and their well-being on college campuses has primarily focused on White, heterosexual, male, Christian, able-bodied upper-middle-class students, with much of this research taking place about predominantly White institutions (PWIs). In recent years, there has been an emerging body of literature that is focused on racial/ethnic minority students on college campuses. While there is a small but growing body of research that explores the experiences of Black students attending Historically Black Colleges and Universities (HBCUs), there is little empirical research that explicitly examines the experiences of Black lesbian, gay, bisexual, transgender, queer, gender nonconforming (sexual and gender minority [SGM]) students attending HBCUs (Mobley & Johnson, 2015). The acronym SGM is not limited to lesbian, gay, bisexual, transgender, queer, and questioning; rather, the term is used throughout the chapter in an effort to be inclusive of and capture the wide range of sexual orientation and gender identities and experiences of people in this group. Black SGM students experience unique challenges as a result of their sexual orientation, gender identity, or gender expression (Rankin, 2005). A few studies have examined the experiences of African American gay or bisexual men (B. Carter, 2013; Means & Jaeger, 2013; Patton, 2011; Strayhorn & Scott, 2012), and lesbian students (Patton & Simmons, 2008). However, much more research is needed to better understand the lived experiences of Black SGM students on HBCUs (Patton & Simmons, 2008).

The purpose of this chapter is to provide a contextual discussion in which to understand African American SGM students who attend HBCUs. This group represents a diverse, intersected group of people. Generally, the literature has discussed and researched "African American/Black" and "SGM" individuals as if they belonged to two separate, independent groups. An artificial separation of race and sexual orientation/gender and sexual identity has been created in psychological research and discourses and obscures the lived experiences of African American SGM people. Moreover, by merely discussing and researching race and sexual orientation/gender identity separately, it oversimplifies and further marginalizes the lives of individuals with intersecting identities, particularly those individuals with multiple categories of social group membership. Cole (2009) asserted that "intersectionality makes plain that gender, race, class, and sexuality simultaneously affect the perceptions, experiences, and opportunities of everyone living in a society stratified along these dimensions" (p. 179). African American SGM students belong to at least three multidimensional social groups (e.g., race, gender, sexual orientation); each group identity is inextricably bound by the other (Reid, 2002). Each social group to which the individual belongs has unique cultural socialization experiences, and each has separate and simultaneous implications related to privilege, oppression, and stigma for the individual.

How people view and understand their social identity(ies) is unique and individual. Although members of respective social groups may share similarities, they also experience their respective social identities differently. The focus of this chapter is on African American SGM college students; however, it is understood that these terms encompass a large, diverse group of people. The terms African American or Black SGM are used interchangeably throughout the chapter. It is acknowledged that African American SGM group members are not a monolithic or homogenous group, but a very diverse group with their own contextual experiences that may have similarities and/or differences with another group that falls within the broad category of racial and sexual/gender minorities. Although SGM group members face numerous barriers and sources of discrimination, respective groups (e.g., Black cisgender gay men) experience unique types of barriers, sources of discrimination, and at times privilege when compared with another group (e.g., transgender Black women). This chapter is not intended to minimize, subordinate, or marginalize any one SGM, and cannot capture the wide, broad, and varied lived experiences of people who identify as African American or Black and SGM. Due to the limited space and scope of the chapter, Black/African American SGMs will be discussed as a collective to highlight the social and psychological complexities that may exist as they navigate living on minority-serving, (cis)heterosexually based HBCU campuses.

The campus climate for Black SGM students at HBCUs is understudied, and very little empirical research has explored Black students' experiences on HBCUs (Gates et al., 2017; Tatum, 2004; Van Camp et al., 2009), and even less has focused on Black SGM students on these college campuses. The chapter will discuss some of the broad issues Black SGM students face in college settings, including invisibility/visibility issues, the absence of a visible SGM community, campus administrators, faculty, staff, and student body who view Black SGM negatively, and the complicit condoning of a heteronormative, homophobic campus climate. The chapter will also include a discussion of the social, personal, interpersonal, academic, and psychological experiences and stressors of Black SGM students who attend HBCUs. Black SGM students live in a contextual world, in which their lives reflect cultural and social messages of both race and sexual/gender identities. As such, it is impossible to discuss Black SGM students without discussing both racial/race-related and sexual/gender identity cultural factors that exist in their lives.

The chapter begins by discussing the creation and existence of HBCUs. It would be remiss to discuss the experiences of African American SGMs on HBCUs without providing an historical context of how HBCUs are located within African American history in this country. African American SGMs are a part of this history and share in the benefits of these educational institutions. Thus, the first section of the chapter will describe the historical context of HBCUs, as they have been instrumental in providing educational opportunities for African Americans. Despite the heteronormative and cissexist climate that exists on HBCU campuses, many African American SGMs elect to attend these colleges and universities. The next section of the chapter will discuss campus climate and college/university selection factors for African Americans; as well as focus on some of the lived experiences of African American SGM students at HBCUs. A final section will discuss ways in which HBCUs can transform their policies and campus climates to be more supportive and embracing of African American SGM students.

## HISTORICALLY BLACK COLLEGES AND UNIVERSITIES

This section is focused on the contextual experience of African American SGM students attending HBCUs. HBCUs have a rich, and significant history, as they were initially created and solely dedicated to educating newly freed African Americans. Although this chapter is not specifically focused on providing or discussing a historical analysis of HBCUs, some discussion of the sociopolitical context and mission of HBCUs is relevant regarding its importance in the Black community. During slavery, all southern states barred enslaved Black people from learning to read and write. After the post-Civil War era, few universities promoted or advocated in their mission a goal to educate Black people. It was during this time that the Freedman's Bureau and several other northern church missionaries (some affiliated with northern White denominations, some affiliated with Black churches) began establishing formal educational campuses for freed African Americans (Gasman et al., 2010).

HBCUs allowed Black men and women to pursue the same educational opportunities as their White counterparts (Albritton, 2012). Mbajekwe (2006) noted, "When the Civil War erupted in 1861 at least 90% of all African Americans were illiterate, and only 28% had received college-or-university-level training from any American institution" (p. 7). Thereafter, several more universities and colleges were founded primarily due to the existence of long-standing discrimination at PWIs that stood against enrolling African Americans in those educational systems. One of the first HBCUs was Cheney University in Pennsylvania, founded in 1837, approximately 3 decades before the Emancipation Proclamation. Today, there are 106 HBCUs in the United States, including both public and private institutions; 27 offer doctoral programs, 52 schools offer master's programs, 83 colleges offer bachelor's degree programs, and 38 schools offer associate degrees.

Despite the long sociohistorical and educational significance of HBCUs, there is a paucity of research that examines African American students' experiences on these campuses. There is even less research focused on examining the experiences of Black SGM students attending HBCUs. Considerably more research has focused on the educational and social experiences of African American students who attend predominantly White institutions (PWIs; Karkouti, 2016; Solórzano et al., 2000; Taylor et al., 2012). Many PWIs have been criticized for having campus climates that are oppressive to and unwelcoming to students of color (Hurtado et al., 1999). The campus environment plays a significant role in a student's sense of belonging, adjustment, educational achievement, mental health, and retention (Brown et al., 2005; Johnson et al., 2007). The selection of a college and/or university is an important step in an individual's life. The student affairs literature has examined factors that influence students' college selection choices; however, much of that literature has focused on the experiences of White students. Although a small body of empirical research has examined students of color's reasons for attending colleges and universities, little is known about what factors influence racial/ethnic minority students' college selection decisions (Smith & Fleming, 2006; Van Camp et al., 2010). Some researchers have suggested that among the many reasons Black students choose a college, race-related reasons do indeed play a role in college choice (Van Camp et al., 2010). Several researchers have found that HBCUs offer greater exposure for students to have Black role models, experience less racial discrimination and racial strain, and feel validated (Berger & Milem, 2000; Fries-Britt & Turner, 2002).

HBCUs have been described as nurturing and affirming of Black students, who in turn feel a greater sense of connection with themselves, each other, and the university. However, while HBCUs may affirm Black students' racial identity collectively, and reduce race-related emotional strain, they have also been criticized for "compel[ling] students who identify as gay or lesbian to suppress these identities while on campus" (Mobley & Johnson, 2015, p. 79), and thus create emotional strain related to their sexual orientation and/or gender identity. Consequently, students who identify as SGM do not always feel welcomed or safe in these spaces.

## CAMPUS CLIMATE

The campus environment plays a significant role in the way in which SGM students experience their academic and personal lives at college (Evans & Broido, 1999). Rankin (2005) defined campus climate as, "the cumulative attitudes, behaviors and standards of employees and students concerning access for, inclusion of, and level of respect for individual and group needs, abilities and potential" (p. 17). Campus climate is an integral factor regarding student academic success, psychological wellness, involvement in athletics, connection to peers and faculty, and campus activities, particularly for students from marginalized communities (Pascarella & Terenzini, 2005). Campus climates are often a microcosm of the larger sociopolitical context, and, as such, they can reflect many of the same types of hostility, prejudice, and oppression that are demonstrated in the larger society. HBCUs are unique and distinctive from predominantly White institutions in that they generally have high enrollments of Black students and they provide a validating race-centered campus environment for African American students. Attending an HBCU can be very empowering for African American students and allows them to encounter less race-related stress, thereby reducing the deleterious effects of racism (e.g., low self-esteem, depression, lowered life satisfaction, anxiety). Although much of this literature does not specifically and intentionally include Black SGM students, they also may experience racial empowerment as well as respite from the negative effects of racism and race-related stress.

HBCUs foster a climate of racial inclusivity, affirmation, and pride for many Black students collectively; however, Black SGM students who attend HBCUs don't always feel that they belong and/or sometimes experience a sense of otherness. Similar to many PWI colleges and universities in the United States, HBCUs impose a heteronormative campus climate. Heteronormativity is a ubiquitous ideal that creates expectations about cisgender sexual attraction/orientation, romantic attraction, sexual and gender expression, and relationship dynamics (Boyer & Lorenz, 2019; Jackson, 2006; Robertson, 2014). Consequently, heterosexuality and heteronormativity privilege and legitimize cisgender heterosexual ideals, values, attractions, and relationships as natural or acceptable, and therefore those who do not conform to this ideal in its entirety are viewed and treated in negative, sometimes physically and verbally abusive, ways (Lewis & Ericksen, 2016).

Many HBCU campus environments are not prepared to meet the diverse needs of SGM students, and as such have not initiated efforts toward assisting them (Patton & Simmons, 2008). Although some campuses have focused on structural diversity, Hurtado (1992) asserted that campuses also need to attend to the other dimensions of the campus climate to create more inclusive environments for SGM students, faculty, and staff.

## INTEGRATION OF INNER AND OUTER PERCEPTIONS OF ONESELF AS A BLACK SEXUAL AND GENDER MINORITY STUDENT

African American SGM students are tasked with negotiating multiple marginalized identities both on- and off-campus. On-campus, they may be negotiating their experience of "otherness" such that although they may feel a part of a Black racial collective, they also may simultaneously feel isolated and marginalized due to their SGM identity. Given these intersecting identities, African American SGM students must negotiate: (a) the salience of any one cultural group identity and group membership in relation to other group memberships; (b) invisibility/visibility concerns and issues; (c) the salience of any one cultural context in relation to sexuality, family, and social relationships; and (d) concurrent forms and experiences of oppression (Fukuyama & Ferguson, 2000).

Due to the continued daily process of negotiating the integration and intersection of multiple, marginalized group identities and multiple forms of oppression, Black SGM students are often at higher risk of experiencing psychological stressors than their White SGM counterparts, as well as their heterosexual racial/ethnic counterparts (Cochran et al., 2003; Hatzenbuehler, 2009). These stressors can result in internalized negative feelings about oneself, membership in and affiliation with one or more social groups, as well as toward members of any one of their respective social identity groups.

## Intersectionality

Much of the literature/research has led researchers, practitioners, academics, and theorists to think of identity from a single, monolithic dimension, "speak[ing] as if race is something Blacks have, sexual orientation is something gays and lesbians have, gender is something women have, ethnicity is something so-called 'ethnics' have" (Gates, 1996, p. 3, as cited in Ferguson & Howard-Hamilton, 2000, p. 284). Consequently, this viewpoint has obscured the complexity of the ways in which individuals navigate multiple group memberships and multiple forms of oppression. Intersectionality research helps analyze how people are located in terms of social structures that capture the power relationship implied by those structures (Stewart & McDermott, 2004). Heterosexuality is positioned as central on most campuses, whether they are PWIs or HBCUs; race is positioned differently on HBCUs than it is on PWIs, such that African American cultural identities are privileged. In this way, Black SGM students can experience privilege based on race on campus, but may also experience marginalization based on sexual orientation or gender/sexual identity. They are in a constant state of maintaining a sense of inner balance and self-concept.

African American SGM students often experience proximal (internalized homophobia, internalized racism) and/or distal stress (e.g., discriminatory events based on race, gender or sexual and/or gender identity); they do not merely contend with a single form of oppression in isolation but rather they contend "with a fluid contextual sexualization of race and racialization of sexuality" (Narváez et al., 2009, p. 65). Thus, Black SGM students do not split their identities but experience them in fluid, intersecting ways. No one identity has primacy over the other; however, the saliency of one or more identities may depend on the environment within which the individual is interacting, the type of oppression(s) the individual experiences at a particular point in time, and/or "intersectional invisibility," which Purdie-Vaughns and Eibach (2008) defined as "the general failure to fully recognize people with intersecting identities as members of their constituent groups" (p. 381). Consequently, Black SGM students can feel marginalized within and outside of their constituent social groups (e.g., feeling visible in their respective racial group but invisible in their SGM identity), thereby simultaneously experiencing being an ingroup and outgroup member in the same space. Hence, on an HBCU, a Black SGM student may at the same time feel empowered and less stigmatized as a Black person, but also feel the stress of stigmatization and marginalization as an SGM person. As one of the participants recounted in Duran's (2019) qualitative study about being a gay Black man in higher education settings:

> Sometimes it feels like I'm an outsider in a niche group. . . . It feels like I'm not accepted anywhere. With People of Color, I'm gay. With gay people, I'm a Person of Color. I'm always different even when I'm around people who I'm supposed to be like. It's hard to find your people. Hard to get through. (p. 1)

## Stigma, Discrimination, and Microaggressions

African American SGM students may experience simultaneous forms of discrimination (e.g., sexism, heterosexism, genderism, homophobia, transphobia) in a variety of ways. Institutional practices, policies, and structures may indirectly perpetuate a hostile, unwelcoming environment, while fellow collegians, faculty, and staff may directly express overt and covert negativity and hostility toward African American SGM students (Collins & Bilge, 2016).

While HBCUs have historically been at the forefront in championing controversial issues in Black communities (Mobley & Johnson, 2015), many "have long struggled with a reputation of being unwelcoming, if not overtly hostile, to gays and lesbians" (McMurtrie, 2013, p. 1). Many Black SGM students navigate proximal (e.g., internalized heterosexism) and distal (e.g., heterosexist events) stressors on college campuses and often live invisible lives (Boykin, 1996; Squire & Mobley, 2015). Depending on the way(s) in which their social identities have developed, some may be more vulnerable to experiencing significant psychological and physical symptoms due to the chronic and cumulative stress as a result of persistent pernicious attacks on some aspect of their identity(ies). Some researchers have suggested that African American SGM students' voices and experiences are silenced and that they live in the "margins" (Squire & Mobley, 2015). One consequence of experiencing the stress and stigmatization connected to living in the "margins" is concealment. Some African American SGM students may conceal their SGM identity relative to their contextual interactions with others. Ferguson et al. (2014) suggested that when negotiating multiple identities, SGM individuals must determine the costs and benefits of invisibility versus visibility. Although the purposeful concealment of one's sexual orientation, sexual identity, or gender expression may result in protection from insidious forms of oppression, it also "has the potential to disempower the individual and to relegate this identity as secondary or tertiary relative to other more visible identities" (Ferguson et al., 2014, p. 55). By concealing their SGM identity, African American SGM collegians may feel included among their racial group but may also experience feelings of depression, anxiety, or difficulty establishing friendships and romantic relationships, as they may still be exposed to blatant or microaggressive exchanges with others.

A similar but different consequence that may result from enduring chronic stress and stigmatization is fragmentation. Ferguson et al. (2014) noted that sexual minorities of color may attempt to protect themselves from the dissonance of incongruous multiple identities by creating clear boundaries between separate aspects of their identities to create a sense of psychological safety. Consequently, African American SGM students may find themselves concealing their SGM identity as a strategy to buffer themselves against hostile, discriminatory, prejudicial actions from faculty and other students. However, fragmentation has the potential to create psychological distress for the student given the constant vigilance and monitoring needed to ensure that their respective identities remain discrete and separate from one another (Ferguson et al., 2014). This kind of psychological distress and vigilance has the potential to cause African American SGM students to be isolated, engage in risky behaviors (e.g., drug and alcohol use), experience academic distress and/or failure, find difficulty in establishing social relationships, or develop physical problems (e.g., weight gain/loss; insomnia).

Depending on how an individual's respective identities develop (i.e., unacceptance to acceptance), a heteronormative and cissexist campus may not feel especially negative. It is important to consider that an individual's respective social identity may have emerged in terms of salience and centrality at different ages in their life, may have evolved unevenly, and likely influenced the manner in which the individual engages in friendships, family, and with sexual/romantic partners (Ferguson et al., 2014). Thus, for individuals whose sexual and gender identity is not very advanced or salient, heteronormative and cissexist messages may not adversely affect their sense of self and desire to refrain from disclosing that specific identity.

## CAMPUS SUPPORT AND AWARENESS

HBCU campus environments are spaces where Black students can openly explore, examine, and affirm their racial identity. Senior leadership on HBCUs can also make their campuses supportive of their SGM students and engage the entire campus to address and ameliorate the negative effects of SGM discrimination and the pervasive heterosexism and cissexism. Some HBCUs have begun implementing new initiatives to make their campuses more SGM-inclusive; however, the interventions that have been created "are oftentimes limited in either scope or visibility" (Mobley & Johnson, 2015, p. 80). In addition, many institutions have yet to create and implement policies that protect and support SGM students, faculty, staff, and administrators (Messinger, 2009). Hurtado et al. (1999) conceptualized racial climate as a multidimensional phenomenon that included an interchange "between external forces (governmental policy and sociohistorical factors) and internal forces (the respective racial context of the institution)" (Lewis & Shah, 2021, p. 2). HBCU leaders can use a similar conceptualization when looking at campus diversity about SGM students and strategically examine (in terms of both external and internal factors) how their campuses are inclusive and rejecting of various aspects of diversity to make systemic changes for SGM students, faculty, and staff. This kind of strategy must include discussions among and between all levels of the campus community (i.e., campus administrators, students, faculty, and staff).

### Structural/Administrative Interventions

One way that higher education administration has traditionally addressed diversity has been to develop various diversity and inclusion initiatives. HBCU senior leadership (e.g., president, provosts) can develop and implement policies that prohibit discrimination and harassment based on sexual orientation and gender/sexual identity for students, faculty, and staff (Robin & Hamner, 2000). These policies demonstrate the university's effort to affirm SGM individuals on campus, as well as convey the institution's stance against discriminatory behavior toward SGM people. The policies should be visible and easily accessible for the entire campus community (e.g., student, faculty, and staff handbooks; university catalogs and brochures; university website), with procedures for reporting grievances and anti-LGBTQ+ crimes to university personnel and/or campus and local authorities to ensure that university policies are upheld and enforced.

Although policies and initiatives are ways that HBCUs can begin to create a safe, secure, and welcoming campus environment for SGM students, "campus administrations must examine the roles they play in reinforcing and perpetuating heteronormative practices that privilege some while marginalizing others" (Mobley & Johnson, 2015, p. 82). This examination can include discussions that address possible stereotypes, stigmas, and biases campus leaders may have about the SGM community. Given that these discourses can be challenging, trainings and workshops led by off-campus consultants may facilitate these types of conversations. Additionally, attendance at leadership meetings such as the HBCU Diversity and Inclusion Leadership Summit (https://www.hrc.org/resources/hbcu-diversity-and-inclusion-leadership-summit) for university presidents and senior executives can be useful in helping campus leaders strategically examine how their existing policies and traditions may implicitly and explicitly impose heteronormative practices in residence life, student activities, athletics, student organizations, religious services, curricular offerings, and employment benefits and health care. Student leaders (e.g., officers of sororities, fraternities, clubs and organizations, team captains) should also be included in the strategic examination of their respective traditions, practices, and policies that may perpetuate heteronormative biases.

Senior leadership can provide many of the structural policies that are needed for campus climate change; student affairs personnel (e.g., residence life, university counseling center, health center, student activities, chaplain services) are strategically positioned within university leadership to examine whether and how various aspects of campus and student life are inclusive of SGM collegians. Student development is a primary function for student affairs professionals, and because they are often the leaders on campus responsible for creating and coordinating student programs and services, their respective offices can provide the internal forces component of campus climate change. With this in mind, student affairs staff should remain attentive to the needs of SGM students, particularly in the areas of admissions and retention services, student life programming, student organizations, student governance, counseling services, residence life, health centers, religious services, and public safety offices.

### Student Affairs Interventions

Each office of student affairs can engage in SGM workshops and trainings that focus on three specific areas: awareness, knowledge, and skills. Topical discussions can address:

- *Awareness*: What information or misinformation do staff members have about Black SGM individuals? How was this information shaped or learned?

- *Knowledge*: What kind of knowledge is important to have when thinking about Black SGM individuals (e.g., language, sexuality, gender, identity development, intersectional identities)? How does implicit bias influence attitudes, perceptions, and decision-making relative to Black SGM individuals?
- *Skills*: How can individuals develop skills when interacting with Black SGM students, such as pronoun usage, awareness of microaggressions, advocacy training, sexual harassment, or intimate partner violence (IPV) among same-sex couples?

Being equipped to understand SGM students from an awareness, knowledge, and skills position will help staff in these offices address some of the longstanding heteronormative practices and traditions on their campuses, as well as examine their own assumptions and the biases they may hold about these collegians. For example, many structural aspects of the campus, as well as student activities and organizations are separated by (cis)gender; "any segregation of students by gender presents a problem for individuals who transcend gender. Restrooms, sports teams, and some student organizations are segregated by gender" (K. Carter, 2000, p. 275). Respective student affairs staff (e.g., resident life, student activities and organization, athletics) will have the awareness, knowledge, and skills to develop institutional changes to be inclusive of SGM students. Additionally, SGM collegians are not a monolithic/homogenous group, therefore the needs of cisgender gay men may be very different from the needs of transwomen or gender-nonconforming collegians. Having this kind of awareness and knowledge will lead to more appropriate changes on campus.

Student affairs leadership can create task forces comprised of staff, students, and faculty to examine campus traditions and practices. Discussions can include examination and exploration of how privilege and oppression exist on campus; how various forms of "isms" may exist on campus that affect all students; how implicit bias influences attitudes and perceptions of students, staff, and faculty; where to create safe spaces on campus (e.g., SGM resource center, SGM student club/organization); and how ally training will be conducted with student groups, faculty, and campus staff. Members of the task force should be diverse, representative, and inclusive of SGM individuals and allies in the campus community. For campuses in which SGM students or staff are reluctant to disclose their sexual minority identity, the task force may need to consult with a community resource that can reflect the voice(s) of Black sexual minorities. It is important to be mindful that all forms of oppression affect not only one group but all groups. Oppression is complex and intersected; those who perpetuate "isms" have as much to learn as those who are the recipients of "isms." Task forces such as these are not only important for information gathering, but also for creating informal networks and allies throughout the campus.

Campus-wide workshops seminars, intergroup dialogues, and discussions can be organized to reach as many members of the campus community as possible, as well as group-specific workshops (e.g., sororities/fraternities, campus police, student government, faculty, health center). Task forces can help strategize the best ways in which to plan and conduct these workshops, such that all members of the campus community can be engaged in a rich, holistic discourse focused on awareness, knowledge, and skills regarding some of the stressors, issues, and academic challenges SGM students experience on campus.

**Academic and Faculty Interventions**

Academic spaces are not immune from discrimination, microaggressions, and implicit biases from fellow collegians as well as from faculty members. Depending on the academic discipline, some faculty may assume that "those students" (SGM) are not in their classrooms. Other faculty may not see the importance or relevance of gaining awareness, knowledge, or skills when interacting with and teaching SGM students. The academic life of students is an important aspect of knowledge acquisition, as well as student interaction. Integrating coursework, research, course readings, and discussions related to SGM can help foster awareness and understanding about the SGM community for all students. Moreover, by not acquiring SGM awareness, knowledge, and skills, faculty potentially perpetuate the invisibility, separation, discrimination, and oppression that SGM students experience. For example, in the social science disciplines, infusing an intersectional lens about SGM individuals in course content and readings helps prepare students to develop competence when working with diverse populations, as well as develop social justice acumen. Providing examples of SGM individuals within academic disciplines provides SGM students with opportunities to feel empowered and develop a sense of pride.

Much of the academic culture is heteronormative, and for HBCUs the academic culture may also project a great deal of Black pride, discussions of Black historical figures, and class examples that may only include Black cisgender people, often creating classroom spaces that may be "chilly climates" for SGM students. Some faculty may not conceive or be mindful of using class examples that are inclusive of Black SGM historical figures. Hegemonic forms of power position diverse marginalized minority groups differently, thereby privileging some identities over others. Hence, African American SGM students may find that their intersections of oppression differ significantly from the intersections of oppression for their heterosexual cisgender classmates. For gender nonconforming SGM students, their preferred pronoun may be ignored or used intermittently by faculty. These microaggressive omissions also contribute to a chilly classroom climate. Consequently, SGM students' voices may be silenced for fear of disclosing their sexual orientation or sexual/gender identity or feeling that their comments and viewpoints will be invalidated, devalued, or perceived as irrelevant by fellow collegians and/or by the faculty. Additionally, SGM students may compartmentalize their identities, thereby only revealing an identity(ies) that allows them to feel safe in the classroom. However, given that African American SGM students' intersecting identities are diverse, engaging in compartmentalization may not be desirable or an option. Consequently, the classroom space may become a hostile, toxic, alienating environment for some SGM students.

Faculty can play a significant role in cultivating an inclusive, engaging, and welcoming classroom for SGM students. Garvey et al. (2019) found that the students in their study felt more affirmed when classes were offered that pertained to LGBT and queer studies, as well as when classroom discussions included topics that addressed race, sexuality, and gender. Some faculty have had training in pedagogy, but fewer have been trained to teach from an intersectional position and to be mindful of students with multiple marginalized identities. Deans and chairpersons will need to be intentional about structurally dedicating time to schedule workshops and trainings for faculty and graduate assistants that focus on (a) awareness of their own assumptions and biases that serve as barriers to effectively creating an inclusive classroom climate; (b) knowledge of Black SGM readings, course materials, and assignments they can use in the classroom; (c) knowledge of microaggressive language and behaviors; and (d) skill development of pedagogy that will assist them in their teaching approach. Strategically introducing and integrating nonheteronormative material in class discussions, assignments, and didactic material is a way to facilitate students' critical self-reflection, and to support, challenge, and expand students' current realities. The faculty member assumes the responsibility of facilitating and maintaining a safe and respectful classroom environment that acknowledges and supports discussions of difference, as well as similarities (Goldberg & Allen, 2018).

## CONCLUSION

The Black community is very diverse, and SGM individuals are a part of this large racial group. HBCUs continue to provide an essential, relevant environment in which African Americans can experience racial pride and affirmation. However, HBCUs that ignore the intersected identities of some of its students within this racial group perpetuate oppressive ideas, attitudes, and behaviors that are contrary to the social justice ideals and aspirations African Americans before them fought so hard for. Black SGM students walk a narrow and sometimes slippery slope in trying to find a sense of belonging within their respective racial/cultural groups. While being on an HBCU campus can bring these students a great sense of racial connectedness, they can also experience a deep sense of isolation and disconnection. The oppressive structures of heterosexism and homophobia prevent Black SGM students from achieving their full academic potential, fully participating in campus activities, and fully engaging in developing social and romantic relationships. Rankin (2005) stated that faculty, staff, and administrators can also suffer the negative effects of heterosexism and homophobia, which can prevent them from mentoring and supporting Black SGM students.

Unacknowledged privilege exists on many HBCU campuses; senior leadership needs to be intentional and have a sustainable long-term organizational commitment to creating an inclusive, safe, and welcoming environment for Black SGM students, faculty, and staff. Systemic passivity due to concerns that the discourse will be disquieting to the majority population will not sustain campus-wide changes intended to create inclusive spaces, dialogue, perceptions, and attitudes. Life on college campuses presents opportunities for academic, personal, spiritual, and social growth for its students. "As HBCUs celebrate the spirit of a shared cultural identity, the notion of highlighting diversity within the Black community offers an exciting and enriching opportunity for students to better understand the contours and unlimited possibilities of identity" (Greenfield et al., 2015, p. 45).

## DISCUSSION QUESTIONS

1. What initiatives, policies, and actions need to occur to create sustainable change on your campus to support/advocate for Black SGM students?
2. What are the unique characteristics and challenges that African American SGM students experience on your campus?
3. What initiatives are needed on your campus to address heterosexism, cissexism, homophobia, and transphobia on your campus?
4. What systems of power exist on your campus that marginalize Black SGM students, and what can be done to equip educators to address these systems?
5. What factors impact African American SGM students' perceptions of inclusion and exclusion at an HBCU?

**TABLE 2.1. Resources**

| Resource name | Description | Source | Helpful for: |
| --- | --- | --- | --- |
| Defining a Common Language | Exercises to gain awareness and common understanding of sexuality, sexual orientation, gender identity terms. | *Teaching for Diversity and Social Justice*, edited by M. Adams, L. A. Bell, and P. Griffin (1997). Routledge. | • Student Affairs<br>• Students<br>• Faculty |
| Gay and Lesbian Medical Association (GLMA) | Organization of lesbian, gay, bisexual, and transgender physicians, medical students, and their supporters to maximize the quality of health services for lesbian, gay, bisexual, and transgender people. | https://www.glma.org | • Student Affairs<br>• Students<br>• Faculty<br>• Health care |

**TABLE 2.1. Resources (*Continued*)**

| Resource name | Description | Source | Helpful for: |
|---|---|---|---|
| *Guidelines for Psychotherapy With LGB Clients* and *Guidelines for Psychological Practice With Transgender and Gender Nonconforming People* | Practice guidelines provide psychologists with a frame of reference for affirmative, culturally competent, developmentally appropriate, and trans affirmative psychological practice with gay, lesbian, bisexual, transgender, and gender non-conforming (TGNC) people across the lifespan. They also provide knowledge and referenced scholarship in the areas of affirmative intervention, assessment, identity, relationships, diversity, education, training, advocacy, and research. | https://www.apa.org | • Student Affairs<br>• Mental health |
| National Black Justice Coalition | A civil rights organization dedicated to the empowerment of Black lesbian, gay, bisexual, transgender, queer, and same-gender-loving (LGBTQ/SGL) people. NBJC's mission is to end racism, homophobia, and LGBTQ/SGL bias and stigma. | https://www.nbjc.org | • Administrators<br>• Student Affairs<br>• Students<br>• Faculty<br>• Law schools |
| National Consortium of Directors of LGBT Resources in Higher Education | Organization dedicated to achieving higher education environments in which lesbian, gay, bisexual, and transgender students, faculty, staff, administrators, and alumni have equity in every respect. | https://www.lgbtcampus.org | • Administrators<br>• Student Affairs<br>• Faculty |

(*continues*)

**TABLE 2.1. Resources (*Continued*)**

| Resource name | Description | Source | Helpful for: |
|---|---|---|---|
| TransWomen of Color Collective (TWOCC) | A national organizing collective led by trans women of color created to uplift the narratives, leadership, and lived experiences of trans folks of color. Historically, has been the catalyst of change for social justice movements. | https://www.twocc.us/ | • Student Affairs<br>• Students<br>• Faculty |
| Human Rights Campaign (HRC) | Human Rights Campaign strives to end discrimination against LGBTQ people and realize a world that achieves fundamental fairness and equality for all. | https://www.hrc.org | • Administrators<br>• Student Affairs<br>• Students<br>• Faculty |
| National LGBTQ Bar Association | A national association of lawyers, judges, and other legal professionals, law students, activists, and affiliated lesbian, gay, bisexual, and transgender legal organizations. The LGBT Bar promotes justice in and through the legal profession for the LGBTQ+ community in all its diversity. | https://lgbtbar.org | • Student Affairs<br>• Students<br>• Faculty<br>• Law school |
| LGBTQ National Help Center | Serving the lesbian, gay, bisexual, transgender, queer, and questioning community by providing free and confidential peer support and local resources. | http://www.glnh.org | • Student Affairs<br>• Mental health<br>• Students<br>• Faculty |

**TABLE 2.1. Resources (*Continued*)**

| Resource name | Description | Source | Helpful for: |
|---|---|---|---|
| Lambda Legal Defense and Education Network | A nonprofit national organization committed to achieving full recognition of the civil rights of lesbians, gay men, bisexuals, transgender people, and everyone living with HIV through impact litigation, education, and public policy work. | https://www.lambdalegal.org | • Student Affairs<br>• Students<br>• Faculty |
| Black and LGBTQ: Approaching Intersectional Conversations | Approaches to consider before, during, and after difficult conversations with people who are uninformed about race, queer identities, or the intersection of both. | The Trevor Project<br>http://www.thetrevorproject.org | • Administrators<br>• Student Affairs<br>• Students<br>• Faculty |

## REFERENCES

Adams, M., Bell, L. A., & Griffin, P. (Eds.). (1997). *Teaching for diversity and social justice*. Routledge.

Albritton, T. J. (2012). Educating our own: The historical legacy of HBCUs and their relevance for educating a new generation of leaders. *The Urban Review, 44*(3), 311–331. https://doi.org/10.1007/s11256-012-0202-9

Berger, J. B., & Milem, J. F. (2000). Exploring the impact of historically Black colleges in promoting the development of undergraduates' self-concept. *Journal of College Student Development, 41*(4), 381–394.

Boyer, S. J., & Lorenz, T. K. (2019). The impact of heteronormative ideals imposition on sexual orientation questioning distress. *Psychology of Sexual Orientation and Gender Diversity, 7*(1), 91–100. https://doi.org/10.1037/sgd0000352

Boykin, K. (1996). *One more river to cross: Black & gay in America*. Doubleday.

Brown, A. R., Morning, C., & Watkins, C. (2005). Influence of African American engineering student perceptions of campus climate on graduation rates. *The Journal of Engineering Education, 94*(2), 263–271. https://doi.org/10.1002/j.2168-9830.2005.tb00847.x

Carter, B. A. (2013). "Nothing better or worse than being Black, gay, and in the band": A qualitative examination of gay undergraduates participating in historically Black college or university marching bands. *Journal of Research in Music Education, 61*(1), 26–43. https://doi.org/10.1177/0022429412474470

Carter, K. A. (2000). Transgenderism and college students: Issues of gender identity and its role on our campuses. In V. A. Wall & N. J. Evans (Eds.), *Toward acceptance: Sexual orientation issues on campus* (pp. 261–282). University Press of America.

Cochran, S. D., Sullivan, J. G., & Mays, V. M. (2003). Prevalence of mental disorders, psychological distress, and mental health services use among lesbian, gay, and bisexual adults in the United States. *Journal of Consulting and Clinical Psychology, 71*(1), 53–61. https://doi.org/10.1037/0022-006X.71.1.53

Cole, E. R. (2009). Intersectionality and research in psychology. *American Psychologist, 64*(3), 170–180. https://doi.org/10.1037/a0014564

Collins, P. H., & Bilge, S. (2016). *Intersectionality* (2nd ed.). Wiley & Sons.

Duran, A. (2019, September 16). "Outsiders in a niche group": Using intersectionality to examine resilience for queer students of color. *Journal of Diversity in Higher Education, 14*(2), 217–227. https://doi.org/10.1037/dhe0000144

Evans, N. J., & Broido, E. M. (1999). Coming out in college residence halls: Negotiation, meaning making, challenges, supports. *Journal of College Student Development, 40*(6), 658–668.

Ferguson, A. D., Carr, G., & Snitman, A. (2014). Intersections of race–ethnicity, gender and sexual minority communities. In M. L. Miville & A. D. Ferguson (Eds.), *Handbook of race–ethnicity and gender in psychology* (pp. 45–63). Springer. https://doi.org/10.1007/978-1-4614-8860-6_3

Ferguson, A. D., & Howard-Hamilton, M. (2000). Addressing issues of multiple identities for women of color on college campuses. In V. A. Wall & N. J. Evans (Eds.), *Toward acceptance: Sexual orientation issues on campus* (pp. 283–297). University Press of America.

Fries-Britt, S., & Turner, B. (2002). Uneven stories: Successful Black collegians at a Black and a White campus. *The Review of Higher Education, 25*(3), 315–330. https://doi.org/10.1353/rhe.2002.0012

Fukuyama, M. A., & Ferguson, A. D. (2000). Lesbian gay, and bisexual people of color: Understanding cultural complexity and managing multiple oppressions. In R. M. Perez, K. A. DeBord, & K. J. Bieschke (Eds.), *Handbook of counseling and psychotherapy with lesbian, gay and bisexual clients* (pp. 81–105). American Psychological Association. https://doi.org/10.1037/10339-004

Garvey, J. C., Mobley, S. D., Summerville, K. S., & Moore, G. T. (2019). Queer and trans* students of color: Navigating identity disclosure and college contexts. *The Journal of Higher Education, 90*(1), 150–178. https://doi.org/10.1080/00221546.2018.1449081

Gasman, M., Lundy-Wagner, V., Ransom, T., & Bowman, N., III. (2010). *Unearthing promise and potential: Our nation's Historically Black Colleges and Universities*. Josey-Bass.

Gates, T. G., Quinn, C. R., & Phillips, M. L., Jr. (2017). LGBTQ-affirmative teaching at historically Black colleges and universities: Understanding program directors' views. *The Journal of Baccalaureate Social Work, 22*(1), 131–142. https://doi.org/10.18084/1084-7219.22.1.131

Goldberg, A. E., & Allen, K. R. (2018). Teaching undergraduates about LGBTQ identities, families, and intersectionality. *Family Relations, 67*(1), 176–191. https://doi.org/10.1111/fare.12224

Greenfield, D. F., Innouvong, T., Aglugub, R. J., & Yusuf, I. A. (2015). HBCUs as critical context for identity work: Reflections, experiences, and lessons learned. *New Directions for Higher Education, 2015*(170), 37–48. https://doi.org/10.1002/he.20130

Hatzenbuehler, M. L. (2009). How does sexual minority stigma "get under the skin"? A psychological mediation framework. *Psychological Bulletin, 135*(5), 707–730. https://doi.org/10.1037/a0016441

Hurtado, S. (1992). The campus racial climate. *The Journal of Higher Education, 63*(5), 539–569. https://doi.org/10.1080/00221546.1992.11778388

Hurtado, S., Milem, J., Clayton-Pedersen, A., & Allen, W. R. (1999). *Enacting diverse learning environments: Improving the climate for racial/ethnic diversity in higher education*. Jossey-Bass.

Jackson, S. (2006). Gender, sexuality and heterosexuality: The complexity (and limits) of heteronormativity. *Feminist Theory, 7*(1), 105–121. https://doi.org/10.1177/1464700106061462

Johnson, D. R., Soldner, M., Leonard, J. B., Alvarez, P., Inkelas, K. K., Rowan-Kenyon, H., & Longerbeam, S. (2007). Examining sense of belonging among first-year undergraduates from different racial/ethnic groups. *Journal of College Student Development, 48*(5), 525–542. https://doi.org/10.1353/csd.2007.0054

Karkouti, I. M. (2016). Black students' educational experiences in predominantly White universities: A review of the related literature. *College Student Journal, 50*(1), 59–70.

Lewis, K. R., & Shah, P. P. (2021). Black students' narratives of diversity and inclusion initiatives and the campus racial climate: An interest-convergence analysis. *Journal of Diversity in Higher Education, 14*(2), 189–202. https://doi.org/10.1037/dhe0000147

Lewis, M. W., & Ericksen, K. S. (2016). Improving the climate for LGBTQ students at an historically Black university. *Journal of LGBT Youth, 13*(3), 249–269. https://doi.org/10.1080/19361653.2016.1185761

Mbajekwe, C. O. W. (2006). Introduction. In C. O. W. Mbajekwe (Ed.), *The future of Historically Black Colleges and Universities: Ten presidents speak out* (pp. 3–42). McFarland & Co.

McMurtrie, B. (2013, October 28). Spurred by activists, HBCUs expand their services for gay students. *The Chronicle of Higher Education.* https://www.chronicle.com/article/spurred-by-activists-hbcus-expand-their-services-for-gay-students/

Means, D. R., & Jaeger, A. J. (2013). Black in the rainbow: "Quaring" the Black gay male student experience at historically Black universities. *Journal of African American Males in Education, 4*(2), 124–141.

Messinger, L. (2009). *Creating LGBTQ-friendly campus: How activists on a number of campuses eliminated discriminatory policies.* American Association of University Professors. http://www.aaup.org/article/creating-lgbtq-friendly-campuses

Mobley, S. D., Jr., & Johnson, J. M. (2015). The role of HBCUs in addressing the unique needs of LGBT students. *New Directions for Higher Education, 2015*(170), 79–89. https://doi.org/10.1002/he.20133

Narváez, R. F., Meyer, I. H., Kertzner, R. M., Ouellette, S. C., & Gordon, A. R. (2009). A qualitative approach to the intersection of sexual, ethnic, and gender identities. *Identity, 9*(1), 63–86. https://doi.org/10.1080/15283480802579375

Pascarella, E. T., & Terenzini, P. T. (2005). *How college affects students: A third decade of research* (Vol. 2). Jossey-Bass.

Patton, L. D. (2011). Perspectives on identity, disclosure, and the campus environment among African American gay and bisexual men at one historically Black college. *Journal of College Student Development, 52*(1), 77–100. https://doi.org/10.1353/csd.2011.0001

Patton, L. D., & Simmons, S. L. (2008). Exploring complexities of multiple identities in a Black college environment. *Negro Educational Review, 59*(3–4), 197–215. https://eric.ed.gov/?id=EJ835225

Purdie-Vaughns, V., & Eibach, R. P. (2008). Intersectional invisibility: The distinctive advantages and disadvantages of multiple subordinate-group identities. *Sex Roles, 59,* 377–391. https://doi.org/10.1007/s11199-008-9424-4

Rankin, S. R. (2005). Campus climates for sexual minorities. *New Directions for Student Services, 2005*(111), 17–23. https://doi.org/10.1002/ss.170

Reid, P. T. (2002). Multicultural psychology: Bringing together gender and ethnicity. *Cultural Diversity & Ethnic Minority Psychology, 8*(2), 103–114. https://doi.org/10.1037/1099-9809.8.2.103

Robertson, M. A. (2014). "How do I know I am gay?": Understanding sexual orientation, identity and behavior among adolescents in an LGBT youth center. *Sexuality & Culture, 18,* 385–404. https://doi.org/10.1007/s12119-013-9203-4

Robin, L., & Hamner, K. (2000). Bisexuality: Identities and community. In V. A. Wall & N. J. Evans (Eds.), *Toward acceptance: Sexual orientation issues on campus* (pp. 245–259). University Press of America.

Smith, M. J., & Fleming, M. K. (2006). African American parents in the search stage of college choice: Unintentional contributions to the female to male college enrollment gap. *Urban Education, 41,* 71–10. https://www.naspa.org/images/uploads/main/SmithM-FlemingM_2006_African_American_parents_in_search_stage_of_college_choice.pdf

Solórzano, D., Ceja, M., & Yosso, T. (2000). Critical race theory, racial microaggressions, and campus racial climate: The experiences of African American college students. *The Journal of Negro Education, 69*(1–2), 60–73. https://www.jstor.org/stable/2696265

Squire, D., & Mobley, S. D., Jr. (2015). Negotiating race and sexual orientation in the college choice process of Black Gay Males. *The Urban Review, 47,* 466–491. https://doi.org/10.1007/s11256-014-0316-3

Stewart, A. J., & McDermott, C. (2004). Gender in psychology. *Annual Review of Psychology, 55*(1), 519–544. https://doi.org/10.1146/annurev.psych.55.090902.141537

Strayhorn, T. L., & Scott, J. A. (2012). Coming out of the dark: Black gay men's experiences at historically Black colleges and universities. In R. T. Palmer & J. L. Wood (Eds.), *Black men in college: Implications for HBCUs and beyond* (pp. 26–40). Routledge.

Tatum, B. (2004). The road to racial equality. *Black Issues in Higher Education, 21*(10), 34–35. https://eric.ed.gov/?id=EJ704927

Taylor, M. J., Austin, C. C., Perkins, J. D., & Edwards, J. L. (2012). Sociohistorical privilege in higher education: Implications for African American student psychological adjustment, resiliency, and success at predominately White institutions. In S. R. Notaro (Ed.), *Health disparities among underserved populations: Implications for research, policy and praxis* (pp. 241–261). Emerald Group Publishing Limited. https://doi.org/10.1108/S1479-358X(2012)0000009015

Van Camp, D., Barden, J., & Sloan, L. R. (2010). Predictors of Black students' race-related reasons for choosing an HBCU and intentions to engage in racial identity—Relevant behaviors. *The Journal of Black Psychology, 36*(2), 226–250. https://doi.org/10.1177/0095798409344082

Van Camp, D., Barden, J., Sloan, L. R., & Clarke, R. (2009). Choosing an HBCU: An opportunity to pursue racial self-development. *The Journal of Negro Education, 78*(4), 457–468.

# Planning and Building New Foundations

*Developing Proposals for Creating LGBTQI+ Resources at Community Colleges*

Emalinda L. McSpadden, Leilani Massey, and Ines I. Almarante

### KEY KNOWLEDGE AREAS

- Few community colleges in the United States provide dedicated spaces on campus for service provision and programming for lesbian, gay, bisexual, transgender, queer, intersex, and all other sexual or gender nonbinary minority (LGBTQI+) students, despite evidence that such spaces and programming are beneficial to student mental health and academic success.
- LGBTQI+ students at community colleges historically have diverse identities across sexual orientation, gender identity, race, culture, and socioeconomic status that make enhanced campus-based LGBTQI+ resources more crucial.
- A proposed strategy for planning, proposing, and implementing LGBTQI+ resource spaces on community college campuses calls for research exploring a campus's cultural climate and attitudes toward LGBTQI+ issues, as well as the specific needs of queer-identifying students.

This chapter explores the lack of LGBTQI+ spaces and resources on community college campuses in the United States, as well as the pressing reasons why such resources are necessary in these settings. Following a brief review of the issues currently facing community college students who identify as LGBTQI+, the chapter focuses on the processes through which dedicated LGBTQI+ spaces can be made a reality on community college campuses that have never housed such spaces before. A framework is then proposed for creating proposals to

---

https://doi.org/10.1037/0000281-004
*Affirming LGBTQ+ Students in Higher Education*, D. P. Rivera, R. L. Abreu, and K. A. Gonzalez (Editors)
Copyright © 2022 by the American Psychological Association. All rights reserved.

establish dedicated LGBTQI+ spaces, including recommendations for approaches to campus climate assessment, organization of campus-based stakeholders, and the components of the proposal itself. The chapter concludes with suggestions for how to proceed in establishing an approved LGBTQI+ space and associated programming, including ongoing assessment for the purposes of enhancing sustainability of these valuable spaces and their crucial work.

While the practice is by no means widespread across all 2-year institutions, many community college campuses across the United States do provide at least limited LGBTQI+ services for their students, ranging from basic informational materials to more developed resource offices or centers on campus. It is not at all common, however, for a community college campus to have a dedicated physical space for LGBTQI+ service provision on the premises, although such services might be provided through other established offices, such as women's centers or student life hubs. Generally, there is a lack of well-developed services on community college campuses for LGBTQI+ students, and likewise, there is a lack of research on LGBTQI+ service provision on 2-year campuses (Nguyen et al., 2018). As such, there are no best practices established for outlining processes for establishing LGBTQI+ spaces on community college campuses.

Commonly employed practices leading to creating dedicated LGBTQI+ spaces on 2-year campuses include various styles of needs assessment, collaborations between established stakeholders, and expanding extant non-LGBTQI+ resources to begin including services for LGBTQI+ students. Despite a lack of universality in methods and strategies for making LGBTQI+ resource spaces possible on community college campuses, there is often no shortage of well-intentioned personnel, ranging from service provision staff and administrators to on-site mental health professionals and teaching faculty, who would very much like to see and contribute to the establishment of such spaces. It is therefore crucial to begin formally considering what methods might best serve to enable campus administrators, staff, faculty, and students in the creation of LGBTQI+ spaces at community colleges.

## NEED FOR LGBTQI+ CENTERS AT COMMUNITY COLLEGES

There are approximately 200 campus based LGBTQI+ student centers in the United States, the majority of which are at 4-year institutions (Valosik, 2015). In community college contexts, students rely on campus service elements for both interpersonal and academic support, and LGBTQ+ student resource centers, when they actually exist on 2-year campuses, are crucial sources of such assistance (Pitcher et al., 2018). LGBTQI+ students on community college campuses are members of a marginalized minority, facing numerous socioemotional difficulties due to their LGBTQI+ status, both on and off campus. A majority of LGBTQI+ college students in the United States report experiencing verbal and physical harassment, and often consider the social climate on their campuses as unwelcoming and hostile toward LGBTQI+ individuals (Kisch et al., 2005; Taylor, 2015). Specific to community college students who identify as LGBTQI+, the research literature and research endeavors exploring the needs and experiences of this group are sorely lacking (Ivory, 2005; Leider, 2012). The existing research demonstrates that classroom experiences among students are major determinants of their wider perceptions of overall LGBTQI+ community college campus climate, and first-generation LGBTQI+ students are more likely to have a more hostile campus climate experience (Garvey et al., 2015). Students on 2-year campuses commonly seek support for both interpersonal and academic needs, and LGBTQI+ resource centers are crucial sources of such support for students (Pitcher et al., 2018). LGBTQI+ resource spaces can serve to familiarize students with queer-supportive job opportunities, scholarships, paid and unpaid internships, health clinics, off-campus mental health resources, housing hospitable to LGBTQI+ students who are homeless, and income insecurity resources (McSpadden, 2020).

Nationwide, 2-year institutions may not realize the full extent of the challenges faced by their LGBTQI+ students, since they often fail to provide adequate LGBTQI+ resources or support and visibility for this silent student demographic. Currently, fewer than half of college-based counseling center websites make any explicit mention of psychotherapeutic services available to LGBTQI+ students; fewer than 10% of college counseling center websites mention any programming on LGBTQI+ issues, offer LGBTQI+ support groups, or provide informational pamphlets on LGBTQI+ topics (McKinley et al., 2015).

It would be helpful if the LGBTQI+ members of community college campuses could engage in a free and open dialogue with their institution's administrators about their needs, but often this discourse is not so easily fostered on commuter campuses. Between the time constraints applicable to any community college student experience that limit such social interactions, a lack of readily visible LGBTQI+ campus presence and a still-developing sense of personal identity for many individuals, students seeking queer-specific support or community are often reluctant to come forward (Ivory, 2005). Likewise, proposals for new LGBTQI+ initiatives and dedicated resource offices are rare, due in large part to a lack of clear institutional support for such efforts. Indeed, dedicated LGBTQI+ spaces could serve to support the established equity and diversity mission of most urban 2-year colleges, yet surprisingly few campuses move to significantly enhance such supports. Furthermore, many faculty and staff who would otherwise be highly motivated to spearhead such initiatives may not find themselves sufficiently supported to do so in light of their own employment demands and security, making even writing a proposal or creating a dedicated LGBTQI+ space more difficult. If such work does not fall directly within the scope of one's work obligations, it may serve to harm one's employment standing rather than enhance it; undertaking responsibilities outside one's official duties can sometimes be frowned upon by supervisors, and many faculty and staff are indeed already overtaxed. This could result in a general reluctance to take on these challenges in meaningful ways.

Because many LGBTQI+ community college students, especially younger ones, are in the early stages of understanding or acknowledging their LGBTQI+ identities, they are less likely to disclose their queerness, and, as a result, it is extremely difficult to track these communities by colleges (Mundy, 2018). It also proves difficult to determine which initiatives and services would be best suited to a given campus population, as well as the best methods with which to undertake those efforts. Based on recent contributions to research on microaggressions and other subtle discrimination toward sexual minority students (Nadal et al., 2011; Woodford et al., 2018), an understanding is beginning to form regarding LGBTQI+ student experience, particularly in the realm of fear, anxiety, and impacts on subsequent mental health (Rankin et al., 2019; Woodford et al., 2015). Among students who identify as members of both sexual and racial minority groups, their intersectionalities of identities call for more focused and appropriately attentive campus-based supports (Jones & McEwen, 2000). Any LGBTQI+ initiatives on 2-year campuses serving large numbers of students of color, as is the case at many community colleges in the United States, must maintain a clear focus on creating programming and services for LGBTQI+ students that also prominently feature race. Since many LGBTQI+ students of color struggle with cultural complexities when coming to terms with their own frameworks of race, gender, and sexuality, it is crucial that all identity intersectionalities receive equal space in college-based support dialogues (Lenning, 2017). LGBTQI+ students report experiencing a lack of accessibility and general promotion of services targeting their needs, while also very much wanting to maintain their privacy and confidentiality around their queer identities (Schaller, 2011). Given these complexities of student experience, providing a campus-based resource space for LGBTQI+ students must reflect an awareness of the full spectrum of queer student experiences. Such spaces must also represent the efforts of the campus itself to support LGBTQI+ student needs by promoting the campus's affirming and nondiscrimination policies (Pitcher et al., 2018). A lack of visible and actionable institutional support for LGBTQI+ students has been linked to negative impacts on mental health and well-being (Russell & Fish, 2016). By creating dedicated spaces and programming focused on LGBTQI+ student well-being, campuses add a crucial and valuable component to their already available student support resources, specifically those that positively affect student success and retention (Nguyen et al., 2018).

Since the need to support LGBTQI+ students on community college campuses is so crucial to students and colleges alike, the methods for doing so within each individual campus context must become an area of more effortful focus. Approaches to creating LGBTQI+ programming and dedicated spaces in community college settings must be relevant and appropriate to a given campus context, including each campus's climate toward LGBTQI+ issues, administrative logistics, any already existing relevant programming or services, and potential obstacles to the resource development process. When more broadly considering the elements of context relevant to any campus, the geographic location and surrounding community landscape also require careful attention. Given that 2-year colleges are overwhelmingly commuter campuses, the impact of attitudes toward LGBTQI+ people and issues within the surrounding community can be directly felt in the campus climate. In urban settings, less space may be available to add physical resource areas to an already crowded student support infrastructure on campus. With all of these contextual elements to consider, creating LGBTQI+ campus spaces is often met with challenges that include cultural stigma within the surrounding community, any specific needs of LGBTQI+ students of racially/ethnically minoritized status, a general scarcity of physical space, lack of financial support, and barriers to communication between crucial campus individuals or offices. On that note, one of the most vital elements to the success of an LGBTQI+ resource space is the presence of clear administrative and institutional support, and some administrative contexts may be more supportive of such innovations than others (Yoakam, 2007), often depending on assumptions of projected costs associated with launching and maintaining a new support space (Sanlo, 2004).

With so many complexities involved in creating new LGBTQI+ support spaces on community college campuses, it is understandable that few campuses take on the challenge, especially going so far as to create a full-time staff position to coordinate the services in question, a move that is particularly rare (Taylor, 2015). However, a convincing amount of research has shown that having school policies and practices in place that promote an inclusive campus climate, including the visible institutional presence of an LGBTQI+ resource space, results in enhancement of general student well-being, greater endorsement of feeling safe, higher levels of academic achievement, and increased mental health quality (Russell & Fish, 2016). Hardships around developing safe spaces for LGBTQI+ students are therefore well worth confronting, given the potential benefits to students in great need of support. Regardless of who undertakes the efforts of resource space development, a systematic process for doing so can serve to both make the work more effective and more efficient. Since this kind of work is often done by individuals already working in other sectors of the community college campus, such as staff or faculty, efficiency is of utmost importance. Moving forward with a clearly organized framework can serve to streamline efforts among stakeholders, ensuring that each stage of the process receives the necessary attention to ensure effective program development and longevity.

## THE LGBTQI+ CAMPUS ASSESSMENT FRAMEWORK

The following is a proposed process framework that draws from the work of several researchers and practitioners (Fine, 2012; Fox & Ore, 2010; McSpadden, 2020; Taylor, 2015; Young & McKibban, 2014) and that can be adapted for the needs of a community college seeking to create new LGBTQI+ resource programming and space on campus. This framework is divided into four phases of development according to various focus domains inclusive of planning, proposing, and implementing a new LGBTQI+ resource space.

## Phase I: Preliminary Research

There are countless origin stories to LGBTQI+ initiatives in community college campus contexts, and no two begin in quite the same way. Numerous campuses see their processes begin when concerned staff, faculty, or student members of the campus community commit to creating programming with longevity beyond a regular event series or student club. This work is ordinarily voluntary, aiming to establish a campus climate within which LGBTQI+ students can feel accepted, affirmed, and safe. Once the individuals or groups undertaking the work of creating a new LGBTQI+ space and resources are established, it is strategically wise to systematically identify any existing LGBTQI+ services on campus. This preliminary research includes gaining an understanding of how already existing LGBTQI+ programming functions within the larger college infrastructure. The following are some guiding questions to consider when exploring already existing programs and resources and how to move beyond those offerings to a dedicated space and programming initiative:

- Who are the current LGBTQI+ related stakeholders and partners within the institution?

- What are the basic LGBTQI+ related needs of the institution, and what is currently being done to fill any of these needs?

- What entities on campus have decision-making power around creating these initiatives?

- Who can provide data or conduct research to inform the work of creating a new LGBTQI+ space?

**Identifying Campus Stakeholders and Partners for LGBTQI+ Initiatives**
A stakeholder within this planning and implementation framework is any member of the campus community who either provides or would utilize supportive services to LGBTQI+ individuals on campus. This should naturally include members of the campus community who themselves identify as LGBTQI+ and are either already involved in queer-specific initiatives or are eager to participate in their inception. This should also include faculty with LGBTQI+ interests, student clubs, staff who spearhead queer-specific activities, etc. In addition, it is also helpful to consider LGBTQI+ initiatives that are no longer active, as well as any stakeholders who were previously involved, in order to better understand potential factors impacting any implementation's success or failure. This is also a time when anyone who is not yet a part of the planning and early implementation process toward a new LGBTQI+ resource space can be identified and recruited to the work at hand. Such individuals can serve on steering committees, taking part in those elements of the process for which they are best suited and in which they might be willing or able to assist.

**Conducting a Preliminary LGBTQI+ Campus Needs Assessment**
This initial exploration of campus needs can draw primarily from discussions with identified stakeholders with LGBTQI+ campus interests and concerns.

Speaking to LGBTQI+ student club members and advisors, mental health professionals, professors and researchers on queer issues, and student life/student success offices can go far to inform this process. Data collected at this point can include practical and financial issues, both in terms of benefit and hindrance, as well as perceptions of student needs, barriers, and rates of involvement with currently available resources. This type of preliminary data can provide crucial information on relevant infrastructural elements enabling such programming, thereby paving the way for better planning for a long-term space and subsequent programming for the service of LGBTQI+ issues on campus.

### Identifying the Appropriate Proposal Audience

Early in the overall planning process, it is important to identify specific administrators and campus offices who are responsible for making final decisions approving any new resource space allocation. This knowledge helps determine the tone of any proposal materials, the route of proposal submission, and the most sensible timing for such a submission. If, for instance, a proposal will be presented to the office of the college president, then the decision process will likely include an additional leadership body with a predetermined meeting schedule. Proposal materials can therefore be planned to be completed and submitted based on that timeline.

### Identifying Data Sources and/or Researchers to Conduct Additional Needs Assessments

Data should be collected to help establish a case for creating an LGBTQI+ space; data are the most important content when justifying expenditure for a new program. Data can include any statistics collected by the college on LGBTQI+ students, although data of this type are rarely collected at the institutional level and only perhaps collected for informing specific inquiries. If no such records exist, then data must be collected independently for the purposes of informing the proposal process. Researchers who undertake this work can be professors, staff, students, or research professionals recruited from off-campus. Regardless of who collects the data, it is imperative that appropriate data collection methods are used (and supervised by someone with relevant research experience).

### Phase II: Needs Assessment Research

While there is technically no gold standard for what methodology should be used or what type of data should be collected, there is a strong argument to be made for at least some element of qualitative data and analysis for this type of campus needs assessment. Due to the reluctance to self-report among LGBTQI+ students, it is difficult to collect reliable numbers that provide a clear understanding of how many LGBTQI+ students are registered at any given time. While it is true that some administrative audiences may historically prefer quantitative approaches, a research approach should be selected based more on its appropriateness for the campus climate situation and the nature of inquiry. Both quantitative and qualitative approaches are effective when performing a needs assessment toward establishing an LGBTQI+ space, since both are capable of and effective at providing evidence of how variables in student experience can be linked to relevant indicators of student success and retention. It can also be helpful to collaborate with institutional research offices on campus to perhaps initiate practices or regular data collection by the institution specific to LGBTQI+ students. The following are some reflective questions to help guide the needs assessment research process:

1. What evidence-based research methods are most appropriate and practical?
2. How will the research explore the specific needs of LGBTQI+ stakeholders and institutional LGBTQI+ culture/climate?
3. How will the findings be communicated to the proposal's target audience, highlighting the benefits of an LGBTQI+ resource space to student success and retention?

**Selecting Appropriate and Practical Research Methods**
If researchers have particular skill sets in one method or another, this will inevitably influence the decision of what methods to use, but qualitative elements will go a long way to allow for explorations of student experiences and meaningful interview quotes as raw data. Both the data collection methods and types of data will impact the strength of arguments used to support creating a new or enhanced LGBTQI+ space and initiative. For instance, since it might be hard to collect quantitative data on the actual number of LGBTQI+ students attending a given community college, carefully collected and analyzed qualitative data collected from a smaller, representative group of student participants can be meaningful and compelling.

**Designing Research to Address a Specific Campus**
Addressing the logistics of data collection, particularly when negotiating the difficulties presented by collecting LGBTQI+ information, will require creativity and dexterity. Whether utilizing archival data, interviews, focus groups, or surveys, identifying and recruiting participants might present some challenges. LGBTQI+ members of the campus community would prove invaluable to recruit for assistance when considering strategies for how to best access and collect data on sensitive issues surrounding sexual orientation and gender identity. It may also prove effective to seek out data from not only LGBTQI+ participants but also heterosexual, cisgender students, staff, and faculty; this could provide an opportunity to evaluate campus climate in terms of how non-LGBTQI+ community members view queer-centric campus policies and programming, classroom environments, and overall attitudes.

When collecting data to better understand LGBTQI+ stakeholder needs on campus along with the institutional LGBTQI+ culture and climate, a combination of different methods might prove useful. The use of both focus groups and individual interviews, for example, could capture nuanced perspectives. It might also prove helpful to collect data from faculty and staff, who might be not be able or willing to participate in focus groups but would be more likely to answer anonymous surveys or short-answer questionnaires.

### Communicating Findings for a Compelling Supportive Argument to the Target Audience

Based on the findings of the completed research, the tone of a proposal can begin to take shape in an effort to depict the most compelling rationale for establishing a long-term LGBTQI+ space on a community college campus. Unlike some types of proposals for service provision, calling for an LGBTQI+ space has a specific set of challenges at the proposal stage. First, as mentioned previously, accurate numbers of students identifying as LGBTQI+ are exceedingly difficult to capture, meaning that even national estimates specific to community colleges can seem speculative. Second, because there are so few LGBTQI+ resource offices on community college campuses nationwide, it is difficult to base a compelling argument on precedent at similar institutions. Third, especially in older institutions, it may prove difficult to advocate for an LGBTQI+ space where no such provision has ever been made or called for previously, so the additional burden of communicating the timeliness of the request falls upon the tone of the proposal and the data therein. For these reasons, exploring the sociocultural dynamics at a particular community college context can prove so necessary. The need for an LGBTQI+ office on a particular campus to serve the entire campus community (and not just LGBTQI+ students) must be clearly communicated, supported by whatever data are presented (and rationale for methodological choices), along with whatever projected benefits can be expected with successful implementation, and all in the service of depicting how the creation of an LGBTQI+ resource space can result in measurable and meaningful student success and retention.

### Phase III: Proposal Structure

Besides the data and arguments for the benefits an LGBTQI+ space could bring to the college community, a successful proposal for such a resource must be more than a call to action to do what's right for the students, antithetical though it may seem to prioritize anything above that. At the core of a completely persuasive proposal is a fundamental alignment with the core guiding mission of the college as an institution, and the data and rationale for any resource space must be solidly set within the institution's conceptual mission framework. All stakeholders who have been a part of the proposal planning process should have an opportunity to read over the proposal draft and offer feedback, so that different domains of the college are accurately represented in the initiative. During the creation of the final proposal, the following questions can be used to guide the process:

- How do research findings support arguments for a new long-term LGBTQI+ space?
- What parts of the institution are represented within the membership of the proposing stakeholder group, and how will they contribute to the space?
- What additional supports can be included?
- What is the implementation timeline?

### Using Findings From Research to Shape Primary Arguments

The data and findings used in the proposal compose the very backbone of the entire endeavor; without strong data, the request for a dedicated LGBTQI+ space on any campus has no reasonably secure grounding. It is therefore of primary importance that all major arguments in support of creating a resource space draw directly from the data. Besides the rationale for an LGBTQI+ space needing to align solidly with the college mission, the presentation of research data and subsequent findings is the most important aspect of the proposal, so much so that it shapes everything else within it.

### Creating a Diverse Stakeholder Group

All participating core stakeholders identified early in the planning process are likely already deeply involved in the work of creating the proposal, but the point during which the proposal is written can be a good time to invite additional stakeholders to join the initiative. Some individuals might find it difficult to take part in the earlier planning stages, yet have an easier time contributing once the research and major planning elements have already taken shape. Diversity from across the campus community will create a compelling image of wide collaboration within the proposal, as well as provide various viewpoints to shape the final vision of what an LGBTQI+ space should be. The inclusion of additional students, staff, faculty, and administrators, queer-identified or non-queer allies, from as many disciplines or roles on campus as possible, will serve to build a powerful coalition leading into eventual implementation of proposed programming. This will demonstrate wide support and personnel investment in both creating and maintaining an LGBTQI+ space, with a higher likelihood of enduring beyond a brief or momentary collaboration.

### Drawing from Additional Supporting Documents

In addition to the core thematic elements of aligning with the college mission and relying on data to support rationale, a proposal for an LGBTQI+ dedicated space would benefit greatly from several other types of materials, if available. These can include any letters of support from college personnel, outside LGBTQI+ service providers (and potential partnering organizations once the resource space is established), various types of LGBTQI+ organizations, and government officials from the local community (a strategy that can be especially helpful for publicly funded college settings). Any members of the campus community willing to provide testimonials or other personal statements in support of the initiative would also lend weight to the proposal; student signatures could also be collected via a supporting petition for inclusion as a powerful appendix.

### Implementation Timeline

Once the stakeholder group has established a general vision for the space and its purpose, a projected timeline for a fully viable LGBTQI+ resource space must also be developed and clearly depicted. Expectations must be realistic, not only for the projected timeline to prepare both space and programming but also for the capacity of an administration to provide the necessary resources required to meet that timeline. For the purposes of being both realistic and expedient, preliminary conversations with administrators who might be able to inform the process with knowledge of previous resource launch timelines or current infrastructure capacities, would be highly useful. Projections can be offered as subject to change, but a proposal is much stronger if timeline projections can be offered with relative certainty.

Just as there is no one method by which to achieve the successful launch of a resource space on a community college campus, there is also no set template for what a proposal should contain. What is offered here is a structure based on a successful proposal model (McSpadden, 2020) that by no means claims to be the only one likely to succeed. Structuring a proposal may rely heavily on the strengths of the stakeholders taking part in the construction of the document, and individual college contexts might call for specific writing approaches or emphasis on certain elements versus others. While one campus might benefit from a proposal heavily advocating for the particular elements of the physical space in question, or the mental health needs of the LGBTQI+ student population on campus, others might be more effective focusing on staffing and budgetary needs.

The structure of a proposal for an LGBTQI+ dedicated campus space might consist of the following:

1. an introduction that includes alignment with the college strategic plan and mission;
2. background on the proposal inception and process;
3. research details and findings;
4. a statement of need and benefits based on research;
5. the resulting vision for the LGBTQI+ resource space, including physical facility, personnel, budget, programming, and timeline;
6. a summary and acknowledgments of stakeholders and their campus roles; and
7. any additional materials, such as letters of support, petition signatures, etc.

## Phase IV: Proposal Acceptance and Creation of an LGBTQI+ Resource Space

Once the necessary permissions and approvals have been granted, the real work can finally begin of providing crucial services to LGBTQI+ students on campus. Depending on what elements of the proposal were accepted, stakeholders may be facing anything from installing new dedicated staff and materials, to simply having received access to a space without any funding or staffing budget. In either case, the following questions can guide next steps:

- What monetary/personnel resources are available for use?
- What are viable programming opportunities considering available resources, including any collaborations possible with on-campus or off-campus entities?
- What outcome assessments will be used?

## Determining Resource Availability

Since so many community college campuses are already struggling with finding enough space and funding, receiving space for serving the needs of LGBTQI+ students can sometimes feel, in itself, a bit miraculous. Nevertheless, the work of such a space can only be effective and impactful with the expenditure of time and money, wherever those might come from. If there is a funding source allocated to the space, the first priority is learning how to access it; if such moneys are not available, then other resources must be called upon, perhaps independent of or external to the campus system.

When identifying resources beyond those internal to the campus, it may prove necessary to employ some creativity within whatever constraints exist in a given community college's administrative financing structure. Crowdsourcing, alumni donations, and private funding have been utilized at both 2-year and 4-year institutions to support LGBTQI+ student emergency funds, scholarships, and other programming initiatives (Choudhuri & Curley, 2019), demonstrating the potential types of sponsorship available to sustain this kind of work. However, these types of support are often hard to come by in communities where resources are already sparse. There are student-targeted funding opportunities available via foundations such as the National Gay and Lesbian Task Force, the Point Foundation, the Fund for Lesbian and Gay Scholarships, and the Transgender Scholarship and Education Legacy Fund, but funders specifically seeking to support campus-based initiatives to support LGBTQI+ programming at community colleges are not readily available. Programs can apply for funding on a case-by-case basis to foundations seeking to support student success, even those without an explicitly LGBTQI+ focus.

## Creating Viable Programming

Once the actual new space is attained and its limits more fully understood, appropriate programming can be planned (which may differ from the original proposal). Beyond events, workshops, trainings, and so on, the very space itself is an arm of programming, and must therefore be appropriately outfitted. Furniture, technology, and any other element of comfortable use of the space may or may not be provided by the campus. If the space is managed through an office of student life or student success, then the proper channels for gaining support from that office must be identified, and relatively quickly, as these offices will likely be instrumental in the initial outreach and marketing for the new LGBTQI+ space on campus. Outreach efforts for publicity and marketing go beyond merely advertising the resource space and its events; outreach also means organizing messaging for the purpose of coordination with all the other service-providing offices on campus and their respective programming strategies. Many community college students struggle to find time for extracurricular enrichment activities, given they usually have more outside responsibilities than students at 4-year residential campuses. Strong marketing and collaborative programming is fundamental to ensuring community college students can access events and services. Given the intersectionalities lived by LGBTQI+ students on an urban community college campus, a space devoted to serving them must create programming that draws from the successes of other offices with whom students already effectively interact. Because students at 2-year colleges attend these institutions for a relatively brief time, remaining conscious of intersectionalities of identity and experience among students is imperative, as it can help to shape more meaningful and impactful programming. This is also necessary when exploring collaborations with partnering entities or agencies, both on and off campus; it is possible that some of these might have been identified during proposal development and more will become known through the process of space development. However, the full scope and capacity of partnering groups and offices cannot be fully realized until an LGBTQI+ space begins taking shape and making its presence known on campus. Once partners are identified, individual and ongoing partnership opportunities can be formulated and scheduled.

**Defining and Utilizing Assessment Strategies**
Research is once again called upon to enhance dialogue with administrators regarding the mission of the LGBTQI+ resource space and its function on campus. Just as for the proposal, it is important to collect ongoing data regarding programming. Methods could include records of room or event attendance, feedback from students who use the space, for example. These data will serve to inform ongoing programming adjustments and can be presented in support of maintaining effective programming approaches. Data collected toward program and resource assessment are essential to securing funding from internal or external grant opportunities, and provides necessary information 1to support any proposed future expansions to service offerings or physical space.

It is also crucial to carefully attend to the privacy needs and comfort levels of anyone using the space or taking part in related programming. Many individuals on college campuses are in the process of exploring and understanding their own identities and expressions, and would prefer to do so without much outward demonstration. Similarly, there are students who may be very much aware of their sexuality or gender but still not wish to express it openly on campus, and some students might fear experiencing social bias if seen interacting with explicitly LGBTQI+ programming. Finally, some students experience legitimate concern and anxiety about their physical safety on campus due to being exposed as LGBTQI+ by interacting with spaces or programs that would potentially imply their membership in the queer community. Whatever the motivations of students to maintain privacy, it falls on the resource space to assist students in that aim, including the creation of procedures and policies in the space and at related events that keep participant privacy in mind. The location of the space itself could benefit from being somewhat removed from high traffic areas on campus to encourage students to seek services without fear of being widely seen, and offering one's identifying information at workshops and other events can be made optional. Guidelines for how to create feelings of security around privacy issues can be formed in collaboration with other service providing offices on campus with similar concerns, including mental health counseling offices and campus health clinics.

## Additional Resources to Consider at the Opening of a Campus Based LGBTQI+ Resource Space

A quick online search will lead to various examples of proposals for new college LGBTQI+ spaces, including the University of California, San Diego; Hendrix College; and Weber State University. When comparing these different proposals, it becomes evident that there is no "best" proposal style; each proposal must be mindful of and appropriate for its own campus culture. So, too, the makeup and function of the actual LGBTQI+ resource space must reflect the needs and concerns of the students for which it was created. That is not to say that any number of materials and practices utilized by other resource spaces cannot be borrowed from, including training manuals, job description templates, and other tools intended for daily operations.

## CASE STUDY: BRONX COMMUNITY COLLEGE

Bronx Community College in New York City used all of the major techniques and strategies described in this chapter, particularly the reliance on qualitative research for the purposes of providing evidence of campus need for a resource space and collaborations with stakeholder partners to reinforce the proposal.

Prior to the creation of their LGBTQI+ Resource Room in fall 2018, there was an LGBTQI+ support group and Rainbow Alliance student club on campus, both maintained by staff member advisors, which met with sparse and inconsistent involvement from members of the campus community. A Safe Space ally training program also existed on campus, but events were poorly attended, and formal trainings eventually faded into smaller talks or workshop events once per semester.

A steering committee of 29 staff, faculty, and students met monthly and collaborated online to write the proposal for the resource room. A faculty member and two student research assistants conducted focus-group research among students and interviews with faculty and staff to determine campus climate regarding LGBTQI+ people and issues. It was impossible to determine exact numbers of LGBTQI+ students, faculty or staff due to a general reluctance to report, as determined through the on-campus research, and in keeping with other research findings (Mundy, 2018). Research findings also uncovered overwhelmingly ignorant attitudes on campus relating to LGBTQI+ issues and experiences, so the argument for a new resource space covered not only serving LGBTQI+ students but also educating the entire campus community.

The proposal included the basic argument for creating a dedicated space for LGBTQI+ services on campus, supported by a brief literature review, the findings of the internal LGBTQI+ campus climate research, a proposed function plan and budget for the space, recommendations for staffing and timeline for opening the resource office, a petition signed by students, staff and faculty in favor of creating the space, and letters of support from department chairs, community-based service providers, and local government officials. The proposal was submitted in June 2018, and the new space was established and ready to serve the campus community at the start of the next semester that August.

Numerous challenges arose; for instance, the resource space was not granted funding by the college, nor were any staffing positions designated for the space. Instead, a faculty member took on the coordinator position, overseeing a student staff member hired through a federal work study program. Another challenge was creating a foothold in the student service landscape in a way that could solidify the role of the resource space on campus among other service provision offices; being such a new entity, it took a full year for different offices on campus to understand that the space existed, let alone what it was designed to do. Despite these obstacles, however, the space proved successful, both as a lounge environment for students to convene and establish community, and a physical hub for all major LGBTQI+ programming on campus.

The previously existing Rainbow Alliance student club and LGBTQI+ support group saw increasing and sustained membership for the first time, and additional student clubs and events grew from rising student interest and involvement. The Safe Space ally training program also grew to include more events, as well as customized training options on demand for different campus offices and departments. Despite lacking a budget or a more traditional staffing structure, the space has proven successful in these areas, establishing that LGBTQI+ students have a place on campus they can consider their own and that the campus community is concerned enough with inclusion and equity to open and promote such a space. With more financial and infrastructural support, perhaps over time the space will be further enabled to do even more to benefit not only queer-identifying students but also the campus and its LGBTQI+ climate as a whole.

In the event that a proposal for an LGBTQI+ dedicated space does not at first receive approval, it is important to remember that this type of rejection is not necessarily a complete rejection of the concept in its entirety. Feedback received upon rejection might provide valuable insights into what adjustments can be made to ensure the item passes upon resubmission. Upon receiving a rejection to a proposal, feedback may initially be either scant or lacking completely, which would then require active inquiry to determine the factors at the root of the refusal. Then, when the timing is right to reassert the efforts of everyone initially involved in the proposal project, the work can continue, informed with valuable responses to what can now be considered a first draft.

## CONCLUSION

Perhaps the most important thing to remember is that, while still rare, LGBTQI+ resource spaces do exist on community college campuses and can be used as models for anyone trying to achieve the same in their own campus contexts. Reaching out to established programs on community college campuses to learn more will most likely result in an eagerness to support efforts to create more LGBTQI+ dedicated spaces. The benefit to students in creating these spaces is well worth whatever efforts are necessary to successfully create safe, validating, affirming, and educational spaces for LGBTQI+ students. A slowly increasing number of community college campuses are realizing that the need for dedicated LGBTQI+ spaces is undeniable, especially if queer-identifying students are to be genuinely afforded the opportunity to take part in the college experience with the same sense of community and inclusion more commonly and readily available to their heterosexual, cisgender peers. By continuing the valuable dialogue that evolves from more and more campuses engaging in this continuously developing area of student services, the social scientists, student life administrators, and all others invested in enhancing their campus environments for LGBTQI+ students will enhance the chances of making more affirmative and inclusive community college campuses a more common reality.

## DISCUSSION QUESTIONS

1. How might LGBTQI+ resource spaces on community college campuses differ from those located on the campuses of 4-year colleges?
2. What needs might first-semester queer-identifying students have that an LGBTQI+ resource space could potentially address?
3. How can a resource space serving LGBTQI+ students also serve non-LGBTQI+ students, faculty, and staff?
4. What are some ways an LGBTQI+ resource space can contribute to creating an inclusive campus climate for all the students at a community college?
5. What roles might students serve in planning, creating, and maintaining an LGBTQI+ space on a community college campus?

## RESOURCES

- Campus Pride Index (https://www.campusprideindex.org)—a listing of registered 2-year and 4-year college campuses available, including ratings of LGBTQI+ inclusivity, services, clubs, etc.
- Campus Pride (https://www.campuspride.org)—a resource for students and groups wishing to foster safer college campuses for LGBTQI+ students.
- Consortium of Higher Education Lesbian Gay Bisexual Transgender Resource Professionals (https://www.lgbtcampus.org)—includes resources and information on running resource spaces and creating LGBTQI+ programming.

## REFERENCES

Choudhuri, D. D., & Curley, K. (2019). Multiplicity of LGBTQ+ identities, intersections, and complexities. In E. M. Zamani-Gallaher, D. D. Choudhuri, & J. L. Taylor (Eds.), *Rethinking LGBTQIA students and collegiate contexts* (pp. 3–16). Routledge. https://doi.org/10.4324/9780429447297-1

Fine, L. (2012). The context of creating space: Assessing the likelihood of college LGBT center presence. *Journal of College Student Development, 53*(2), 285–299. https://doi.org/10.1353/csd.2012.0017

Fox, C. O., & Ore, T. E. (2010). (Un)covering normalized gender and race subjectivities in LGBT "Safe Spaces." *Feminist Studies, 36*(3), 629–649.

Garvey, J. C., Taylor, J. L., & Rankin, S. (2015). An examination of campus climate for LGBTQ community college students. *Community College Journal of Research and Practice, 39*(6), 527–541. https://doi.org/10.1080/10668926.2013.861374

Ivory, B. (2005). LGBT students in community college: Characteristics, challenges, and recommendations. *New Directions for Student Services, 2005*(111), 61–69. https://doi.org/10.1002/ss.174

Jones, S. R., & McEwen, M. K. (2000). A conceptual model of multiple dimensions of identity. *Journal of College Student Development, 41*(4), 405–414.

Kisch, J., Leino, E. V., & Silverman, M. M. (2005). Aspects of suicidal behavior, depression, and treatment in college students: Results from the spring 2000 national college health assessment survey. *Suicide & Life-Threatening Behavior, 35*(1), 3–13. https://doi.org/10.1521/suli.35.1.3.59263

Leider, S. J. (2012). LGBTQ people on community college campuses: A 20-year review. *Community College Journal of Research and Practice, 36*(7), 471–474. https://doi.org/10.1080/10668926.2012.664084

Lenning, E. (2017). Unapologetically queer in unapologetically Black spaces: Creating an inclusive HBCU campus. *Humboldt Journal of Social Relations, 39*, 283–293.

McKinley, C. J., Luo, Y., Wright, P. J., & Kraus, A. (2015). Reexamining LGBT resources on college counseling center websites: An over-time and cross-country analysis. *Journal of Applied Communication Research, 43*(1), 112–129. https://doi.org/10.1080/00909882.2014.982681

McSpadden, E. L. (2020). Creating LGBTQI+ programing in urban higher education: Considering the creation process of a campus resource room. *Journal of Gay & Lesbian Social Services, 32*(3), 310–327. https://doi.org/10.1080/10538720.2020.1752873

Mundy, D. E. (2018). Identity, visibility & measurement: How university LGBTQ centers engage and advocate for today's LGBTQ student. *Journal of Public Interest Communications, 2*(2), 239–263. https://doi.org/10.32473/jpic.v2.i2.p239

Nadal, K. L., Issa, M., Leon, J., Meterko, V., Wideman, M., & Wong, Y. (2011). Sexual orientation microaggressions: "Death by a thousand cuts" for lesbian, gay, and bisexual youth. *Journal of LGBT Youth, 8*(3), 234–259. https://doi.org/10.1080/19361653.2011.584204

Nguyen, D. J., Brazelton, G. B., Renn, K. A., & Woodford, M. R. (2018). Exploring the availability and influence of LGBTQ+ student services resources on student success at community colleges: A mixed methods analysis. *Community College Journal of Research and Practice, 42*(11), 783–796. https://doi.org/10.1080/10668926.2018.1444522

Pitcher, E., Camacho, T., Renn, K., & Woodford, M. (2018). Affirming policies, programs, and supportive services: Using an organizational perspective to understand LGBTQ college student success. *Journal of Diversity in Higher Education, 11*(2), 117–132. https://doi.org/10.1037/dhe0000048

Rankin, S., Garvey, J. C., & Duran, A. (2019). A retrospective of LGBT issues on US college campuses: 1990–2020. *International Sociology, 34*(4), 435–454. https://doi.org/10.1177/0268580919851429

Russell, S. T., & Fish, J. N. (2016). Mental health in lesbian, gay, bisexual, and transgender (LGBT) youth. *Annual Review of Clinical Psychology, 12*(1), 465–487. https://doi.org/10.1146/annurev-clinpsy-021815-093153

Sanlo, R. (2004). The LGBT campus resource center director: The new profession in student affairs. *NASPA Journal, 37*(3), 485–495. https://doi.org/10.2202/1949-6605.1113

Schaller, S. (2011). Information needs of LGBTQ College Students. *Libri, 61*(2), 100–115. https://doi.org/10.1515/libr.2011.009

Taylor, J. (2015). Call to action: Embracing an inclusive LGBTQ culture on community college campuses. *New Directions for Community Colleges, 2015*(172), 57–66. https://doi.org/10.1002/cc.20163

Valosik, V. (2015). Supporting LGBT international students. *International Educator, 24*(2), 48–51. https://www.nafsa.org/sites/default/files/ektron/files/underscore/ie_marapr15_fsa.pdf

Woodford, M. R., Kulick, A., & Atteberry, B. (2015). Protective factors, campus climate, and health outcomes among sexual minority college students. *Journal of Diversity in Higher Education, 8*(2), 73–87. https://doi.org/10.1037/a0038552

Woodford, M. R., Weber, G., Nicolazzo, Z., Hunt, R., Kulick, A., Coleman, T., Coulombe, S., & Renn, K. A. (2018). Depression and attempted suicide among LGBTQ college students: Fostering resilience to the effects of heterosexism and cisgenderism on campus. *Journal of College Student Development, 59*(4), 421–438. https://doi.org/10.1353/csd.2018.0040

Yoakam, J. R. (2007). Resources for gay and bisexual students in a Catholic college. *Journal of Men's Studies, 14*(3), 311–321. https://doi.org/10.3149/jms.1403.311

Young, S. L., & McKibban, A. R. (2014). Creating safe places: A collaborative autoethnography on LGBT social activism. *Sexuality & Culture, 18*(2), 361–384. https://doi.org/10.1007/s12119-013-9202-5

# 4

# LGBTQ Students in Nonaffirming Religious Institutions

Theresa Stueland Kay and Joshua R. Wolff

**KEY KNOWLEDGE AREAS**

- Intersectional identities involving sexual orientation, gender identity, religion, and spirituality for sexual and gender minority (SGM) college students.

- How such intersections may create unique challenges and tensions for SGM students who attend nonaffirming religious universities/colleges (NARUs).

- Foundational religious tenets that inform subsequent behavioral policies toward SGM people at NARUs.

- Rates (and risk) of mental health disparities, stigma, and discrimination toward SGM students who attend NARUs.

- Implications and recommendations for the U.S. Department of Education, the American Psychological Association, and other professional accreditors in resolving conflicts between diversity/civil rights standards versus protecting religious freedoms.

Many faith-based universities teach that sexual and gender minority (SGM) identities (e.g., LGBTQ) are sinful (i.e., morally wrong) and substandard to heterosexual and cisgender identities (Wolff & Himes, 2010). For clarity, we refer to these institutions more specifically as nonaffirming religious universities (NARUs). In this chapter, we provide an overview of how NARU policies and campus climates affect SGM students, and we describe the legal context that

---

https://doi.org/10.1037/0000281-005
*Affirming LGBTQ+ Students in Higher Education*, D. P. Rivera, R. L. Abreu, and K. A. Gonzalez (Editors)
Copyright © 2022 by the American Psychological Association. All rights reserved.

allows these policies to exist, as well as the role of government agencies and accrediting organizations within the larger regulatory environment. Then, we provide recommendations for improving campus climate and SGM student outcomes while reducing barriers and health disparities for SGM students who attend NARUs. It is important to note that there are a wide variety of beliefs, policies, and climates within NARUs and among the faculty, staff, and students who work for or attend them. Thus, conclusions in this chapter may not be generalizable to all NARUs or all individuals who work for them.

NARUs adhere to conservative (or sometimes referred to as "traditional") religious beliefs about gender and sexuality that have significant implications for campus policies and behavioral standards (Wolff & Himes, 2010; Wolff et al., 2017). For example, NARUs are likely to hold the theological tenets that humans are created only as cisgender male or female, sex and gender are immutable, and sexual relationships should only take place between one cisgender male and female pair within the context of marriage (Looy & Bouma, 2005). Moreover, individuals whose behavior and/or presentation deviates from this belief system are considered to be sinning (i.e., violating God's commands) and/or disordered (Bockting & Cesaretti, 2001).

Consequently, it is common for NARUs to develop policies that forbid most (if not all) behaviors or other expressions that deviate from the norms described above. For example, Coley (2018) surveyed religious colleges in the United States and found at least 211 that prohibited same-sex relationships and sexual behavior. However, Coley also noted that "because of the ambiguity of the language [in these prohibition statements], it could theoretically be applied against two people of the same sex engaged in behaviors such as hand-holding" (p. 427). While policies that explicitly address transgender and gender nonconforming (TGNC) individuals have been less common, they have started to emerge with greater frequency. For example, Biola University (2016) developed a formal policy that states, "We do not affirm attempts to change one's given biological birth sex via medical intervention in favor of the identity of the opposite sex or of an indeterminate identity," adding "we will make institutional decisions in light of this policy regarding employment, hiring, retention, and other employment matters" (i.e., TGNC employees who transition can be fired). Additionally, a growing number of media reports document that SGM students and faculty experience significant obstacles within NARU campus climates (e.g., denial of housing consistent with students' gender identity, expulsion/termination of employment) after they reveal their identities or are outed against their will (e.g., Hunt & Pérez-Peña, 2014; Pulliam Bailey, 2013; Rokos, 2014). Moreover, many NARUs forbid SGM-affirming student organizations such as gender/sexuality alliances (GSAs), sometimes despite students' efforts to form them (McEntarfer, 2011).

Consequences of SGM expressions or "behaviors" can include academic probation, mandatory psychotherapy (which may have the goal of changing sexual orientation and/or gender identity to comply with religious norms), restrictions of on-campus privileges, suspension, and expulsion (Craig et al., 2017; Wolff & Himes, 2010). A recent study by the Religious Exemption Accountability Project

(REAP) and College Pulse (2021) found that nearly one in 10 (8%) transgender/nonbinary students and 4% of sexual minority students who attend NARUs reported that their college "suggested sexual orientation or gender identity change efforts" (p. 24). A chilling example of enforcement of behavioral codes within a NARU is described by a male-identified student participant from a study by Craig et al. (2017), who said,

> I was slated in the end to be put on a 40 day fast of bread and water because I loved another man. I am diabetic. If I had submitted to the fast I would have died. I left them instead. (p. 8)

Though this specific experience may not be generalizable, it illustrates the fear, pain, and potential harm that some SGM students may experience. Further, the recent study by REAP/College Pulse (2021) found that 12% to 30% of students who attend NARUs identify as SGMs or reported experiencing non-heterosexual attraction—suggesting this topic may be of widespread importance for many SGM students. To reduce and prevent negative outcomes toward SGM students who attend NARUs, it is important to understand the legal context in the United States that allows them to occur.

## POSTSECONDARY ACCREDITATION AND LEGAL OVERVIEW

To better understand how discriminatory policies continue to exist at NARUs accredited by the American Psychological Association (APA), a brief historical lens and legal overview is essential. In the United States' higher education system, postsecondary educational institutions must be accredited by regional, national or institutional entities (e.g., the Higher Learning Commission) to receive federal funds (Council for Higher Education Accreditation, 2002). At the state level, additional programmatic accreditation is required for training programs in many fields (e.g., health service psychology) for graduates to obtain licensure or various forms of employment. Both regional/national and programmatic accreditors have the authority to set various requirements related to student admission and retention policies (e.g., diversity, equity, inclusion). Within its Standards of Accreditation for doctoral health-service psychology programs, the APA Commission on Accreditation (CoA) explicitly allows faith-based institutions to claim exemption from diversity requirements by giving preference to applicants from the same faith tradition in hiring and admissions processes (APA, 2019). Many NARUs have interpreted (and continue to interpret) this language as granting them permission to deny admission to and dismiss SGM students. In 2001, the CoA considered removing or altering this language due to concerns about discrimination toward SGM students (Biaggio, 2014). However, the U.S. Department of Education (ED), under President George W. Bush, essentially threatened to remove APA's accreditation authority, leading APA to retain this language (Biaggio, 2014). Similarly, regional (institutional) accrediting bodies may be bound to similar constraints.

Due to guidelines established by Congress, religiously affiliated institutions in the United States are exempt from various civil rights enforcement mechanisms (e.g., Title IX) that have been used to prohibit discrimination against SGM students (United States Department of Education, 2021). To qualify for these religious exemptions to Title IX, universities have historically written to ED asking for them (United States Department of Education, n.d.). Such letters in recent years have been submitted by NARUs to exempt themselves from compliance with ED's interpretation that Title IX protects transgender and nonbinary students from discrimination at any educational institution that receives federal funding (e.g., student loans). Numerous NARUs also sought exemptions related to sexual orientation as well as gender identity to maintain their code of conduct policies and hiring and admission practices that they argued are grounded in their religious doctrine. In 2015, ED began publishing Title IX exemption request letters from NARUs on its website (United States Department of Education, n.d.). This public record appears to have been prompted by concerns about the welfare of SGM students who attend NARUs and in response to calls from members of Congress for greater transparency (Wolff et al., 2019).

These regulatory protections offered through Title IX were abruptly halted in February 2017 when the Trump Administration withdrew the previous Obama-era guidance on protections for transgender students (Green, 2017). However, in early 2021, President Biden signed an executive order reinstating Title IX protections for SGM students at facilities that receive federal funding (The White House, 2021). This is a promising policy reversal that may be used to extend limited protections to SGM students at NARUs. However, it is nearly certain that this Title IX executive order will be challenged in court, creating a very uncertain legal landscape—that may or may not afford legal protections—for SGM students who attend Title IX exempt institutions.

## CAMPUS CLIMATE

Nonaffirming beliefs regarding SGM individuals and their identities extend into the overall campus climate in several ways. Craig et al. (2017) found that SGM students observed various class and chapel sessions that focused on how SGM identities and behaviors were sinful and/or signs of psychopathology. Moreover, students' perception of these teachings was that they rejected scientific findings that indicate that such identities are in fact normative and an important area of diversity. Across higher education, Beemyn (2011), Hurtado et al. (1998), Meyer et al. (2011), and Rowell (2009) have noted that SGM individuals commonly witness and experience derogatory remarks as well as social isolation (e.g., not being invited to social gatherings). Based on student descriptions, this may be even more explicit and/or common in NARU environments. For example, a student who attended a NARU reported, "I was appalled my senior year when two professors made jokes in the classes about homosexuals. Of course, everyone thought this was funny. Students were allowed to bash homosexuals" (Craig et al., 2017, p. 12). Additionally, the recent REAP/College Pulse survey (2021) found that only 31% of LGBTQ+ students felt like their opinions were welcomed in classes, as compared to 52% of heterosexual students.

Further, several studies suggest that SGM students at NARUs may experience greater risk for verbal harassment and physical violence compared with their heterosexual or cisgender peers or that these may occur in blatant ways (e.g., Craig et al., 2017). For example, the REAP/College Pulse study (2021) found that 22% of gender minority students at NARUs felt harassed or bullied, and 14% reported being sexually assaulted on campus (compared with 5% and 2% of cisgender students, respectively). At least one transgender participant in the Wolff et al. (2017) qualitative study reported that they were concerned for their physical safety while on campus. One study at a Catholic institution found that SGM students who were harassed or threatened were less likely to report being victimized because they feared retaliation or worsening of the situation due to the nonaffirming campus environment (Lockhart, 2013). Again, these results and experiences are not necessarily generalizable to all NARUs, but at minimum raise concerns.

## PSYCHOLOGICAL FUNCTIONING AND HEALTH

Questions remain as to whether the combination of formal disciplinary policies and unique campus climate exact a toll on SGM students' psychological well-being at NARUs. Broadly, across all higher education settings, SGM college students are at significantly higher risk for self-injury and suicidal behavior (Effrig et al., 2014), as well as symptoms of depression and social anxiety (Center for Collegiate Mental Health, 2015; Effrig et al., 2014; Maloch et al., 2013; McAleavey et al., 2011; Woodford et al., 2014), than their cisgender and heterosexual peers. Though these findings have not been replicated in NARUs specifically, various qualitative inquiries suggest that the rates of self-harm or thoughts of hopelessness may be similar (Craig et al., 2017). Further, Craig et al. (2017) found themes that included institutionalized homophobia/transphobia, a culture of fear, marginalization and isolation, coping/resilience, and struggle. Meyer (2003) noted that *minority stress* (i.e., unique stressors experienced by a group due to their socially marginalized status and identities) plays a unique and detrimental role in fostering mental health disparities for SGM individuals. In the same vein, some SGM students at NARUs may be more likely to experience mental health symptoms than their straight and cisgender counterparts. This hypothesis is tentatively supported by emerging qualitative studies. While interviewing transgender and nonbinary NARU students and alumni, Wolff et al. (2017) found themes of invisibility, rejection, and ambivalence/conflict surrounding participants' experiences and religious/SGM identities. Many of the stressors described by SGM students and alumni were unique to SGM students (e.g., difficulty finding trans-affirming medical care on campus), and might not have occurred in a fully affirming campus setting.

Despite these concerns, findings from the Wolff et al. (2016) study did not show a clear difference in depression, social anxiety, and eating concern behaviors among SGM students who attended religiously conservative versus religiously liberal colleges. Thus, the relationship between campus policies and mental health is probably complex and varied, though perhaps still detrimental to some students, especially in the absence of formal social support systems on campus. A recent study by Heiden-Rootes et al. (2020) supports this hypothesis. These authors sampled 384 sexual minority college students and alumni using a mixed-method survey, and concluded that "increased college religious conservatism predicted depression through decreased college acceptance and increased internalized homophobia" (p. 445). Heiden-Rootes et al. also raised the possibility that these symptoms may have lasting effects (independent of age) after graduation for SGM alumni.

## SPIRITUAL DEVELOPMENT AND PROTECTIVE FACTORS

Given the policies and campus climates of many NARUs, some may wonder why SGM individuals apply to and attend NARUs and similar institutions. Biaggio (2014) and Wolff et al. (2019) explained that various complex factors may compel SGM students to attend NARUs. For example, prospective SGM applicants may wish to attend a university that allows them to fully embrace their faith and religious customs in an educational setting. Other individuals may want training in the integration of their faith and course content (e.g., applied clinical skills). Still other prospective students may not yet be aware of their SGM identities, or they hope that going to a NARU will help them change their SGM identities, expressions, and/or attractions.

Several studies (Wolff et al., 2017; Yarhouse et al., 2015) have noted cases in which SGM students at NARUs found positive support as they navigated their spiritual and SGM identity development. For example, some participants found affirming therapists and professors, as well as GSAs (or their equivalent) on campus (Wolff et al., 2017). Also, Yarhouse et al. (2015) reported that some of their participants observed openness to discuss SGM identities and the presence of "pockets of safety" (p. 23) on campus. Similarly, over half of the participants in the Wolff et al. (2016) study reported having told at least one other person on campus about their sexual orientation, suggesting the possibility of feeling safe within one or more interpersonal relationships. Other studies have portrayed the presence of faculty who were supportive of SGM students (Wolff et al., 2017; Yarhouse et al., 2009). Further, some SGM students reported a deepening sense of spirituality and meaning while attending a NARU, despite negative experiences with religion (Wolff et al., 2017). In this same vein, another study suggests that NARUs can be helpful spaces that allow for SGM students to explore their identities and beliefs within their faith communities (Stratton et al., 2013). Thus, experiences on campus can be positive for some SGM students and congruent with their values, making it difficult to offer conceptual models that are widely generalizable.

## CONCEPTUAL MODEL

The factors surrounding SGM student experiences, campus climate, psychological well-being, and spiritual development at NARUs are complex and varied. Using a conceptual model to understand SGM student risk factors at NARUs, Wolff et al. (2017) incorporated White Hughto et al.'s (2015) *social-ecological model of transgender stigma*. They proposed that SGM students may experience stigma at structural, interpersonal, and individual levels at NARUs. *Structural stigma* consists of campus policies, lack of resources, and nonaffirming religious teachings. *Interpersonal stigma* includes harassment, physical violence, and fear of rejection by peers, friends, and/or family. *Individual stigma* involves psychological conflict and ambivalence between individuals' SGM and religious identities. These varying types of stigma can stand alone, but also intersect to create unique barriers, challenges, and risks for SGM students who attend NARUs. But as noted earlier, there may also be protective factors at NARUs that buffer or negate some of the detrimental experiences reported by some SGM students and alumni. With this concept in mind, we move to recommendations aimed at addressing concerns at the individual, interpersonal, and structural levels.

## RECOMMENDATIONS FOR BEST PRACTICES AND INTERVENTIONS

Wolff et al. (2019) proposed a four-pronged advocacy and intervention strategy for preventing and reducing harm to SGM students who attend NARUs, which consists of (a) changes to internal campus policies, (b) development and expansion of campus resources, (c) oversight from accreditation agencies, and (d) enforcement of civil rights protections and oversight of compliance from ED and state higher education agencies. The following section details recommendations aligned with the above categories.

### Changing Campus Policies

There is likely strong common ground between NARU administrations/boards/faculty and SGM advocates in eliminating bullying or harassment of SGM students, regardless of differences in theological interpretation or religious views. Thus, an important starting point is to explicitly add language to NARU nondiscrimination and antiharassment policies that includes gender identity and sexual orientation. Importantly, this language sends a message to the entire campus community that bullying of SGM students will not be tolerated. Further, it signifies to SGM students that there are policies in place that allow them to report bullying and obtain help from qualified campus personnel (e.g., student affairs, Title IX coordinators). Some NARUs have already added this language to their antidiscrimination policies (e.g., George Fox University, n.d.). NARUs that make these additions to their antidiscrimination policies are enacting a reasonable and positive step in creating safer campus environments while holding onto their religious convictions. However, for students to feel safe in reporting allegations of harassment or bullying, NARUs must protect SGM individuals who make reports from retaliation. For instance, an SGM student who discloses their transgender identity while reporting gender-based harassment should not subsequently be disciplined or outed if their gender identity violates the campus code of conduct (i.e., the student's sexual/gender identities should remain confidential throughout the investigative process).

**Develop, Enhance, and Distribute Resources**

Health care providers (e.g., physicians, psychologists, counselors) who work for NARUs must be equipped to deliver clinical services that can address the complex intersection of gender identity, sexual orientation, and religion/spirituality for SGM students. This difficult task warrants significant institutional investment into training and educational opportunities for staff. Various professional associations, including the APA, American Medical Association (AMA), and the American Counseling Association (ACA), offer detailed guidelines to mental health and medical providers who provide care to SGM individuals. Consistent with these guidelines, NARU health care providers need to be trained on principles of client self-determination, stigma and discrimination toward LGBTQ people broadly and within higher education specifically, and various risk factors (e.g., suicidal ideation) that are more prominent and require proper screening in these settings (APA, 2000). The guidelines also call on providers to examine their own sources of bias (which, at NARUs, could be rooted in religious beliefs), as this may damage the therapeutic relationship and progress.

We urge NARU mental health providers to review the APA's *Guidelines for Psychotherapy With Lesbian, Gay, and Bisexual Clients* (APA, 2000) and the APA's *Guidelines for Psychological Practice With Transgender and Gender Nonconforming People* (APA, 2015) for detailed guidelines and assistance. These providers have a particularly heavy responsibility to maintain confidentiality and provide informed consent up-front about the limits thereof, since disclosure of an SGM student's identities at a NARU could result in the student's dismissal, ostracism, or other consequences (Wolff & Himes, 2010). Relatedly, only appropriately trained clinicians should have access to confidential client records at health and counseling centers. When referring to off-site providers, NARUs should implement screenings to ensure provider competence in working with SGM individuals as well as adherence to established professional guidelines. For example, questions posed to referral sources could include: (a) Do you practice sexual orientation/gender identity change efforts, otherwise referred to as "conversion therapy"? (b) What types of formal trainings have you completed in regard to working with SGM people? (c) Can you describe the theoretical model or guidelines you follow in working with SGM clients?

Another essential resource for students includes opportunities for social support. GSAs can provide many potential benefits for SGM students who attend NARUs, including assistance for working through identity concerns, social support, decreased negative identities, and decreased religious incongruence (Heiden-Rootes et al., 2020; Lockhart, 2013). GSAs can also provide resources to decrease bullying/harassment, improve perceptions of campus safety and belonging, educate via campus outreach, improve GPAs, and act as a protective factor against depression and substance abuse for SGM students (Heck et al., 2014; Ioverno et al., 2016; Poteat et al., 2013; Seelman et al., 2015). Because some SGM students who attend NARUs may not identify with labels such as "gay" or "lesbian" (Yarhouse et al., 2009), other descriptors may be needed (see Biola University, 2018). Thus, such groups can provide possible protective factors for SGM students while maintaining the school's religious tenets. Importantly, the identity of group members should be protected and internal communications safeguarded against disclosure or retaliation.

Creating safe spaces for SGM students is likely challenging in environments that may lack expertise in implementation of SGM resources or programs. Thus, we believe it is important for professional associations (e.g., APA) to work collaboratively with NARUs to develop resources, modify existing resources, and help implement them for SGM students. Given that many NARUs have programs already accredited by various associations, in addition to faculty/staff who hold membership, this pairing seems like a natural fit. NARUs, government agencies, private funders, and professional associations could provide funding for research on SGM student experiences and health on NARU campuses. Such data could be useful in evaluating the efficacy of various resource implementations.

Resources must also be infused into campus curriculum for effective teaching in the classroom environments and larger campus climate. NARUs are encouraged to develop clear action plans that address SGM diversity in course curriculum, establish appropriate housing for gender minorities (e.g., community housing that creates safe spaces for transgender students), and continually assess their climate toward SGM people. Existing centers, such as The Stonewall Center at the University of Massachusetts Amherst (Beemyn, 2011), provide helpful resources and guidelines for best practices that could be modified by NARUs to create safer campus climates. A broader, more comprehensive list of resources could be created by ED and made widely available to NARUs and other colleges. A list of resources is provided in Table 4.1, though it is by no means exhaustive.

Regardless of investment, it seems quite plausible that some SGM students might fear retaliation or not feel adequately supported on campus given disallowing policies. Thus, an external resource could be developed by regional or professional accreditors. For example, a confidential consultation phone number could be offered for students in accredited programs, which should not be limited to NARU programs. Such a resource could widely benefit students and staff from other marginalized identities (e.g., students of color) who also experience educational discrimination at both religious and nonreligious postsecondary educational institutions (Wolff et al., 2019).

Since NARUs often receive significant funding from private donors, administrators may be concerned that these donors will withhold money if they make any of the changes suggested here. It may be helpful to frame such changes as being consistent with Jesus' example of helping people marginalized by society (e.g., women and those living in poverty). Also, given the negative press that many NARUs have received, making these changes may help these institutions appear more welcoming and inclusive.

**Enhance Oversight From Accrediting Bodies**

As argued earlier, the research and anecdotal evidence suggests that campus policies that single out and uniquely target SGM people might put some students at risk for harm (e.g., bullying, victimization, mental health problems), especially when linked to support-seeking behaviors (e.g., disciplinary consequences for transgender students who seek medical care) and lack of formal social support systems (Heiden-Rootes et al., 2020; Wolff et al., 2017). Such practices are flagrantly at odds with nondiscrimination and campus/program climate standards set for forth by almost every accrediting body (e.g., APA, Higher Learning Commission). We are very skeptical that campus climates at NARUs can ever truly be safe for SGM students when harsh consequences and retaliatory policies are in place. Thus, we share Wolff et al.'s (2019) position that accreditors should prohibit NARUs from *uniquely targeting* sexual and gender minority identities as linked to disciplinary consequences. We say "uniquely targeting" because SGM students are seemingly held to a more stringent standard that is unequal compared with their cisgender and heterosexual peers (Coley, 2018; Wolff & Himes, 2010). For example, a student in a same-sex relationship who is sexually abstinent could still be dismissed for holding hands with someone of the same sex. We are extremely doubtful that a different-sex couple would be similarly scrutinized at NARUs. We also share the concerns raised by Wolff et al. (2019) regarding the need to protect SGM students from being forced or pressured to out themselves, which violates many accreditation standards as well as APA (2017) ethical codes. That said, we affirm NARUs in their right to maintain their own distinctive religious belief systems and traditions (Smith & Okech, 2016), while holding all students *equally accountable* to the standards. For example, if heterosexual students can be reprimanded for having premarital sexual intercourse, then it seems reasonable that same-sex couples who are not married could be held to the same expectations. In this situation (assuming all else is held equal), sexual orientation is not a determining factor in assigning reprimand; rather, the focus is on explicit policies against premarital sexual intercourse. That said, this would require NARUs to recognize students who are in same-sex marriages, which many do not. Perhaps one way to remedy this dilemma is for NARUs to distinguish between the legal rights of married SGM people, without having to condone the rights theologically (e.g., married same-sex coupled students would not be dismissed, but space on campus cannot be used to perform same-sex weddings). In the second author's observations from visiting multiple religious universities, this is one of the ways that Roman Catholic institutions attempt to remedy these apparent conflicts. But in their current state at many NARUs, these policies illustrate how SGM students are placed in double-binds and held to more stringent standards of conduct.

APA accreditation standards (2016) explicitly state that faculty must be granted full academic freedom. We agree that this is a central protection needed for an academic institution to flourish, in that it allows faculty, students, and staff to hold open dialogue, complete unbiased research, and disseminate knowledge, even when the data may be contrary to that of the institutional positions. Policies that attach disciplinary consequences (e.g., employment termination) to faculty/staff who develop affirming views of SGM identities clearly violate such accreditation requirements and therefore warrant oversight from accreditors. Similarly, we call upon institutional and regional accreditors (e.g., Middle States Commission on Higher Education) to strengthen their standards for diversity, equity, and inclusion of SGM students.

## Government Enforcement of Civil Rights Protections and Improved Transparency

A relatively simple (and seemingly noncontroversial) starting point would be to enhance transparency, which was implemented by the previous Obama-era U.S. Department of Education in publicizing the requests of NARUs wanting to legally discriminate against SGM students via Title IX exemption (United States Department of Education, n.d.). We call on ED to require formal exemption request letters from NARUs, and to continue to publish these. This may help prospective students select a college or university that is the right "fit" for them considering their values, gender identity, and/or sexual orientation. Similarly, regional (e.g., Higher Learning Commission) and professional accreditors (e.g., APA) should follow ED's lead and publish searchable public lists of accredited programs that have requested exemptions from diversity, admission, hiring, and retention standards related to SGM identities. Further, concerns by ED or an accreditor about any program's diversity (or lack thereof) should be made public. While publicly available information could help some SGM students, it is unlikely to be useful to SGM students who did *not* identify as SGM prior to entering their program (Wolff et al., 2019). Thus, we raise a critical question: Who protects SGM students who are already enrolled at NARUs and may have experienced harm due to their sexual/gender identities? As outlined above, current legal exemptions under Title IX policies offer very little (if any) protection for SGM students at NARUs. We share the concerns raised by the Society for the Psychology of Sexual Orientation and Gender Diversity (APA Division 44, 2021) that this is unacceptable, and that the U.S. government has a moral and fiduciary responsibility to investigate allegations of harm—equally and regardless of whether a university is religious or not—that are filed by SGM students.

## CONCLUSION

Faith-based education plays an important—and sometimes positive—role in the lives of many SGM students who attend such postsecondary institutions. Yet the current body of research, combined with numerous media and anecdotal reports, suggests that some SGM students encounter adverse consequences from unique policies and campus climate issues at NARUs. In the absence of providing enforceable protections for these students, accrediting organizations and government agencies have contributed to these problems by making exceptions and providing exemption from accreditation standards. Improving SGM student experiences and health outcomes at NARUs should incorporate multistakeholder, systemic changes within these institutions, including (but not limited to): (a) staff trainings on SGM identities; (b) enforcement of diversity standards and nondisclosure ethical guidelines (e.g., student confidentiality) by accrediting organizations; (c) governmental agencies working to promote transparency; and (d) commitments from professional associations such as the APA to provide resources that tackle head on the discrimination and health disparities that are fostered in religious environments toward SGM students, while also maintaining respect for and understanding of religious views and diversity.

## DISCUSSION QUESTIONS

1. What are some of the challenges that SGM students could face in a religious college or university that does not affirm their identity and/or expressions?
2. How can religious colleges and universities maintain their belief systems while also creating safe campus climates for SGM students?
3. How might religion and spirituality be important in the lives of many SGM people?
4. Similarly, how can these beliefs and identities be better supported? What biases might SGM students who are religious also experience?
5. How can students and faculty who are allies to the SGM community support such students on campus?
6. What responsibilities, if any, do professional associations, accreditors, and the government have in assisting SGM students who attend NARUs?

## FURTHER READING

- *Rescuing Jesus: How People of Color, Women, and Queer Christians are Reclaiming Evangelicalism,* by Deborah Jian Lee (2015). Beacon Press.
- *Torn: Rescuing the Gospel from the Gays-vs.-Christians Debate,* by Justin Lee (2012). Jericho Books.

**TABLE 4.1. Resources for Nonaffirming Religious Colleges and Universities**

| Resources and samples | Strategies and recommendations | Role |
|---|---|---|
| NCAA's LGBTQ Non-discrimination Policy Guide<br><br>American Council on Education (ACE)<br><br>NORC at the University of Chicago | Create safe spaces for SGM students to find social support and obtain resources<br><br>Add sexual orientation and gender identity to nondiscrimination policies<br><br>Remove policies and codes of conduct that hold SGM students to greater scrutiny than their heterosexual, cisgender peers<br><br>Support institutional research on campus climate and diversity | Administrators, deans, and boards of directors |
| APA's *Guidelines for Psychotherapy With LGB Clients; Guidelines for Psychotherapy With Transgender and Gender Diverse People*<br><br>ACA's *Counseling LGBTQ Adults Throughout the Lifespan*<br><br>World Professional Association of Transgender Health (WPATH) | • Obtain training in working with SGM populations<br>• Protect student's privacy in not disclosing sexual orientation and gender identities<br>• Explore own biases that could affect the therapeutic relationship<br>• Screen for increased risk factors associated with SGM identities that are correlated with increased social stigma and discrimination<br>• Offer trainings and outreach on campus to faculty and student affairs staff | Campus medical and behavioral health providers |
| The Stonewall Center at University of Massachusetts Amherst | • Create inclusive classroom environments that respect diversity<br>• Be allies to SGM students and advocate on their behalf<br>• Show respect for students' religious identities and SGM identities | Faculty and other staff |
| OneWheaton<br>OneGeorgeFox<br>Brave Commons | Reach out and find support from people who will affirm and support your various identities<br><br>Know you are not alone! | Students |
| The Reformation Project<br>Q Christian Fellowship | Create welcoming spaces that help students explore their various identities and beliefs<br><br>Offer students resources to help them synthesize their identities, including differing perspectives | Campus clergy and spiritual directors |

*Note.* NCAA = National Collegiate Athletic Association; APA = American Psychological Association; ACA = American Counseling Association; SGM = sexual and gender minority.

## REFERENCES

American Psychological Association. (2000). *Guidelines for psychotherapy with lesbian, gay, and bisexual clients.* https://www.apa.org/practice/guidelines/glbt.pdf

American Psychological Association. (2015). Guidelines for psychological practice with transgender and gender nonconforming people. *American Psychologist, 70*(9), 832–864. https://doi.org/10.1037/a0039906

American Psychological Association. (2017). *Ethical principles of psychologists and code of conduct* (2002, amended June 1, 2010, and January 1, 2017). http://www.apa.org/ethics/code/index.aspx

American Psychological Association. (2019). *Standards of accreditation for health service psychology* (2015, Revisions Approved August 2017; June 2018; November 2019). http://www.apa.org/ed/accreditation/about/policies/standards-of-accreditation.pdf

American Psychological Association Division 44: Society for the Psychology of Sexual Orientation & Gender Diversity. (2021). *Professional psychology groups urge the U.S. Department of Education to protect LGBTQ+ students at religious colleges and universities.* https://www.apadivisions.org/division-44/news-events/religious-university-lgbtq-discrimination.pdf

Beemyn, G. (2011). *How might the needs of transgender people differ from the needs of cisgender (non-transgender) lesbian, gay, and bisexual (LGB) people?* The Stonewall Center, University of Massachusetts Amherst. https://www.umass.edu/stonewall/sites/default/files/Infoforandabout/transpeople/the_needs_of_transgender_people.pdf

Biaggio, M. (2014). Do some APA-accredited programs undermine training to serve clients of diverse sexual orientations? *Psychology of Sexual Orientation and Gender Diversity, 1*(2), 93–95. https://doi.org/10.1037/sgd0000027

Biola University. (2016, March). Institutional statements on human sexuality and trans-sexualism and transgenderism. *Biola University Employee Handbook* (Section 3.21, 1).

Biola University. (2018). *The dwelling.* https://studenthub.biola.edu/the-dwelling

Bockting, W. O., & Cesaretti, C. (2001). Spirituality, transgender identity, and coming out. *Journal of Sex Education and Therapy, 26*(4), 291–300. https://doi.org/10.1080/01614576.2001.11074435

Center for Collegiate Mental Health. (2015). *2014 Annual report.* https://eric.ed.gov/?id=ED572852

Coley, J. S. (2018). Theologies of exclusion: Christian universities and discrimination against sexual minorities. *Sociological Spectrum, 38*(6), 422–437. https://doi.org/10.1080/02732173.2018.1564097

Council for Higher Education Accreditation. (2002, September). *The fundamentals of accreditation: What do you need to know?* https://www.chea.org/fundamentals-accreditation-what-do-you-need-know

Craig, S. L., Austin, A., Rashidi, M., & Adams, M. (2017). Fighting for survival: The experiences of lesbian, gay, bisexual, transgender, and questioning students in religious colleges and universities. *Journal of Gay & Lesbian Social Services, 29*(1), 1–24. https://doi.org/10.1080/10538720.2016.1260512

Effrig, J. C., Maloch, J. K., McAleavey, A., Locke, B. D., & Bieschke, K. J. (2014). Change in depressive symptoms among treatment-seeking college students who are sexual minorities. *Journal of College Counseling, 17*(3), 271–285. https://doi.org/10.1002/j.2161-1882.2014.00063.x

George Fox University. (n.d.). Discrimination, bias and harassment. http://www.georgefox.edu/grad-sps-policies/harassment-discrimination.html

Green, E. (March 6, 2017). The Trump administration may have doomed Gavin Grimm's case. *The Atlantic.* https://www.theatlantic.com/politics/archive/2017/03/the-trump-administration-may-have-doomed-gavin-grimm/518676/

Heck, N. C., Livingston, N. A., Flentje, A., Oost, K., Stewart, B. T., & Cochran, B. N. (2014). Reducing risk for illicit drug use and prescription drug misuse: High school gay–straight alliances and lesbian, gay, bisexual, and transgender youth. *Addictive Behaviors, 39*(4), 824–828. https://doi.org/10.1016/j.addbeh.2014.01.007

Heiden-Rootes, K., Wiegand, A., Thomas, D., Moore, R. M., & Ross, K. A. (2020). A national survey on depression, internalized homophobia, college religiosity, and climate of acceptance on college campuses for sexual minority adults. *Journal of Homosexuality, 67*(4), 435–451. https://doi.org/10.1080/00918369.2018.1550329

Hunt, J., & Pérez-Peña, R. (2014, July 24). Housing dispute puts Quaker university at front of fight over transgender issues. *The New York Times.* http://www.nytimes.com/2014/07/25/us/transgender-student-fights-for-housing-rights-at-george-fox-university.html

Hurtado, S., Carter, D. F., & Kardia, D. (1998). The climate for diversity: Key issues for institutional self-study. *New Directions for Institutional Research, 1998*(98), 53–63. https://doi.org/10.1002/ir.9804

Ioverno, S., Belser, A. B., Baiocco, R., Grossman, A. H., & Russell, S. T. (2016). The protective role of gay–straight alliances for lesbian, gay, bisexual, and questioning students: A prospective analysis. *Psychology of Sexual Orientation and Gender Diversity, 3*(4), 397–406. https://doi.org/10.1037/sgd0000193

Lee, D. J. (2015). *Rescuing Jesus: How people of color, women, and queer Christians are reclaiming evangelicalism.* Beacon Press.

Lee, J. (2012). *Torn: Rescuing the Gospel from the gays-vs.-Christians debate.* Jericho Books.

Lockhart, J. (2013, April 17). *Sexual & gender minority students speak out: A campus climate survey* [Paper presentation]. Fordham University Undergraduate Research Symposium.

Looy, H., & Bouma, H., III. (2005). The nature of gender: Gender identity in persons who are intersexed or transgendered. *Journal of Psychology and Theology, 33*(3), 166–178. https://doi.org/10.1177/009164710503300302

Maloch, J. K., Bieschke, K. J., McAleavey, A. A., & Locke, B. D. (2013). Eating concerns in college women across sexual orientation identities. *Journal of College Counseling, 16*(3), 275–288. https://doi.org/10.1002/j.2161-1882.2013.00042.x

McAleavey, A. A., Castonguay, L. G., & Locke, B. D. (2011). Sexual orientation minorities in college counseling: Prevalence, distress, and symptom profiles. *Journal of College Counseling, 14*(2), 127–142. https://doi.org/10.1002/j.2161-1882.2011.tb00268.x

McEntarfer, H. K. (2011). "Not going away": Approaches used by students, faculty, and staff members to create gay–straight alliances at three religiously affiliated universities. *Journal of LGBT Youth, 8*(4), 309–331. https://doi.org/10.1080/19361653.2011.607623

Meyer, I. H. (2003). Prejudice, social stress, and mental health in lesbian, gay, and bisexual populations: Conceptual issues and research evidence. *Psychological Bulletin, 129*(5), 674–697. https://doi.org/10.1037/0033-2909.129.5.674

Meyer, I. H., Ouellette, S. C., Haile, R., & McFarlane, T. A. (2011). "We'd be free": Narratives of life without homophobia, racism, or sexism. *Sexuality Research & Social Policy, 8*(3), 204–214. https://doi.org/10.1007/s13178-011-0063-0

Poteat, V. P., Sinclair, K. O., DiGiovanni, C. D., Koenig, B. W., & Russell, S. T. (2013). Gay–straight alliances are associated with student health: A multischool comparison of LGBTQ and heterosexual youth. *Journal of Research on Adolescence, 23*(2), 319–330. https://doi.org/10.1111/j.1532-7795.2012.00832.x

Pulliam Bailey, S. (2013, September 23). Transgender theology professor leaves Christian college. *Christianity Today.* http://www.christianitytoday.com/gleanings/2013/september/transgender-professor-azusa-pacific-heath-adam-ackley.html?paging=off

Religious Exemption Accountability Project, & College Pulse. (2021). *The LGBTQ+ student divide: The state of sexual and gender minority students at taxpayer-funded Christian colleges.*

Rokos, B. (2014, July 11). Cal Baptist wins on most claims in suit by transgender student. *The Press Enterprise.* http://www.pe.com/articles/javier-697433-baptist-university.html

Rowell, E. H. (2009). Promoting dialogue on the transgender experience in college courses through films and literature. *Human Architecture, 7*(1), 87–92. https://scholarworks.umb.edu/humanarchitecture/vol7/iss1/9/

Seelman, K. L., Forge, N., Walls, N. E., & Bridges, N. (2015). School engagement among LGBTQ high school students: The roles of safe adults and gay–straight alliance characteristics. *Children and Youth Services Review, 57*, 19–29. https://doi.org/10.1016/j.childyouth.2015.07.021

Smith, L. C., & Okech, J. E. A. (2016). Ethical issues raised by CACREP accreditation of programs within institutions that disaffirm or disallow diverse sexual orientations. *Journal of Counseling and Development, 94*(3), 252–264. https://doi.org/10.1002/jcad.12082

Stratton, S. P., Dean, J. B., Yarhouse, M. A., & Lastoria, M. D. (2013). Sexual minorities in faith-based higher education: A national survey of attitudes, milestones, identity, and religiosity. *Journal of Psychology and Theology, 41*(1), 3–23. https://doi.org/10.1177/009164711304100101

United States Department of Education. (n.d.). *Other correspondence*. Office of Civil Rights. https://www2.ed.gov/about/offices/list/ocr/correspondence/other.html

United States Department of Education. (2021, March 8). *Exemptions from Title IX*. https://www2.ed.gov/about/offices/list/ocr/docs/t9-rel-exempt/index.html

The White House. (2021, March 8). *Executive order on guaranteeing an educational environment free from discrimination on the basis of sex, including sexual orientation or gender identity* [Presidential action briefing]. https://www.whitehouse.gov/briefing-room/presidential-actions/2021/03/08/executive-order-on-guaranteeing-an-educational-environment-free-from-discrimination-on-the-basis-of-sex-including-sexual-orientation-or-gender-identity/

White Hughto, J. M., Reisner, S. L., & Pachankis, J. E. (2015). Transgender stigma and health: A critical review of stigma determinants, mechanisms, and interventions. *Social Science & Medicine, 147*, 222–231. https://doi.org/10.1016/j.socscimed.2015.11.010

Wolff, J. R., Atieno Okech, A. E., Smith, L. C., & Southwick, P. J. C. (2019). Protecting sexual and gender minorities in academic institutions with disallowing policies: Psychological, ethical, and accreditation concerns. *Training and Education in Professional Psychology, 14*(3), 249–256. https://doi.org/10.1037/tep0000272.

Wolff, J. R., & Himes, H. L. (2010). Purposeful exclusion of sexual minority youth in religious higher education: The implications of discrimination. *Christian Higher Education, 9*(5), 439–460. https://doi.org/10.1080/15363759.2010.513630

Wolff, J. R., Himes, H. L., Soares, S. D., & Miller Kwon, E. (2016). Sexual minority student experiences in non-affirming religious higher education: Mental health, outness and identity. *Psychology of Sexual Orientation and Gender Diversity, 3*(2), 201–212. https://doi.org/10.1037/sgd0000162

Wolff, J. R., Stueland Kay, T., Himes, H. L., & Alquijay, J. (2017). Transgender and gender nonconforming student experiences in Christian higher education: A qualitative exploration. *Christian Higher Education, 16*(5), 319–338. https://doi.org/10.1080/15363759.2017.1310065

Woodford, M. R., Han, Y., Craig, S., Lim, C., & Matney, M. M. (2014). Discrimination and mental health among sexual minority college students: The type and form of discrimination does matter. *Journal of Gay & Lesbian Mental Health, 18*(2), 142–163. https://doi.org/10.1080/19359705.2013.833882

Yarhouse, M. A., Dooling, H., Watson, K., & Campbell, M. C. (2015). Experiences of students and alumni navigating sexual identity in faith-based higher education: A qualitative study. *Growth: The Journal of the Association for Christians in Student Development, 14*(14), 16–27.

Yarhouse, M. A., Stratton, S. P., Dean, J. B., & Brooke, H. L. (2009). Listening to sexual minorities on Christian college campuses. *Journal of Psychology and Theology, 37*(2), 96–113. https://doi.org/10.1177/009164710903700202

# 5

# One Model, Multiple Locations
*The Salisbury University Safe Spaces Program*

Diane S. Illig, Michèle M. Schlehofer, and Tara Taylor

**KEY KNOWLEDGE AREAS**

- Trainings that close the policy-practice gap can help institutions of higher education better align student experiences with stated diversity commitments.

- Workshops that address macro- and mesosystems, in addition to individual ally competencies, have the potential to change institutional structures.

- Workshops developed from an intersectional framework can be used across multiple institutional contexts with similar impact.

Many higher education institutions state a commitment to diversity, yet take a superficial approach to creating inclusive environments (Chun & Evans, 2016). This results in student experiences that often fall short of institutional goals (Chun & Evans, 2016). Institutions of higher education are not always inclusive of lesbian, gay, bisexual, transgender, and queer (LGBTQ+) students. For instance, the majority (73%–80%) of students describe their campus as "homophobic" (Rankin, 2005), and over 50% report hearing LGBTQ+ slurs (Mathies et al., 2019). Many LGBTQ+ students remain closeted in such environments. This is particularly true for transgender and genderqueer students, up to 67% of whom conceal their identity on campus (Goldberg et al., 2019). LGBTQ+ students attending community colleges are also more likely to be closeted (Garvey et al., 2015). Community college students are more likely to

---

https://doi.org/10.1037/0000281-006
*Affirming LGBTQ+ Students in Higher Education*, D. P. Rivera, R. L. Abreu, and K. A. Gonzalez (Editors)
Copyright © 2022 by the American Psychological Association. All rights reserved.

still live at home, reducing their opportunities for LGBTQ+ identity exploration and making it harder to find or develop LGBTQ+ affinity groups on campus (Garvey et al., 2015). A transformative paradigm, which addresses power relationships and dynamics, has the potential to better align institutional missions with student experiences (Nunez et al., 2015).

## THEORETICAL FRAMEWORKS

According to the minority stress model (Hendricks & Testa, 2012; Meyer, 2003), LGBTQ+ people experience consistent, lifelong exposure to stigma and discrimination. This combination of stigma and discrimination shares commonalities with challenges faced by other groups (e.g., racial, ethnic, or religious minorities) but also contains additional stressors. These stressors include an increased risk of being a target of a hate crime, as well as experiences and expectations of family rejection. Stigma can lead to internalized homophobia and concealing one's identity (Lewis et al., 2003; Meyer, 2003). For LGBTQ+ students, stigma results in lower satisfaction, lower GPA, and less academic persistence (Garvey et al., 2018; Mathies et al., 2019; Morris & Lent, 2019), all of which are common indicators used by institutions to measure student success (Kim, 2017).

LGBTQ+ racial and ethnic minorities are multiplicatively stigmatized (Meyer, 2003). The experiences of LGBTQ+ students vary based on race, ethnicity, and institution. For instance, Black LGBTQ+ students face unique obstacles in institutions of higher education. Black LGBTQ+ students who attend Predominantly White Institutions (PWIs) report feeling unwelcomed and excluded (Goode-Cross & Tager, 2011). LGBTQ+ spaces on PWI campuses are perceived as "White" spaces in which Black LGBTQ+ students will experience racial microaggressions. And the small number of Black LGBTQ+ students on a PWI campus means that there are limited opportunities to develop friendships and romantic relationships with other Black LGBTQ+ students (Goode-Cross & Tager, 2011). Although Historically Black Colleges and Universities (HBCUs) have a long history of providing exceptional support for Black students by centering Black identity, pride, and culture, HBCUs have been slow to adopt policies and practices that are inclusive of LGBTQ+ people (Lenning, 2017; Lewis & Ericksen, 2016). Black LGBTQ+ students who attend HBCUs may remain closeted and feel that they must make being LGBTQ+ a secondary identity to being Black, rather than having a fully supported, integrated Black LGBTQ+ identity (Lewis & Ericksen, 2016).

These effects can be ameliorated by developing allies: cisgender, heterosexual people who, largely motivated by social justice concerns (Edwards, 2006), offer support to LGBTQ+ people (Harper et al., 2013). Institutions of higher education have increasingly focused on developing training programs to promote ally identities and competency in working with LGBTQ+ people (Rivers & Swank, 2017). These trainings have been effective in their aims (Rivers & Swank, 2017). Trainings typically consist of an overview of LGBTQ+ communities, including terminology and discussion of misconceptions and privilege.

Rivers and Swank (2017) suggested that LGBTQ+ people themselves benefit from going through such training, as it could increase their feelings of acceptance and connection to their peers. Sexual orientation and gender identity are complex, and being LGBTQ+ does not guarantee ally competencies in all LGBTQ+ identities.

Crenshaw (1989, 1991) coined the term *intersectionality* to refer to the unique ways that Black women experience discrimination. Discrimination against Black women differs both from standard narratives of "sexism" and "racism." Intersectionality suggests oppression is interactive, rather than additive (Daley et al., 2007; Salem, 2018). An additive model of oppression perceives the experiences of someone who is marginalized on two social localities, such as a Black, gay male, as "double jeopardy" or "race + sexual orientation" (Daley et al., 2007). An intersectional approach characterizes their oppression as racialized homophobia (race × sexual orientation). Unfortunately, intersectionality is often reduced to merely a "multiple identities" approach (Grzanka & Miles, 2016; Salem, 2018). This has resulted in erasing structural inequalities, negating the potential of intersectionality to thwart oppression (Salem, 2018). A true intersectional approach recognizes that social identities are interlocking and reflect systems of power and oppression (e.g., Bowleg, 2012). By focusing attention on systems, intersectionality is potentially institutionally transformative.

## SAFE SPACES: A STRATEGY FOR CHANGING CAMPUS CLIMATE

Orienting ally training to an intersectional framework shifts the focus to a direct deconstruction of structural systems that contribute to the oppression of LGBTQ+ people. This includes an analysis of federal and state laws that protect or marginalize this population, as well as institutional practices and individual-level marginalizing behaviors. It is from this perspective that Salisbury University's *Creating LGBTQ+ Safe Spaces—Being an Ally* (henceforth referred to as Safe Spaces) program operates.

Safe Spaces, offered in partnership between Salisbury University and the Maryland Commission on Civil Rights' Education and Outreach Department, is a 3.5-hour workshop that helps shift institutions of higher education from places that are unwelcoming and hostile to ones that are inclusive, welcoming, and affirming. In the workshop, participants—consisting of students, faculty, staff, and upper administration—problem-solve and strategize a variety of situations and objectives in order to implement changes at the personal, departmental, and organizational levels. The program has been implemented across multiple, diverse institutions of higher education. Each institution has to craft its own diversity and inclusion plan to address institutional inequalities. Safe Spaces provides opportunities to start these conversations, brainstorm short- and long-term actions, identify key stakeholders, and assume personal accountability for implementing changes. This is accomplished by providing a foundation relevant to all audiences (e.g., language and symbols, recent data and examples of discrimination, laws, policies and practices). Since every institution of higher education is also a workplace, information on workplace issues is included. For instance, during the workshop, participants score their campus climate using a checklist of LGBTQ+ inclusivity indicators.

Each workshop is facilitated by two to three trainers. Trainers are diverse across race, gender, sexual orientation, age, and other socio-localities, and we intentionally recruit Black and other trainers of Color. All trainers complete a 2-day (16 hour) training that covers content and strategies for delivery, so that the workshop is presented similarly across institutional contexts. Facilitators engage their cultural competencies when reading a room—for example, observing where marginalized people sit, physical comfort, if participants are friendly with one another, and so forth. These all inform content delivery and provide opportunities to engage attendees in active reflection. Trainers move participants to ensure racial and ethnic integration in the room, and provide copies of the slides in large print for visually impaired attendees.

The workshops are designed to best serve 25 to 35 people, with a minimum of 15 and a maximum of 40. Keeping attendance within this range ensures participants benefit by the comments and experiences of others in attendance, and that discussions do not feel rushed. Upon completion, each participant receives a 45-page resources booklet and can sign an ally commitment to receive a Safe Spaces sticker to prominently display. Stickers are only given to people willing to sign the ally commitment.

The Safe Spaces team works with each host institution to ensure that there is sufficient space and setup for the workshop. Room configuration affects workshop delivery, and large auditorium-style rooms are ineffective for interactions and discussions. When workshops end up in this setting, facilitators direct seating arrangements to ensure that there are small groups and no one is sitting off on their own. Because technology glitches can occur, facilitators are prepared to use a Safe Spaces computer and LCD projector if needed.

Some institutions require attendance at Safe Spaces, whereas at others attendance is optional. Mandatory trainings reach more people, but they can also result in less engagement and more subtle discourtesies like arriving late, leaving early, and using electronic devices. To prepare for potential issues, the Safe Spaces team collects preliminary information on whether the host institution is mandating attendance. To build community, particularly when resistance is anticipated, an opening small-group exercise is used. There is also a "public service announcement" concerning electronic devices that addresses the ineffectiveness of multitasking, as well as what others think of people who use devices in meetings.

Although content is consistent, interactive discussion is tailored to and varies across different institutional contexts. For example, gendered honorifics (e.g., "Ms.," "Mrs.," "Mr.") are prevalent in Black culture (Atang, 2004). Rigid gender roles are part of HBCU culture; for instance, most HBCUs crown a yearly King and Queen, sometimes called Mr. and Miss (Lenning, 2017). As such, there are deeper discussions around gendered honorifics when conducting trainings at HBCUs and schools serving primarily students of Color

(PSOCs) than at PWIs. In religious institutions, as well as in HBCUs—most of which were established by Black churches and thus have a religious culture (Lenning, 2017; Lewis & Ericksen, 2016)—trainers have deeper discussions over the reconciliation of religious teachings with affirmation of LGBTQ+ people. These are two examples of how approaches to solutions are complex.

Although multiple trainings of this nature exist, Safe Spaces is unique in several key ways. First, Safe Spaces differs from other programs as the training addresses competency at multiple ecological levels, including the structural barriers of oppression. In addition to providing an introductory overview to LGBTQ+ people, the Safe Spaces program addresses how to restructure organizational policies and procedures, such as forms, to be more inclusive and affirming towards LGBTQ+ people. Mesosystemic structures (i.e., people and groups who span boundaries between students and the organization) are discussed as pathways for inclusion, and as ways to translate inclusive policies to inclusive practices, helping close the policy to practice gap. As well, both federal and state laws, and the ways in which they can further support or oppress LGBTQ+ people, are discussed. An emphasis on translating laws into practice keeps the focus on changing or mitigating the effects of oppressive systems and structures, rather than on individual-level education and attitude change. This focus has the additional benefit of increasing the likelihood that the workshop is consistently received across a variety of institutional contexts.

## Preliminary Findings Assessing Impact

To date, the Safe Spaces program has been distributed to 1,288 participants in five institutions of higher education spanning across two mid-Atlantic states. These institutions vary in whether they are public or private, religious or secular, located in rural or urban areas, are HBCUs, PSOCs, or PWIs, and whether they are 4-year or 2-year colleges. See Table 5.1 for a summary of institutional characteristics.

**TABLE 5.1. Summary of Characteristics of Higher Education Institutions Receiving Safe Spaces Training**

| Institution ID | 4- or 2-year | Private or public | PWI, PSOC, or HBCU | Religious or secular | Rural or urban | Size of student population | State ID | No. of evals |
|---|---|---|---|---|---|---|---|---|
| 1 | 4 year | Private | PSOC | Religious | Rural | 1,600 | 1 | 28 |
| 2 | 4 year | Public | PWI | Secular | Rural | 8,714 | 2 | 432 |
| 3 | 4 year | Public | PWI | Secular | Urban | 3,000 | 2 | 40 |
| 4 | 4 year | Private | PWI | Secular | Rural | 1,484 | 2 | 67 |
| 5 | 2 year | Public | PSOC | Secular | Urban | 7,160 | 2 | 174 |
| 6 | 4 year | Public | HBCU | Secular | Urban | 7,747 | 2 | 103 |

Note. PWI = Predominantly White Institution; PSOC = Primarily Students of Color in Historically White Institution; HBCU = Historically Black College or University.

## Methodology

A user-driven (Patton, 2008) postworkshop outcomes evaluation was conducted, which was designed to provide both the Safe Spaces team and institutions requesting training with substantive feedback on immediate program impact. All Safe Spaces attendees were asked to complete a short, postworkshop evaluation form. The evaluation form was intentionally brief so as to allow it to be completed on-site. Participants respond to five open-ended questions: (1) Why did you choose the Safe Spaces workshop?; (2) What aspects of the training were most beneficial to you personally? Professionally?; (3) Please tell us one thing you learned in the training which surprised you; (4) Please tell us one thing you would do differently to improve this training; and (5) Additional comments.

Data provided from a total of 844 attendees over a 5-year period were analyzed to assess reactions to and potential impacts of the program. Of specific interest was determining the extent to which feedback was positive versus negative, and whether participants responded similarly to the workshop across participating institutions. Analyzing qualitative data to assess program impact is appropriate, as the goals of qualitative research align with intersectional theory (Syed, 2010).

Responses to each open-ended item were coded by two independent coders. A modified consensual qualitative research (CQR) approach, developed to analyze short qualitative data, was used (Spangler et al., 2012). First, each coder independently read the transcripts and identified possible coding categories. Then, the coders compared notes and developed a potential list of coding categories for each open-ended item. Next, each coder independently coded 20% of the transcripts using the coding scheme. Coding was compared, interrater agreement was calculated, and discrepancies were discussed and resolved by mutual agreement. This process was repeated until interrater agreement reached 85%; after, one coder completed the coding.

## Postworkshop Evaluation Results

Table 5.2 lists the top three themes for each open-ended question. The most common themes across all open-ended questions were positive and indicated that the training was impactful. The next step was to assess the extent to which coded responses to each of the evaluation items were consistent across the institutions where Safe Spaces was implemented. To test this, a series of chi-square goodness-of-fit tests were calculated, comparing the relative frequency in which each code was applied across each institution. Due to the number of codes (83 codes across all five items), a Bonferroni adjustment was applied to control for inflated alpha. Using this more stringent criterion, only nine of the 83 coded themes (or, 11% of the themes) were differentially applicable across institutions.

Of the nine codes that statistically differed across institutions, five pertained to reasons for attending the training. Examination of the pattern of codes found

**TABLE 5.2. Top Three Themes Emerging From Each Evaluation Question**

| Item | Coded theme (n; %) | Description of theme |
| --- | --- | --- |
| 1. Reasons for choosing workshop | Cognition (n = 302; 35.5%) | To learn; be educated; increase personal awareness |
| | Mandatory (n = 267; 31.4%) | Supervisor required attendance |
| | Action (n = 131; 15.4%) | To bring change; create a more inclusive environment |
| 2. Aspects of the training most beneficial | Language (n = 242; 28.4%) | General LGBTQ+ terminology and definitions |
| | General resources (n = 172; 20.2%) | The booklet; statistics; data; examples; information |
| | Interactive (n = 163; 19.2%) | Role play; scenarios; open/honest discussion |
| 3. One surprising thing learned in the training | General terminology (n = 136; 16%) | General terminology was helpful |
| | Abuse statistics (n = 16; 12.5%) | Statistics regarding abuse, assault, hate crimes, etc. |
| | Pronouns (n = 76; 8.9%) | Proper pronoun use; gender-neutral pronouns |
| 4. One thing you would do differently to improve training | No change (n = 197; 23.1%) | No change; excellent; keep it as is |
| | Interactive activities: unspecified (n = 78; 9.2%) | Need additional interactive activities, not specified |
| | Interactive activities: small group discussions/games (n = 49; 5.8%) | Participants requested more small group discussions and small group games |
| 5. Additional comments | Enjoyed training (n = 159; 18.7%) | Good; awesome training; enjoyed; thank-yous |
| | Positive comments on presenters (n = 27; 3.2%) | Presenters great, handled self well, knowledgeable |
| | Increased reach (n = 23; 2.7%) | Make mandatory; more should attend |

*Note.* Comments that occurred too infrequently to categorize into themes were omitted.

that attendees from both the secular PSOC and HBCU were significantly more likely to state that they were either required to attend the training ($\chi^2$ (5) = 77.51, $p < .000$, V = .303), or that it was expected ($\chi^2$ (5) = 19.85, $p < .001$, V = .153), than attendees from the PWIs or religious PSOCs. Almost 50% of attendees from the secular HBCU stated they were required to attend the training, and almost an additional 18% from the secular PSOC said their attendance was expected; attendees from other institutions reported being required or expected to attend at significantly lower rates. Attendees from institutions that reported feeling required or expected to attend were significantly less likely to say they were attending to increase their learning ($\chi^2$ (5) = 40.7, $p < .001$, V = .220), develop skills as an ally ($\chi^2$ (5) = 24.8, $p < .001$, V = .171), or to learn how to create an inclusive environment ($\chi^2$ (5) = 26.43, $p < .001$, V = .177).

Despite differences in their reasons for attendance, attendees across all institutions reported similar impact of Safe Spaces training, as indicated by the fact that the vast majority of coding on open-ended Items 2 through 5 were not statistically different across institutions. The only significant differences were in perceptions that the interactive components were most beneficial to learning: fewer attendees at the secular PSOCs and HBCUs stated that the interactive components were beneficial (ranging from 6%–8% of attendees) than attendees from the PWIs and the religious PSOC institutions (12%–28% of attendees) ($\chi^2$ (5) = 40.35, $p < .001$, V = .219). There were also differences in how surprising attendees found the information on general terminology ($\chi^2$ (5) = 26.92, $p < .001$ V = .179) and pronoun use ($\chi^2$ (5) = 54.59, $p < .001$, V = .254), but there was no discernible pattern to this effect. As such, we can infer that Safe Spaces was largely consistently well-received across all participating institutions, regardless of whether they were public or private, whether the school is an HBCU, PWI, or PSOC institution, religious or secular, located in rural or urban areas, and whether they are 4-year or 2-year colleges.

**Long-Term Impact**

The Safe Spaces team has started to assess longer term impact via follow-up and outreach. The training took place in two states that have LGBTQ+ public accommodation laws, which provided opportunities to problem-solve and strategize both physical changes regarding restrooms and locker rooms and messaging for campus communications. For example, a private religious school participant reported, upon follow-up, that new employees are now "strongly encouraged" to include pronouns on their email signatures. At a public school, blueprints for a new building were adapted to include at least one all-gender restroom.

Allies at institutions in states without legal protections for LGBTQ+ people can leverage their institutional mission and values statements and strategic plans regarding diversity and inclusion as mechanisms for meaningful institutional change. Lofty language often serves as a substitute for transformative change (Chun & Evans, 2016). Each of the institutions participating in the Safe Spaces training had well-crafted, visionary goals and values, yet each struggled to create the inclusive campuses they aspired to. Strengthening ally competencies of people working within mesosystems can result in greater alignment of student experiences with institutional goals. It can also prepare allies for engagement in further institutional advocacy.

Safe Spaces participants leave the training with identified short- and long-term initiatives to move their institution in the direction of its values and goals. For example, at some institutions, participants left with plans to do a thorough review of their employment and student forms to ensure that information collected was both necessary and inclusive. After learning that many organizations and agencies lack adequate procedures to effectively handle complaints of harassment or discrimination by LGBTQ+ individuals, human resources and campus legal counsel participants intended to review their institutional procedures. Follow-up reports show that two institutions were actively working on the language for new procedures for complaints; one named an assistant vice president as the lead for LGBTQ+ campus initiatives.

At the individual level, participants identified a number of simple changes they could make, such as adding pronouns to their email signature, sharing information with colleagues, and committing to being an ally by displaying the Safe Spaces sticker. In a 6-month follow-up, two coaches of women's sports at a rural, private college reported holding team meetings to discuss language use on the field and in the locker rooms and began discussing issues of uniforms and locker room use for trans and gender nonconforming athletes with administrators.

## CONCLUSION

LGBTQ+ students at institutions of higher education face significant barriers to educational success. This is particularly true for Black LGBTQ+ students, transgender and genderqueer students, and students attending community colleges. These barriers negatively and notably impact student performance, including GPA, retention, and graduation rates—all metrics institutions use to track student success. Individual-level biases and prejudices, unwelcoming organizational frameworks and procedures, inhibitive mesosystems, and discriminatory state and federal laws converge, making academic success a struggle for LGBTQ+ students. Therefore, the creation of supportive spaces for LGBTQ+ students requires exposing components of structural oppression in existing laws and systems, finding work-arounds to mitigate their impact, and closing existing policy-practice gaps.

In this chapter, the Safe Spaces program was presented as one method by which workshops promoting the inclusion of LGBTQ+ people can be developed and implemented from an intersectional approach. Meaningful change requires a multipronged approach to address institutional inequalities. Findings from postworkshop evaluations suggest that, while reasons for attending the training vary across institutions (as a function of whether attendance is required), Safe Spaces is consistently well-received, regardless of institutional context.

## NEXT STEPS

The Safe Spaces 6-month follow-up survey serves as a reminder to participants of the actions they committed to, and provides opportunity to feel good about their accomplishments. For the Safe Spaces program, these data add further evidence of our workshop's effectiveness and provide examples for future trainings. Future evaluations will assess the impact of Safe Spaces on perceptions of student safety and belonging, as well as institutional-level indicators of student success, such as GPA, retention, and graduation rates. Safe Spaces has also launched a website (https://safespacetraining.org) that includes future training dates, tips on being an ally, and links to resources to keep participants and trainers up-to-date.

Given the complexities of institutions of higher education, Safe Spaces is examining ways to target audiences (e.g., campus security, housekeeping and dining services) that are routinely unrepresented at a workshop. We are also developing an advanced training workshop for the faculty and staff who have high levels of LGBTQ+ awareness and competencies, as well as a workshop which addresses the needs of Black LGBTQ+ people. Other future plans include developing a program working with key administrators to focus on the systemic barriers to LGBTQ+ inclusion at their institutions.

Finally, the COVID-19 pandemic presented challenges to the delivery of Safe Spaces. Prior to the pandemic, we required in-person trainings, as webinars do not facilitate the type of interaction needed to develop ally competencies (Pantalone, 2015). However, during the pandemic, we modified Safe Spaces to fit a virtual sphere. This included reducing the workshop length from 3 to 2 hours to prevent "zoom fatigue," and increasing interactive discussion in proportion to trainer-presented content. We will be assessing the impacts of virtual trainings and comparing these with our standard in-person trainings in the months to come.

## DISCUSSION QUESTIONS

1. How does Safe Spaces put intersectionality theory into practice?
2. What makes the Safe Spaces program unique from similar types of trainings?
3. Should institutions require employees attend Safe Spaces training? Why or why not?
4. How could long-term impact of the program be assessed?
5. Would a shorter or longer program have a different impact? How so?

## RESOURCES

1. LGBT Campus Policy Recommendations (https://www.lgbtcampus.org/policy-practice-recommendations)—Provides policy recommendations for supporting LGBTQ+ students in institutions of higher education.

2. Chapter on Providing Trainings from The Community Toolbox (https://ctb.ku.edu/en/table-of-contents/structure/training-and-technical-assistance)—Provides practical suggestions on designing effective trainings and workshops.

3. Cancer Network Guide for Creating LGBTQ+ Competency Trainings (https://cancer-network.org/wp-content/uploads/2017/02/best_practices.pdf)—Provides a detailed framework for developing LGBTQ+ competency workshops, including pointers for trainers and a sample assessment plan.

## REFERENCES

Atang, C. (2004). The pragmatics of Afrocentric communication patterns: Some implications for African Americans. In J. Gordon (Ed.), *The African presence in Black America* (pp. 323–334). Africa World Press.

Bowleg, L. (2012). The problem with the phrase *women and minorities:* Intersectionality—An important theoretical framework for public health. *American Journal of Public Health, 102*(7), 1267–1273. https://doi.org/10.2105/AJPH.2012.300750

Chun, E., & Evans, A. (2016). Rethinking cultural competence in higher education: An ecological framework for student development. *ASHE Higher Education Report, 42*(4), 7–162. https://doi.org/10.1002/aehe.20102

Crenshaw, K. (1989). Demarginalizing the intersection of race and sex: A Black feminist critique of antidiscrimination doctrine, feminist theory and antiracist policies. *University of Chicago Legal Forum, 1989*(1), Article 8. https://chicagounbound.uchicago.edu/cgi/viewcontent.cgi?article=1052&context=uclf

Crenshaw, K. (1991). Mapping the margins: Intersectionality, identity politics, and violence against women of color. *Stanford Law Review, 43*(6), 1241–1299. https://doi.org/10.2307/1229039

Daley, A., Solomon, S., Newman, P. A., & Mishna, F. (2007). Traversing the margins: Intersectionalities in the bullying of lesbian, gay, bisexual and transgender youth. *Journal of Gay & Lesbian Social Services, 19*(3–4), 9–29. https://doi.org/10.1080/10538720802161474

Edwards, K. (2006). Aspiring social justice ally identity development: A conceptual model. *NASPA Journal, 43*(4), 39–60.

Garvey, J. C., Squire, D. D., Stachler, B., & Rankin, S. R. (2018). The impact of campus climate on queer-spectrum student academic success. *Journal of LGBT Youth, 15*(2), 89–105. https://doi.org/10.1080/19361653.2018.1429978

Garvey, J. C., Taylor, J. L., & Rankin, S. R. (2015). An examination of campus climate for LGBTQ community college students. *Community College Journal of Research and Practice, 39*(6), 527–541.

Goldberg, A. E., Kuvalanka, K. A., & Dickey, L. (2019). Transgender graduate students' experiences in higher education: A mixed-methods exploratory study. *Journal of Diversity in Higher Education, 12*(1), 38–51. https://doi.org/10.1037/dhe0000074

Goode-Cross, D. T., & Tager, D. (2011). Negotiating multiple identities: How African-American gay and bisexual men persist at a predominantly White institution. *Journal of Homosexuality, 58*(9), 1235–1254. https://doi.org/10.1080/00918369.2011.605736

Grzanka, P. R., & Miles, J. R. (2016). The problem with the phrase "intersecting identities": LGBT affirmative therapy, intersectionality, and neoliberalism. *Sexuality Research & Social Policy, 13*(4), 371–389. https://doi.org/10.1007/s13178-016-0240-2

Harper, A., Finnerty, P., Martinez, M., Brace, A., Crethar, H. C., Loos, B., Harper, B., Graham, S., Singh, A., Kocet, M., Travis, L., Lambert, S., Burnes, T., Dickey, L. M., & Hammer, T. R. (2013). ALGBTIC competencies for counseling with LGBQQIA individuals. *Journal of LGBT Issues in Counseling, 7*(1), 2–43. https://doi.org/10.1080/15538605.2013.755444

Hendricks, M. L., & Testa, R. J. (2012). A conceptual framework for clinical work with transgender and gender nonconforming clients: An adaptation of the minority stress model. *Professional Psychology, Research and Practice, 43*(5), 460–467. https://doi.org/10.1037/a0029597

Kim, J. (2017, February 16). The 5 most commonly found metrics for student success. *Evisions.* https://evisions.com/resources/blog/5-commonly-found-metrics-student-success/#:~:text=Our%20objective%20here%20is%20to,performance%2C%20and%20tracking%20educational%20goals

Lenning, E. (2017). Unapologetically queer in unapologetically Black spaces: Creating an inclusive HBCU campus. *Humboldt Journal of Social Relations, 1*(39), 283–293.

Lewis, M. W., & Ericksen, K. S. (2016). Improving the climate for LGBTQ students at an Historically Black University. *Journal of LGBT Youth, 13*(3), 249–269. https://doi.org/10.1080/19361653.2016.1185761

Lewis, R. J., Derlega, V. J., Griffin, J. L., & Krowinski, A. C. (2003). Stressors for gay men and lesbians: Life stress, gay-related stress, stigma consciousness, and depressive symptoms. *Journal of Social and Clinical Psychology, 22*(6), 716–729. https://doi.org/10.1521/jscp.22.6.716.22932

Mathies, N., Coleman, T., McKie, R. M., Woodford, M. R., Courtice, E. L., Travers, R., & Renn, K. A. (2019). Hearing "that's so gay" and "no homo" on academic outcomes for LGBQ + college students. *Journal of LGBT Youth, 16*(3), 255–277. https://doi.org/10.1080/19361653.2019.1571981

Meyer, I. H. (2003). Prejudice, social stress, and mental health in lesbian, gay, and bisexual populations: Conceptual issues and research evidence. *Psychological Bulletin, 129*(5), 674–697. https://doi.org/10.1037/0033-2909.129.5.674

Morris, T. R., & Lent, R. W. (2019). Heterosexist harassment and social cognitive variables as predictors of sexual minority college students' academic satisfaction and persistence intentions. *Journal of Counseling Psychology, 66*(3), 308–316. https://doi.org/10.1037/cou0000341

Nunez, A.-M., Hurtado, S., & Galdeano, E. C. (Eds.). (2015). *Hispanic-serving institutions: Advancing research and transformative practice*. Routledge. https://doi.org/10.4324/9781315747552

Pantalone, D. W. (2015). Improving the evidence base for LGBT cultural competence training for professional psychologists: Commentary on "Quality LGBT health education: A review of key reports and webinars." *Clinical Psychology: Science and Practice, 22*(2), 145–150. https://doi.org/10.1111/cpsp.12101

Patton, M. Q. (2008). *Utilization focused evaluation* (4th ed.). Sage.

Rankin, S. R. (2005). Campus climates for sexual minorities. *New Directions for Student Services, 2005*(111), 17–23. https://doi.org/10.1002/ss.170

Rivers, B., & Swank, J. M. (2017). LGBT ally training and counselor competency: A mixed-methods study. *Journal of LGBT Issues in Counseling, 11*(1), 18–35. https://doi.org/10.1080/15538605.2017.1273162

Salem, S. (2018). Intersectionality and its discontents: Intersectionality as traveling theory. *European Journal of Women's Studies, 25*(4), 403–418. https://doi.org/10.1177/1350506816643999

Spangler, P. T., Liu, J., & Hill, C. E. (2012). Consensual qualitative research for simple qualitative data: An introduction to CQR-M. In C. E. Hill (Ed.), *Consensual qualitative research: A practical resource for investigating social science phenomena* (pp. 269–283). American Psychological Association.

Syed, M. (2010). Disciplinarity and methodology in intersectionality theory and research. *American Psychologist, 65*(1), 61–62. https://doi.org/10.1037/a0017495

# II

# STUDENT POPULATIONS

# 6

# Recommendations and Advocacy Strategies for Meeting the Needs of Transgender and Nonbinary Students

Luke R. Allen and lore m. dickey

**KEY KNOWLEDGE AREAS**

- Campus facilities may need modifications to make restrooms and student housing safe places for transgender and nonbinary (TNB)[1] students.

- Student life, including health care services, can provide inclusive activities and programs that address the needs of TNB students.

- TNB students may request changes to their academic record that are reflective of their affirmed identity.

- It is no longer acceptable to ignore the needs of TNB students, as there are more TNB people on college campuses than in previous decades.

The number of students who openly identify as transgender or gender nonbinary on college and university campuses is increasing (G. Beemyn, 2019; G. Beemyn & Rankin, 2016; Nicolazzo et al., 2018; Scott et al., 2011). At the same time, TNB students are the most likely to experience violence and other difficulties (e.g., lack of access to mentors, discrimination) on campus,

---

[1] At the time of writing this chapter, TNB was one way to describe people whose gender identity is different from the sex they were assigned at birth. The authors recognize that the term "TNB" may not fit for all people and may go out of favor over time.

https://doi.org/10.1037/0000281-007
*Affirming LGBTQ+ Students in Higher Education*, D. P. Rivera, R. L. Abreu, and K. A. Gonzalez (Editors)
Copyright © 2022 by the American Psychological Association. All rights reserved.

which can adversely affect educational outcomes (Dugan et al., 2012; Rankin et al., 2010). This chapter outlines the needs of TNB students in higher education and contains recommendations for higher education institutions on how best to meet the needs of TNB students. In addition, we emphasize advocacy strategies and describe the steps to take for addressing TNB student needs in higher education settings.

## UNDERSTANDING THE LANDSCAPE ON COLLEGE CAMPUSES

In this section, we explore areas of interest for TNB students related to college and university campuses based on the extant literature. We focus on facilities, student life including health services, and records and registration.

### Facilities

Historically, many facilities on college campuses were gender segregated. This includes restrooms, locker room facilities, and residence halls. These spaces, when they conform to the gender binary, harm TNB students, especially those with a genderqueer or nonbinary identity (Herman, 2013; Woodford et al., 2017).

### Restrooms

Language is constantly evolving and changing in the trans community, and this includes how to best identify restrooms. Currently, the most affirmative label for restrooms is *all-gender restrooms*. Previous terms used to indicate gender-inclusive restrooms have included *unisex, gender neutral, gender-inclusive,* and *family restroom*. Perhaps the most simplistic language to indicate an all-gender restroom is the word: restroom. More recently, we are beginning to see "all-gender" or "gender-inclusive" restroom signs. To some, using the terms "gender-neutral" or "unisex" is similar to racial colorblindness, where there may be some subtle erasure or denial of one's reality (Ball, 2015). According to the National School Climate Survey conducted by GLSEN, 45.2% of TNB students avoided school restrooms and locker rooms because they felt unsafe or uncomfortable (Kosciw et al., 2020). Research indicates that TNB students who are prevented from accessing appropriate restrooms have a higher likelihood of lifetime suicide attempts (Seelman, 2016; Sutton, 2016).

A primary location for harassment and assault of TNB individuals is public restrooms. Consequently, gender-segregated restrooms threaten the safety of TNB individuals. Gender-segregated restrooms can present health concerns. According to Herman (2013), 54% of TNB respondents reported having some sort of health problem as a consequence of trying to avoid using public restrooms, such as dehydration, kidney infections, and urinary tract infections. Subsequent studies have found similar results (Platt & Milam, 2018; Seelman, 2014b, 2016; Sutton, 2016).

Reminding university administrators of the benefits of single-stall, gender-inclusive restrooms goes beyond the interest and safety of TNB students (Chess et al., 2008). All-gender restrooms help families when a guardian brings a child of a different gender into a restroom. All-gender restrooms are also important for individuals with disabilities who need the assistance of a helper. Moreover, all-gender restrooms are an excellent example of a university's commitment to *universal design*.[2] Nonbinary people do not identify as male or female, hence, they may not be able use a restroom that is appropriate to their gender identity unless an all-gender restroom is provided. It is not uncommon to find single-stall restrooms on college campuses, especially in academic buildings. Sometimes these single-stall restrooms are reserved for faculty. Making these restrooms publicly available will require a significant paradigm shift that will necessarily require support from faculty.

**Locker Rooms and Athletics**

The use of locker room facilities, though not limited to members of athletic teams, merits exploration. In 2011, the National Collegiate Athletic Association (NCAA) published a document that explores the ways that colleges and universities can develop inclusive athletic opportunities for TNB athletes. It is important to note that these recommendations apply only to athletic opportunities that are official NCAA sports. As such, it does not include intramural or other athletic endeavors (even elite teams) where the sport is not a recognized NCAA opportunity. The case for inclusion of TNB athletes includes guiding principles, recommended policy, and additional guidelines. The guiding principles include statements such as "participation in intercollegiate athletics is a valuable part of the education experience for all students," "the integrity of women's sports should be preserved," and "the medical privacy of transgender students should be preserved" (NCAA Office of Inclusion, 2011, p. 10).

The NCAA highlights two areas where policies may need to be developed: the use of banned substances and mixed team status. Testosterone is considered a banned substance by the NCAA unless the athlete has a medical exception. The college or university must request this medical exception before the TNB athlete can compete (NCAA Office of Inclusion, 2011). There is no readily available information about the levels of hormones that are and are not acceptable.

Trans feminine athletes must continue to compete on the men's team for 1 year after initiating hormone treatment, which must include a testosterone blocker (e.g., finasteride, spironolactone). Trans masculine athletes must participate on the men's team after they have initiated hormone treatment. If a trans feminine athlete is within their first year on hormones and wishes to compete on the women's team, the team would be considered a mixed team. The same is true for trans masculine athletes. If they would like to continue on the women's team and have started testosterone, the team would be classified as

---

[2]Often the design is created for the average user. In contrast, Ron Mace (2008) stated, "universal design is the design of products and environments to be usable by all people, to the greatest extent possible, without the need for adaptation or specialized design."

a mixed team. If either of these athletes has yet to initiate hormone treatment, the trans feminine athlete can only compete on a men's team, and the trans masculine athlete can compete on either a men's or a women's team.

Knowing which team a student–athlete is eligible to participate on will help to clarify the use of locker rooms. First and foremost, it is important to speak with the student–athlete about their needs with regard to which locker room to use. Reasons for this include perceived safety of the student–athlete and the availability of resources. In the same ways that it is problematic to suggest that a TNB elementary school student always use the bathroom in the nurse's office, a student–athlete should not be forced to use a facility that is inconvenient or makes them conspicuous as a TNB person. The NCAA (NCAA Office of Inclusion, 2011) makes clear the importance of protecting the student-athlete's right to privacy. As a reminder, the recommendations regarding policy in this section do not apply to team or intramural sports. Colleges and universities are encouraged to develop policies of their own, so that there is less confusion about which team a TNB college student is eligible to participate on.

**Campus Housing**
It is important for college administrators to develop practices that recognize diverse sexual and gender identities and expressions (Lawrence & Mckendry, 2019). In a study by Krum et al. (2013), more than 46% of TNB participants reported that the existence of gender-inclusive housing (GIH) options positively influenced their decision to attend a school. This section discusses options of appropriate housing conditions that may be provided within the context of residential life (housing) programs. Changing the sex designation on housing intake forms, making available a wide selection of housing options, documenting the existence and location of rooms that have their own bathrooms and showers, and regular training workshops for professionals and assistants in residence life all serve to make GIH welcoming for TNB students.

**Forms**
The traditional options of "male" or "female" on an intake form not only fail to recognize the complex nature of gender identity and the multitude of factors that influence sex but also lack sufficient information for roommate assignments. Using the term *transgender* as an option when the item or question only asks for one's *gender identity* or *sexual orientation* can be problematic, as many make a conceptual distinction between *transgender identity, sexual orientation,* and *gender identity* (e.g., American Psychological Association [APA], 2015; Morgan & Stevens, 2008). Instead, the option of transgender could be included on housing forms when asking about any special concerns. When adding choices for gender beyond "male" and "female," the term "other" should never be used. The use of "other" is seen as the objectification of TNB people. Instead of using "other," this entire field may best be a fill-in-the-blank question. Another approach would be to add a category called "another gender." Finally, there is the option of asking (a) What sex were you assigned at birth and (b) What is

your gender identity? For the time being, the answers to the first part would be male or female. The second question should be a fill-in-the-blank answer choice to allow the student autonomy in identifying their gender. You may consider offering answer options to the second question as examples that can assist the responder in devising their answers. If you choose to do so, we recommend "female," "male," "transgender." Finally, administrators need to be aware that they may have students whose driver's license or birth certificate lists the sex/gender with the letter "X." As of March 2021, nineteen states and Washington, DC, allow the use of X as a gender marker on a driver's license (Movement Advancement Project, 2021). Only 13 states allow X as the gender marker on a birth certificate. X is used by some people who do not identify on the gender binary.

There may be a need to develop an interdepartmental working group to address how to develop forms and other sources of student data. Included in this group is the need for representatives from information technology, the registrar, athletics, campus health services, dean of students or campus activities, and academic affairs. This list is not intended to be exhaustive, rather a starting point for those offices that should be included.

Students have the right to privacy concerning their gender identity. Some colleges or universities may require demonstration of need for a particular housing option. If this is the case, then transgender students should be allowed to demonstrate such need through a letter from a health professional without the need for onerous activity on the part of the student. Ideally, students will be able to secure this letter from a provider in the university health services or counseling center. In some cases, colleges have considered writing letters such as this a conflict of interest. Essentially, the argument states that one university office cannot provide a letter that is antithetical to the policy of another department. Nonbinary people may never see a mental health professional or disclose their gender identity to doctors; in such cases, requiring documentation in support of students may be seen as inappropriate.

Although the number of colleges that have GIH has not been exhaustively studied, according to Campus Pride (2021a), more than 250 universities offer GIH (i.e., where students can have a roommate of any gender). When GIH is limited, usually placement priority is given to students requiring accommodations based on their gender identity/expression. In order for priority to be given, it is expected that students who desire such accommodations notify housing services in a timely manner. Krum et al. (2013) outlined a number of possible GIH options:

- *Apartment style*: Students of any sex or gender have a room with a locking door within a larger apartment and share a living room, kitchen, and one or more bathrooms.
- *Self-contained single rooms*: This involves housing students in single rooms (it is unclear whether this option includes bathroom facilities).
- *Same room/different sex pairings*: Allows students to live in the same room with roommates of any sex or gender identity, either with an attached

bathroom, a gender-inclusive bathroom on the hall floor, or one community bathroom.

- *Gender identity assignment*: Students are allowed to request to be housed based on their gender identity instead of their sex as assigned at birth.

- *Evenly split rooms*: A four-person, two-bedroom apartment style option where rooms are evenly divided by "legal sex," such that only students of the same legal sex may share a room and all students share the common spaces.

Preferences for housing in terms of *comfort* and *likeliness to attend an institution* were found between the five different housing options described above. Krum et al. (2013) stated that 34% preferred apartment-style housing, 28.2% preferred self-contained singles, 19.4% preferred same room/different sex pairings, 15.5% preferred gender identity assignment, and 2.9% preferred evenly split groups option.

**Student Life**

The kinds and types of interactions a student has while in college can have a significant impact on quality of life and academic success. In this section, we explore various aspects of student life including health services.

**Health Services**
There is a clear and consistent need for universities to improve access to address the basic health care needs of their TNB students and offer trans-affirmative care (B. G. Beemyn, 2005; Catalano, 2015; Lennon & Mistler, 2010; Santos et al., 2021; Singh et al., 2013). Historically, helping professions have contributed to discrimination against transgender individuals "by being insensitive, inattentive, uninformed, and inadequately trained and supervised to provide culturally proficient services to transgender individuals and their loved ones" (American Counseling Association [ACA], 2010, p. 145). Professional association guidelines for working with TNB individuals acknowledge that language has been used in the past to oppress and discriminate against transgender people (ACA, 2010; APA, 2015). TNB students may be reluctant to disclose their gender identity for fear of how a provider may respond. TNB students report they are not receiving adequate counseling and healthcare services on campuses (Goldberg, Beemyn, et al., 2019; McKinney, 2005; Santos et al., 2021). The lack of adequate healthcare services may have a negative effect on the retention, academic success, and physical and psychological well-being (Dugan et al., 2012; Heath & Wynne, 2019) of these students.

**Counseling Services**
One of the advantages of counseling centers in university settings is that they may not have to work within the confines of insurance companies, which allows for more flexibility with regard to the eligibility and number of sessions allowed (Lennon & Mistler, 2010). One of the challenges for a counseling

center can be to ensure TNB students are aware of the services the center provides, as well as to communicate that the center is an affirming place (Lennon & Mistler, 2010). In a study of 75 transgender students, McKinney (2005) found that only four of the respondents indicated positive interactions with campus counselors. More recently, Santos et al. (2021) identified significant negative experiences between TNB students and campus counseling center providers.

Trans-affirming mental health professionals are needed on campus to help transgender students thrive in spite of intense trans-prejudice, lack of family or peer support, and other obstacles such as institutional barriers (Goldberg, Kuvalanka, et al., 2019; Yarbrough, 2018). Clients may be uncomfortable discussing gender issues during an intake session. It is important to gather information while being sensitive to clients' needs. In a qualitative study by Singh et al. (2013), some participants reported that "the idea 'they needed' counseling" (p. 217) just because they were TNB was frustrating. One participant shared, "There's a difference between 'I need to go to a counselor' and 'I'm trans'" (p. 217). It is important to keep in mind that not all transgender clients come to therapy to discuss issues that have to do with gender (APA, 2015).

Race and cultural background also influence the lives of TNB students and their presenting concerns (see APA, 2015, Guideline 3). In the absence of clear efforts to demonstrate and display a culture of inclusivity and understanding, TNB students of color may be reticent to speak with counselors of a difference race or ethnicity about experiences related to anti-Blackness, xenophobia, or systemic racism. Not only are trans-affirming clinicians needed to reach underserved students, but counseling centers (and institutions) need to have the value of diversity represented through their recruitment, hiring, and retention practices.

Even though there is greater awareness of the needs of TNB students, it is possible that the needs of BIPOC (Black, Indigenous, and People of Color) TNB people's lives have not been part of this discussion. Often, a trainee will be working with a senior-level psychologist. This person may not have much training in work with TNB people. This means that they may be operating from dated approaches to work with TNB clients. As a result, the cultural needs of a client may be dismissed as the supervisor considers the gender concerns to be more important than racial identity. This approach erases the intersectional identities that clients (trainees and staff) bring to the conversation.

**Physical Health**

A provider with a lack of education regarding TNB health care could create serious and potentially life-threatening concerns for their TNB patients. This can be especially true when students require assistance with hormones. At the very least, all physicians in student health care services should have a basic knowledge of the effects of hormone therapy on the body (dickey, 2017). Other difficulties may arise when TNB students must enter a clinic that is described as a "men's" or "women's" clinic. Being required to access care at clinics that reify the gender binary is problematic, as the TNB person will likely be required to access a clinic that conforms with the sex they were assigned at birth. At best, accessing this care may be awkward; at worst, it is likely to be a hostile care facility.

One aspect of physical health is related to sexual and reproductive health. Sexual health for TNB people is not different than it would be for cisgender people. This means that it may be necessary to talk about safer sex practices, the need for sexually transmitted infections (STI) testing and treatment (which should include pre-exposure prophylaxis [i.e., PrEP] and postexposure prophylaxis [PEP]), and options for managing an unplanned pregnancy. Trans masculine people must know that testosterone is not a contraceptive. In fact, a trans masculine person can become pregnant, even if they are no longer menstruating after initiating hormone treatment (Light et al., 2014; Obedin-Maliver & Makadon, 2016).

TNB individuals may choose to preserve their eggs or sperm prior to initiating hormone treatment (Chang et al., 2018; dickey, 2021). There will likely be a cost associated with either process. Preserving sperm is much simpler than preserving eggs. Trans masculine people may have a more difficult time preserving their gametes. In addition to the process being more costly, unfertilized eggs are quite fragile. This means that they may not be viable for later use. Fertilized eggs are less fragile, though the trans person may not know whom they would like to have be the sperm donor. As such, it may be quite difficult for a trans masculine person to preserve fertilized eggs (dickey et al., 2016).

A final consideration with physical health is the availability of culturally competent medical care. A culturally competent medical provider will have a good understanding of the WPATH SOC and other such documents that describe a transition process. Ideally, providers will work from an informed consent or harm reduction approach, thereby reducing the obligation on the part of the student (Chang et al., 2018). Trans masculine students may need to get a regular pelvic exam. If health services only offers this type of care through a "women's clinic," it is unlikely that a trans masculine student will feel safe attending.

**Collaborative Care**
Health professionals operating in college and university health and counseling centers may not work in isolation; rather, they perform their duties as part of a larger system. The work of mental health professionals may directly or indirectly be influenced by policies established through "administrators, state-wide politicians, or religious personnel" (Lennon & Mistler, 2010, p. 235). Their duties can involve varying degrees of interactions with faculty and staff, other departments, health services, and administrators. TNB students may benefit from discussions with administrators and staff in part because the student may not have the full responsibility of advocating for their needs (Ducheny et al., 2017). For instance, counselors and therapists may find that campus health services were unaware of TNB concerns and could then work

to improve them together. TNB students who are denied treatment may choose to purchase hormones online or through gray market sources, due to the lower cost. According to the American College of Obstetricians and Gynecologists' Committee on Health Care for Underserved Women (2011), more than 50% of trans persons have used injected hormones that "were obtained illegally or used outside of conventional medical settings" (p. 1455). There are health risks associated with this, as taking unregulated dosages of hormones without medical supervision may result in dissatisfactory physical development or life-threatening conditions (Giordano, 2008; Mepham et al., 2014). A harm reduction approach would suggest that campus counselors first work with the client to attain proper oversight and medical care from qualified health professionals (Marlatt et al., 2011). If the student continues to self-medicate, the counselor should make a referral to campus or local health services that offer free instruction on how to properly inject medications.

**Records and Registration**

The registrar is the keeper of all records related to a person's academic experience (e.g., grades, enrollment, withdrawal, class rosters). Trans students may need to interact with the registrar, and if the university does not have favorable policies for how trans students can change their name or gender marker in their official record, this can be quite challenging for the student.

**Advising**

Initially, students likely have little choice on whom they are assigned as an academic advisor. This may be a good match from the outset, or it may not (Sheldon et al., 2015). A good advisor will understand some of the academic challenges faced by TNB students and be prepared to advocate for their advisees' needs. This includes working with the student to address challenging interactions with course instructors, such as the failure to use an affirmed name and pronouns. Students are encouraged to work out any differences they might have with their advisor prior to asking for a different advisor. Advisors should be prepared to understand the challenges a TNB person might face in an academic setting that arise from a social and/or medical transition. Referral to appropriate counseling services is critical as mental health counseling is not the role of the academic advisor (Pryor, 2015). Many colleges and universities have robust policies that protect sexual and gender minority (SGM) students and educational and outreach programming that celebrates sexual and gender diversity. Ensuring that academic advisors have access to resources that address the unique needs of SGM students is important. At the same time, some of the experiences that SGM people have on college campuses can be traumatic in nature. Whether this is a "big T" trauma (e.g., rape or sexual assault, violence) or another very difficult interaction or set of interactions in which the TNB student is discriminated against or mistreated in the classroom can have a significant impact on the students' overall success.

## Basic Orientation

Orientation is a time when students are first introduced to services and programs available on campus. Members of the student affairs or dean of students office are encouraged to provide an inclusive orientation program with information on programs that are available to LGBTQ+ students. Allowing TNB students or student organizations to discuss these resources during orientation would be highly appropriate.

## Name Changes

Name changes can be handled in a number of ways. Most colleges and universities have policies in place that allow a change of name only when it has occurred through a legal process (e.g., marriage, court-ordered name change). For TNB students, name changes can be a significant hurdle, making it difficult to present in a manner that is supportive of their identity. The cost for this process alone can be quite significant. Added to that burden is the need to be out to one's parents, if the parents have access to the student record.

At schools where instructors are required to keep attendance records for all classes, this may be an embarrassing time for TNB students. Some schools have created flexible policies or have purchased software that allows a student to make a name change without legal documentation on university records, including changes to course and grade rosters, directories, and other documents such as student ID cards and diplomas (Washington University in St. Louis, n.d.). The reasoning behind these less-restrictive approaches is so that any person in the campus community can be treated with respect, as others will have access to the name they use rather than the one they were given at birth.

The second author worked with a former institution to develop a process for informing course instructors of name and pronoun usage for TNB students. The model for this process is similar to how instructors are notified of classroom accommodations for students with documented disabilities. For TNB students, they register with the LGBTQ+ office (or other such office) and indicate which course instructors should be notified of name and pronoun changes that are not consistent with the official registration system. Students may choose to include all or only some of their course instructors. The LGBTQ+ office will then send letters to course instructors asking them to adhere to the student's wishes regarding the use of names and pronouns in the classroom. This process has the potential to eliminate awkward conversations between students and faculty members. Faculty will be able to make a correction on their roster prior to the start of classes.

## EFFECTING CHANGE ON COLLEGE CAMPUSES

Effecting change on college and university campuses requires support and buy-in from faculty, staff, and administrators across campus, especially at the highest levels. Building this collaboration means the best chance of success in creating the campus environment that allows TNB students to feel safe and supported, so they can focus on their education.

**Nondiscrimination Policies**

TNB students are encouraged to have a good understanding of the nondiscrimination policies that are in place at their college or university. The number of schools that have TNB-inclusive policies continues to grow (over 1,000; Campus Pride, 2021b; Perdue, 2015). It is also possible that different policies apply to different groups of people on campus (e.g., faculty, staff, students).

The second author worked at a midsized southern university, where there were five different nondiscrimination statements. Each statement covered different protected classes, and none of the statements included gender identity or gender expression. Students are encouraged to work with officials in the classroom, campus activities, the workplace, and student affairs to ensure that they have the necessary protection according to university policy in the event that they are the victim of harassment or discrimination.

Much work has been done in recent years within the court system to address discrimination toward TNB people in the workplace. Anecdotally, some would say that the rulings that state that discriminating against TNB people is a form of sex discrimination according to Title IX is sufficient protection for TNB people in the workplace. However, others discuss the importance of having a clear statement that is inclusive of gender identity and gender expression. These statements give a clear signal to current and prospective members of the community that the campus is welcoming, and that there is a safety net to protect them.

**Advocacy**

Advocacy for TNB people can be applied at several levels. This includes individual, institutional, and policy levels of change (Chang et al., 2018). For the purposes of this chapter, we focus on changes at the institutional level.

In meetings with administrators, you may find it useful to know your University's peer institutions. *Peer institutions* are universities that are comparable to one another in relevant ways such as size, enrollment, research activity, type, or association. Peer institutions are the colleges and universities to which your university will most often compare itself. If you do not know your peer institutions, the office for institutional research will have a list of such institutions. You may also be able to find this on the college or university website. Depending on your advocacy aims, it can be helpful to explore what your peer institutions might already have in place. If you are able to identify peer institutions that have already made progress toward the goal for which you are aiming, these may be important to note in meetings, memoranda, letters, and campus newspaper interviews. Highlight where your university might be lagging behind, but also where it is ahead of peer institutions.

The first author advocated for gender-inclusive restrooms at a previous university. He wrote a memorandum directly to higher administration about the need for gender-inclusive restroom facilities. There was no response from higher administration. Although there was support from his faculty advisors and academic department, this support was insufficient to gain the attention of administrators. His mistake in trying to affect change was that he was not inclusive and collaborative from the beginning. That is, he did not formally seek support from others campus offices and groups. Recognizing this mistake, and the lack of response from higher administrators, he changed his approach and was able to garner support from a variety of sources. The university newspaper ran a cover story, which gathered attention, both positive and negative. It was not always easy getting support; however, the more support we had, the easier it was to get more people and organizations on board. In the meantime, through collaboration with the university architect, single-stall restrooms were located, and gendered signs were converted to gender-inclusive restroom signs. The first author helped to change the university's guidelines regarding the construction and maintenance of restrooms (see Appendix 6.1 for sample policies). Although there have been no policy-level changes regarding restroom facilities as of the time of this writing, this issue has risen to the level of university administrators.

**Title IX**
Title IX of the Education Amendments of 1972 prohibits sex discrimination in federally funded education programs and activities in the United States (20 U.S.C. §1681 et seq.). This includes colleges and universities receiving any federal financial assistance (including financial aid). In 2014, new guidance regarding Title IX was issued by the U.S. Department of Education's Office of Civil Rights (OCR) and aimed to protect all students regardless of their sexual orientation or gender identity. The OCR advised: "Title IX's sex discrimination prohibition extends to claims of discrimination based on gender identity or failure to conform to stereotypical notions of masculinity or femininity and OCR accepts such complaints for investigation" (U.S. Department of Education, 2014, p. 2). This guidance significantly broadened the scope of Title IX. However, the Trump administration withdrew the letter described above (U.S. Department of Education Office for Civil Rights, 2017). The withdrawal of the advice does not change Title IX itself nor the fact that it protects transgender people (National Center for Transgender Equality, 2017). It indicated the Department of Education's OCR did not intend to enforce the law in the same manner as did the Obama administration. However, on March 8, 2021, President Biden issued an executive order stating "all students should be guaranteed an educational environment free from discrimination on the basis of sex, including discrimination in the form of sexual harassment, which encompasses sexual violence, and including discrimination on the basis of

sexual orientation or gender identity" (Biden, Jr., 2021, Section 1). Reinterpretations, withdrawal of guidance, and administration changes add to the confusion about the ways in which transgender students, professionals, and allies may advocate for a safer and welcoming environment. Nevertheless, Title IX is still pertinent to the protection and fair treatment of transgender students. At the time of this writing, it is too soon to tell exactly how this new executive order will affect policy and new guidance; however, it likely will be supportive of the needs of TNB students.

### Title VII of the Civil Rights Acts of 1964

In recent years, there has been a change in the ways that Title VII of the Civil Rights Act of 1964 (hereafter Title VII) has been interpreted. There has been less attention focused on Title VII than there has on Title IX. Title VII has a broader focus in that it relates to the rights of people across many domains, whereas Title IX is focused on education settings.

Title VII has been used as a means of addressing employment discrimination (Lee, 2012). Lee (2012) listed the gender nonconformity approach to be the most commonly used defense of a TNB person's rights when they have been discriminated against. Less common are the per se and constructionist approaches to making a claim against an employer. Lee noted that the Price Waterhouse v. Hopkins (490 U.S. 228, 1989) case led to a change in the ways that Title VII was applied. Prior to this, previous actions against employers were found in favor of the employer, as a person's gender identity was not considered to be protected. The courts did not equate gender identity with sex, which was the protected class (Archibald, 2016).

Title IX and Title VII have both been used in recent years to provide protection for TNB people against various forms of discrimination. The challenge with these cases is that there is a significant burden on the trans person to prove they were discriminated against. This is not always easy to prove, in part because many employers have learned not to say "I am firing you because you are trans." Still, we know that TNB people are often mistreated in the workplace and Title IX or Title VII may offer a legal remedy.

## PRACTICE RECOMMENDATIONS

This section lists some practice recommendations that represent a starting place for colleges and universities that wish to increase to safety of their campus for TNB students, faculty, and staff.

### Facilities

The recommendations under this section concern facilities in colleges and universities. This includes general restroom recommendations, residential life, and student life.

## Restrooms

One possible solution to reduce the problem of binary restrooms is the implementation of future-oriented guidelines and policies (see Appendix 6.1 and Appendix 6.2) requiring that all extensively renovated or constructed buildings include at least one single-stall, gender-inclusive restroom. Students and other members of the university community should be able to use any public restroom that corresponds to their gender identity.

Students, faculty, staff, administrators, and organizations who serve TNB people within an institution can form an alliance with the campus facilities and services, the university architect, or building managers to survey and locate existing single occupancy restrooms and request sign changes. Coordinate with student affairs, campus health centers, and LGBTQ+ organizations (when present) to make a list of all-gender restrooms available on your university's website.

## Residential Life

Residential life ("res life") staff should make available the location of rooms and housing options that have their own bathrooms and showers. B. G. Beemyn (2005) suggested that when housing does not have a private restroom for each room, res life staff should document whether the buildings have any gender-inclusive restrooms, and which (if any) shower facilities have lockable stalls, rather than just a shower curtain. Res life offices should provide a GIH option in which a student can have a roommate of any gender. GIH could, in part, be located in an LGBTQ+-themed housing option or an LGBTQ+/ally living–learning community. It is important to note though that LGBTQ+-themed residential housing may not be comfortable for all TNBers. For example, a heterosexual trans man living in LGBTQ+-themed residential housing might feel unwanted pressure to disclose his trans identity. Even though the student made the decision to live in an LGBTQ+-friendly space, not all students want to be open about their gender history. When possible, have a wide selection of housing options. B. Beemyn et al. (2005) provided excellent advice for res life staff regarding how TNB students can interface with res life:

> To inform current and prospective students about how the campus addresses the housing needs of transgender people, colleges and universities should include such information, along with the contact information of a housing staff person who can respond to . . . questions and concerns. (p. 54)

Some universities have taken this advice by outlining frequently asked questions regarding GIH on their websites or providing relevant information in a guide to community living. Other recommendations for res life include:

- The option to self-identify one's gender on housing forms.

- "Your gender is: _____," or multiple choices of "Male," "Female," "Self-Identify: _____" (B. Beemyn et al., 2005, p. 52).

- Only the information needed to fulfill housing requests should be solicited.

- A letter from a medical or mental health professional should be sufficient in demonstrating need for housing accommodations based on a student's gender identity.

- Students should not be required to have changed the gender marker on their birth certificate or driver license in order to receive appropriate, safe housing.

**Health Services**

Professionals working in university counseling and health care clinics need to have additional training to be aware of the specific needs of transgender students (APA, 2015; dickey, 2017). In addition to this awareness, they also need to be able to provide more specialized care. The university should adopt hiring practices such that the campus health and counseling centers employ professionals who are knowledgeable and experienced in serving TNB students. Campus health centers should develop and maintain a list of doctors and counselors who specialize in trans health in case an outside referral is needed.

The following advocacy steps and solutions are drawn from a number of sources (B. G. Beemyn, 2005; Catalano, 2015; Santos et al., 2021; Seelman, 2014a; Singh et al., 2013) and the authors of this chapter.

*Beginning Steps*

- Foster a TNB-friendly climate through visible "safe space" signs.

- Seek input from TNB students about their health care experiences.

- Identify, affiliate with, and publicize the names of community providers who are supportive of TNB students and knowledgeable about trans health concerns.

- Observe Transgender Day of Remembrance (November 20).

- Observe Transgender Day of Visibility (March 31).

- Take advantage of free, on-demand webinars such as those provided by the Fenway Institute (see https://www.lgbthealtheducation.org) or use the campus's electronic library resources to locate relevant journals or journal articles.

- Train counselors to write letters for medical transitions when appropriate.

*Intermediate Steps*

- Provide education on the devastating effects of trans-negativity (e.g., suicidality; substance abuse; and violence, including murder).

- Require all campus health and counseling center staff to attend training about trans health concerns or read books that are designed to provide basic information (see Erickson-Schroth, 2014).

- Offer counseling services that support the coming-out process.
- Enable TNB members of the campus community to identify their affirmed name and gender identity on forms and records.

*Advanced Steps*

- Create a trans health care team to provide comprehensive and collaborative care to TNB students.
- Provide gynecological exams for affirmed-male students.
- Have pharmacies stock hormones and intramuscular and subcutaneous syringes.
- Offer health insurance coverage for hormone therapy, gender-affirming surgeries, counseling services, and other health care needs related to TNB care.

**Records and Registration**

The following are recommendations related to records and registration services, including advising, basic orientation, and name/name changes.

- When a roll call is necessary, instructors should use last names and allow the student to state the name, nickname, and pronouns they use.
- Provide broadly inclusive orientation programming that addresses the unique needs of TNB students.
- Implement policies that allow a student, faculty, or staff member to make a name change without legal documentation on university records.

## CONCLUSION AND FUTURE ENDEAVORS

The number of openly identified transgender and nonbinary students is increasing on college and university campuses. Faculty, staff, and administrators are encouraged to implement the recommendations provided in this chapter. Further, language used by TNB people continues to evolve. By keeping pace with TNB students and their needs, colleges and universities will be able to create an affirming climate. As a result, TNB students will be given the best chance to thrive. Colleges and universities have the capacity to create health, safe, affirming educational environments inclusive of all students regardless of their gender history.

## DISCUSSION QUESTIONS

1. What are actions I can take that would demonstrate support of TNB students?
2. How do I conceptualize the roles of policy and advocacy given my position and job title at my institution?

3. What areas are in need of growth and change at my own institution?
4. How might the needs of TNB students differ based on the state and/or national jurisdiction of the institution?
5. What resources are already available to me and TNB students at my institution?
6. How do I know if I am perceived as being affirmative toward TNB students?

**RESOURCES**

1. *Trans Bodies, Trans Selves*, by L. Erickson-Schroth (2014). Oxford University Press.
2. *Trans People in Higher Education*, edited by G. Beemyn (2019). State University of New York Press.
3. *A Clinician's Guide to Gender-Affirming Care: Working With Transgender and Gender Nonconforming Clients*, by S. C. Chang, A. A. Singh, & l. m. dickey (2018). Context Press.
4. "From Best to Intentional Practices: Reimagining Implementation of Gender-Inclusive Housing," in *Journal of Student Affairs Research and Practice*, by Z. Nicolazzo, S. B. Marine, & R. Wagner (2018).
5. *Supporting Transgender and Non-Binary Students and Staff in Further and Higher Education: Practical Advice for Colleges and Universities*, by M. Lawrence & S. Mckendry (2019). Jessica Kingsley Publishers.
6. *Transgender Mental Health*, by E. Yarbrough (2018). American Psychiatric Association.
7. *The Queer and Transgender Resilience Workbook: Skills for Navigating Sexual Orientation and Gender Expression*, by A. A. Singh (2018). New Harbinger Publications.
8. *A Guide to Transgender Health: State-of-the-Art Information for Gender-Affirming People and Their Supporters*, by R. A. Heath & K. Wynne (2019). Praeger.
9. *Case Studies in Clinical Practice With Trans and Gender Non-Binary Clients: A Handbook for Working With Children, Adolescents, and Adults*, by l. m. dickey (2021). Jessica Kingsley Publishers.
10. *The Gender Quest Workbook: A Guide for Teens and Young Adults Exploring Gender Identity*, by R. J. Testa, D. Coolhart, & J. Peta (2015). Instant Help Books.

## APPENDIX 6.1: SAMPLE GUIDELINES FOR CONSTRUCTION OF SINGLE OCCUPANCY GENDER-INCLUSIVE RESTROOMS

### SINGLE OCCUPANCY GENDER-INCLUSIVE RESTROOMS

1. All buildings shall have a single occupancy gender-inclusive restroom in the following locations:
   a. On the main floor level.
   b. On every floor level other than the main level, except where a single occupancy gender-inclusive restroom exists on the floor above and the floor below.
   c. Where required by code.
2. Every construction project shall consider the location of existing single occupancy gender-inclusive restrooms and shall include the construction of additional single occupancy gender-inclusive restrooms to meet the requirements of the preceding paragraph. No exception is given to any project, except with written approval from [FACILITIES & SERVICES].
3. All single occupancy gender-inclusive restrooms shall meet the requirements of the [NATIONAL ACCESSIBILITIES LAW] and all local and state/province of [STATE] accessibility guidelines.
4. The sign that identifies the single occupancy gender-inclusive restroom shall:
   a. Include the word "Restroom."
   b. See inclusionary sign options below:

5. The restroom door shall use a lock that switches from "vacant" to "occupied" when the lock is activated.
6. Contact [FACILITIES & SERVICES] for signage, plumbing fixtures, restroom accessories, and space requirements.

**Note**: University *guidelines* generally include a higher level of detail than university *policies* (see Appendix 6.2), as is the case here. The process to update guidelines is usually less comprehensive than changing policy.

**Note**: The example guidelines above should be edited, changed, or revised in collaboration with your university's facilities and services unit (or equivalent), as needed.

**Note**: Sometimes, as in the case of low-cost renovations, funding may not be available to create or renovate a restroom. A formula should be constructed in advance for cases such as this (e.g., if the cost of accommodating a bathroom would be more than X% of the total funding).

## APPENDIX 6.2: SAMPLE POLICY LANGUAGE FOR GENDER-INCLUSIVE RESTROOMS

### POLICY STATEMENT:

All buildings shall have a gender-inclusive restroom as is outlined in university guidelines. In keeping with the University's policy of nondiscrimination on the basis of gender identity, any person may use the restroom that corresponds to the individual's gender identity.

### REFERENCES

American Counseling Association. (2010). Competencies for counseling with transgender clients. *Journal of LGBT Issues in Counseling*, 4(3–4), 135–159. https://doi.org/10.1080/15538605.2010.524839

American Psychological Association. (2015). Guidelines for psychological practice with transgender and gender nonconforming people. *American Psychologist*, 70(9), 832–864. https://doi.org/10.1037/a0039906

Archibald, C. J. (2016). Transgender bathroom rights. *Duke Journal of Gender Law & Policy*, 24(1), 1–31. https://scholarship.law.duke.edu/djglp/vol24/iss1/1

Ball, A. L. (2015, November 5). In all-gender restrooms, the signs reflect the times. *The New York Times*. https://www.nytimes.com/2015/11/08/style/transgender-restroom-all-gender.html?_r=0

Beemyn, B., Curtis, B., Davis, M., & Tubbs, N. J. (2005). Transgender issues on college campuses. *New Directions for Student Services*, 2005(111), 49–60. https://doi.org/10.1002/ss.173

Beemyn, B. G. (2005). Making campuses more inclusive of transgender students. *Journal of Gay & Lesbian Issues in Education*, 3(1), 77–87. https://doi.org/10.1300/J367v03n01_08

Beemyn, G. (Ed.). (2019). *Trans people in higher education*. SUNY Press.

Beemyn, G., & Rankin, S. R. (2016). Creating a gender-inclusive campus. In Y. Martinez-San Miguel & S. Tobias (Eds.), *Trans studies: The challenge to hetero/homo normativities* (pp. 21–32). Rutgers Press.

Biden, J. R., Jr. (2021). *Guaranteeing an educational environment free from discrimination on the basis of sex, including sexual orientation or gender identity*. https://www.federalregister.gov/documents/2021/03/11/2021-05200/guaranteeing-an-educational-environment-free-from-discrimination-on-the-basis-of-sex-including

Campus Pride. (2021a). *Colleges and universities that provide gender-inclusive housing.* https://www.campuspride.org/tpc/gender-inclusive-housing/

Campus Pride. (2021b). *Colleges and universities with nondiscrimination policies that include gender identity/expression.* https://www.campuspride.org/tpc/nondiscrimination/

Catalano, D. C. J. (2015). "Trans enough?": The pressures trans men negotiate in higher education. *TSQ: Transgender Studies Quarterly, 2*(3), 411–430. https://doi.org/10.1215/23289252-2926399

Chang, S. C., Singh, A. A., & dickey, l. m. (2018). *A clinician's guide to gender-affirming care: Working with transgender and gender nonconforming clients.* Context Press.

Chess, S., Kafer, A., Quizar, J., & Richardson, M. U. (2008). Calling all restroom revolutionaries! In M. B. Sycamore (Ed.), *That's revolting! Queer strategies for resisting assimilation* (pp. 216–236). Soft Skull.

Committee on Health Care for Underserved Women. (2011). Committee opinion no. 512: Health care for transgender individuals. *Obstetrics & Gynecology, 118*(6), 1454–1458. https://doi.org/10.1097/AOG.0b013e31823ed1c1

dickey, l. m. (2017). Toward developing clinical competence: Improving health care of gender diverse people. *American Journal of Public Health, 107*(2), 222–223. https://doi.org/10.2105/ajph.2016.303581

dickey, l. m. (2021). *Case studies in clinical practice with trans and gender non-binary clients: A handbook for working with children, adolescents, and adults.* Jessica Kingsley Publishers.

dickey, l. m., Ducheny, K. M., & Ehrbar, R. D. (2016). Family creation options for transgender and gender nonconforming people. *Psychology of Sexual Orientation and Gender Diversity, 3*(2), 173–179. https://doi.org/10.1037/sgd0000178

Ducheny, K., Hendricks, M. L., & Keo-Meier, C. L. (2017). TGNC-affirmative interdisciplinary collaborative care. In A. A. Singh & l. m. dickey (Eds.), *Perspectives on sexual orientation and diversity: Affirmative counseling and psychological practice with transgender and gender nonconforming clients* (pp. 69–93). American Psychological Association. https://doi.org/10.1037/14957-004

Dugan, J. P., Kusel, M. L., & Simounet, D. M. (2012). Transgender college students: An exploratory study of perceptions, engagement, and educational outcomes. *Journal of College Student Development, 53*(5), 719–736. https://doi.org/10.1353/csd.2012.0067

Erickson-Schroth, L. (2014). *Trans bodies, trans selves: A resource for the community.* Oxford University Press.

Giordano, S. (2008). Lives in a chiaroscuro. Should we suspend the puberty of children with gender identity disorder? *Journal of Medical Ethics, 2008*(34), 580–584. https://doi.org/10.1136/jme.2007.021097

Goldberg, A. E., Beemyn, G., & Smith, J. Z. (2019). What is needed, what is valued: Trans students' perspectives on trans-inclusive policies and practices in higher education. *Journal of Educational & Psychological Consultation, 29*(1), 27–67. https://doi.org/10.1080/10474412.2018.1480376

Goldberg, A. E., Kuvalanka, K. A., Budge, S. L., Benz, M. B., & Smith, J. Z. (2019). Health care experiences of transgender binary and nonbinary university students. *The Counseling Psychologist, 47*(1), 59–97. https://doi.org/10.1177/0011000019827568

Heath, R. A., & Wynne, K. (2019). *A guide to transgender health: State-of-the-art information for gender-affirming people and their supporters.* Praeger.

Herman, J. L. (2013). Gendered restrooms and minority stress: The public regulation of gender and its impact on transgender people's lives. *Journal of Public Management & Social Policy, 19*(1), 65–80.

Kosciw, J. G., Clark, C. M., Truong, N. L., & Zongrone, A. D. (2020). *The 2019 National School Climate Survey: The experiences of lesbian, gay, bisexual, transgender, and queer youth in our nation's schools.* GLSEN. https://www.glsen.org/sites/default/files/2020-11/NSCS19-111820.pdf

Krum, T. E., Davis, K. S., & Galupo, M. P. (2013). Gender-inclusive housing preferences: A survey of college-aged transgender students. *Journal of LGBT Youth, 10*(1–2), 64–82. https://doi.org/10.1080/19361653.2012.718523

Lawrence, M., & Mckendry, S. (2019). *Supporting transgender and non-binary students and staff in further and higher education: Practical advice for colleges and universities*. Jessica Kingsley Publishers.

Lee, J. (2012). Lost in translation: The challenges of remedying transgender employment discrimination under Title VII. *Harvard Journal of Law & Gender, 35*(2), 423–461. https://harvardjlg.com/wp-content/uploads/sites/19/2012/01/Lee.pdf

Lennon, E., & Mistler, B. J. (2010). Breaking the binary: Providing effective counseling to transgender students in college and university settings. *Journal of LGBTQ Issues in Counseling, 4*(3–4), 228–240. https://doi.org/10.1080/15538605.2010.524848

Light, A. D., Obedin-Maliver, J., Sevelius, J. M., & Kerns, J. L. (2014). Transgender men who experienced pregnancy after female-to-male gender transitioning. *Obstetrics & Gynecology, 124*(6), 1120–1127. https://doi.org/10.1097/AOG.0000000000000540

Mace, R. (2008). *About UD*. The Center for Universal Design. https://www.ncsu.edu/ncsu/design/cud/about_ud/about_ud.htm

Marlatt, G. A., Larimer, M. E., & Witkiewitz, K. (Eds.). (2011). *Harm reduction: Pragmatic strategies for managing high-risk behaviors* (2nd ed.). Guilford Press.

McKinney, J. S. (2005). On the margins: A study of the experiences of transgender college students. *Journal of Gay & Lesbian Issues in Education, 3*(1), 63–76. https://doi.org/10.1300/J367v03n01_07

Mepham, N., Bouman, W. P., Arcelus, J., Hayter, M., & Wylie, K. R. (2014). People with gender dysphoria who self-prescribe cross-sex hormones: Prevalence, sources, and side effects knowledge. *Journal of Sexual Medicine, 11*(12), 2995–3001. https://doi.org/10.1111/jsm.12691

Morgan, S. W., & Stevens, P. E. (2008). Transgender identity development as represented by a group of female-to-male transgendered adults. *Issues in Mental Health Nursing, 29*(6), 585–599. https://doi.org/10.1080/01612840802048782

Movement Advancement Project. (2021). *Snapshot: LGBTQ equality maps*. https://www.lgbtmap.org/equality-maps

National Center for Transgender Equality. (2017). *FAQ on the withdrawal of federal guidance on transgender students*. http://www.transequality.org/issues/resources/faq-on-the-withdrawal-of-federal-guidance-on-transgender-students

NCAA Office of Inclusion. (2011, August). *NCAA inclusion of transgender student-athletes* (Adopted April 2010). https://ncaaorg.s3.amazonaws.com/inclusion/lgbtq/INC_TransgenderHandbook.pdf

Nicolazzo, Z., Marine, S. B., & Wagner, R. (2018). From best to intentional practices: Reimagining implementation of gender-inclusive housing. *Journal of Student Affairs Research and Practice, 55*(2), 225–236. https://doi.org/10.1080/19496591.2018.1399896

Obedin-Maliver, J., & Makadon, H. J. (2016). Transgender men and pregnancy. *Obstetric Medicine, 9*(1), 4–8. https://doi.org/10.1177/1753495X15612658

Perdue, T. J. (2015). Trans* issues for colleges and universities: Records, housing, restrooms, locker rooms, and athletics. *The Journal of College and University Law, 41*, 45–70. https://heinonline.org/HOL/LandingPage?handle=hein.journals/jcolunly41&div=7&id=&page=

Platt, L. F., & Milam, S. R. B. (2018). Public discomfort with gender appearance-inconsistent bathroom use: The oppressive bind of bathroom laws for transgender individuals. *Gender Issues, 35*(3), 181–201. https://doi.org/10.1007/s12147-017-9197-6

Pryor, J. T. (2015). Out in the classroom: Transgender student experiences at a large public university. *Journal of College Student Development, 56*(5), 440–455. https://doi.org/10.1353/csd.2015.0044

Rankin, S., Weber, G. N., Blumenfeld, W. J., Frazer, S., Campus Pride, & Q Research Institute for Higher Education. (2010). *2010 state of higher education for lesbian, gay, bisexual and transgender people*. Campus Pride.

Santos, T. C., Mann, E. S., & Pfeffer, C. A. (2021). Are university health services meeting the needs of transgender college students? A qualitative assessment of a public university. *Journal of American College Health, 69*(1), 59–66. https://doi.org/10.1080/07448481.2019.1652181

Scott, D. A., Belke, S. L., & Barfield, H. G. (2011). Career development with transgender college students: Implications for career and employment counselors. *Journal of Employment Counseling, 48*(3), 105–113. https://doi.org/10.1002/j.2161-1920.2011.tb01116.x

Seelman, K. L. (2014a). Recommendations of transgender students, staff, and faculty in the USA for improving college campuses. *Gender and Education, 26*(6), 618–635. https://doi.org/10.1080/09540253.2014.935300

Seelman, K. L. (2014b). Transgender individuals' access to college housing and bathrooms: Findings from the National Transgender Discrimination Survey. *Journal of Gay & Lesbian Social Services, 26*(2), 186–206. https://doi.org/10.1080/10538720.2014.891091

Seelman, K. L. (2016). Transgender adults' access to college bathrooms and housing and the relationship to suicidality. *Journal of Homosexuality, 63*(10), 1378–1399. https://doi.org/10.1080/00918369.2016.1157998

Sheldon, K. M., Garton, B., Orr, R., & Smith, A. (2015). The advisor quality survey: Good college advisors are available, knowledgeable, and autonomy supportive. *Journal of College Student Development, 56*(3), 261–273. https://doi.org/10.1353/csd.2015.0027

Singh, A. A. (2018). *The queer and transgender resilience workbook: Skills for navigating sexual orientation and gender expression.* New Harbinger Publications.

Singh, A. A., Meng, S., & Hansen, A. (2013). "It's already hard enough being a student": Developing affirming college environments for trans youth. *Journal of LGBT Youth, 10*(3), 208–223. https://doi.org/10.1080/19361653.2013.800770

Sutton, H. (2016). Transgender college students more at risk for suicide when denied bathroom, housing rights. *Campus Security Report, 13*(2), 9. https://doi.org/10.1002/casr.30167

U.S. Department of Education Office for Civil Rights. (2014). *Questions and answers on Title IX and sexual violence.* www2.ed.gov/about/offices/list/ocr/docs/qa-201404-title-ix.pdf

U.S. Department of Education Office for Civil Rights. (2017, February 22). *Dear Colleague Letter* [U.S. Secretary of Education Betsy DeVos Issues Statement on New Title IX Guidance]. http://www2.ed.gov/about/offices/list/ocr/letters/colleague-201702-title-ix.docx

Washington University in St. Louis. (n.d.). *Preferred name policy in student information.* https://registrar.wustl.edu/student-records/ssn-name-changes/preferred-name-policy-student-information/

Woodford, M. R., Joslin, J. Y., Pitcher, E. N., & Renn, K. A. (2017). A mixed-methods inquiry into trans* environmental microaggressions on college campuses: Experiences and outcomes. *Journal of Ethnic & Cultural Diversity in Social Work, 26*(1–2), 95–111. https://doi.org/10.1080/15313204.2016.1263817

Yarbrough, E. (2018). *Transgender mental health.* American Psychiatric Association.

# 7

# Supporting LGBTQ+ College Students Living With Disabilities

Franco Dispenza, Merideth Ray, and Jamian S. Coleman

**KEY KNOWLEDGE AREAS**

- LGBTQ+ college students (undergraduate and graduate) living with disabilities may have visible/apparent or invisible/nonapparent conditions that are either congenital or acquired. Disabilities include mental/behavioral health, developmental, neuropsychological, cognitive, sensory, physical, motor, medical/chronic illness and other physical conditions.

- LGBTQ+ college students living with disabilities encounter ableism, disablism, microaggressions, stigma, oppression, and other minority related stressors from a variety of communities, including the disability, sexual, and gender minority communities.

- LGBTQ+ students living with disabilities are resilient in the face of adversity.

- Strategies, practices, and interventions in higher education should focus on incorporating Universal Design principles, bolstering resilience, easing transitions into college and into the world-of-work, upholding and creating affirming policies, and helping to develop welcoming and inclusive campus environments.

Disability communities are highly diverse in terms of race, ethnicity, nationality, religion, spirituality, language, and socioeconomic status. Undergraduate

---

https://doi.org/10.1037/0000281-008
*Affirming LGBTQ+ Students in Higher Education*, D. P. Rivera, R. L. Abreu, and K. A. Gonzalez (Editors)
Copyright © 2022 by the American Psychological Association. All rights reserved.

and graduate students living with disabilities attending institutions of higher education may hold any number of the aforementioned identities, including diverse sexual orientations, gender identities, and forms of gender expression. Although not focused specifically on college and university students, researchers have found that prevalence rates of disability are higher among sexual minority persons than heterosexual-identified persons living in the United States (Björkenstam et al., 2016; Fredriksen-Goldsen et al., 2012). Similar disability prevalence rates also exist for gender minority persons (e.g., transgender, genderqueer, gender nonconforming; Witten, 2014). In addition to high prevalence rates of disability, Cochran et al. (2017) reported higher rates of functional impairment (e.g., limitations or difficulties that interfere with activities of daily living, such as mobility) among sexual minority persons when compared with heterosexual-identified persons. As normative facets of lifespan development and culture, college and university faculty and staff will encounter LGBTQ+ students living with disabilities.

College and university students may possess a diverse array of disabilities. Disabilities can be congenital, present at birth, or acquired at any point during the lifespan. Disabilities include, but are not limited to, mental/behavioral health (e.g., schizoaffective, bipolar, substance use), developmental (e.g., autism, cerebral palsy), neuropsychological/cognitive (e.g., intellectual, learning, or traumatic brain injury), sensory (e.g., d/Deaf, macular degeneration), medical/chronic illness (e.g., sickle cell, cancer), and other physical (e.g., neuromuscular) conditions (Dispenza, Hunter, & Kumar, 2018). Disabilities also are classified as either visible/apparent or not visible/apparent. In one study, approximately 76% to 86% of all college students registered with disability service offices identified living with a learning, attention, psychiatric, or chronic illness-related disability (Raue & Lewis, 2011). However, it is unknown how many college and university students with disabilities identify as LGBTQ+.

College and university faculty, staff, and administrators will encounter students living with disabilities, as well as LGBTQ+ students, but they also need to understand the psychosocial and academic experiences of LGBTQ+ students living with disabilities. Despite limited but growing research and scholarship on LGBTQ+ college students living with disabilities (Harley et al., 2002; Miller, 2017; Miller et al., 2019), college and university faculty, staff, and administrators need fundamental conceptual strategies—or alternative ways of thinking about nuance and complex issues pertaining to this population. In this chapter, we first discuss how oppression and stigma, disclosure and identity, and resilience impact the lives of LGBTQ+ students living with disabilities. Without being overly prescriptive—due to limited research, policy, or even established standards in higher education—we then provide several considerations for affirmative practice, including universal design, transitions and supports, institution and legal policies, and additional recommendations for campus personnel.

## PSYCHOSOCIAL EXPERIENCES OF LGBTQ+ STUDENTS LIVING WITH DISABILITIES

The lives of LGBTQ+ college students with disabilities are filled with unique psychosocial contexts. They experience multiple forms of oppression and stigma, need to contend with issues of disclosure, and often have to adapt to adversities associated with holding intersecting identities. Each of these contexts is discussed in this section.

### Oppression and Stigma

Persons living with disabilities, as well as LGBTQ+ persons, share experiences of oppression and a history of civil injustice (Drummond & Brotman, 2014). Sexuality, gender, and disability identities are socialized and politicized constructs that marginalize and oppress persons who do not hold dominant identities in a given social space (e.g., heteronormative, cisgender, and able-bodied/minded spaces; Kafer, 2013; McRuer, 2006, 2011). Queer theorists postulate that anything outside of heterosexuality (i.e., lesbian, gay, bisexual, queer identities) can be deemed abnormal, rendering *compulsory heterosexuality* as the fundamental and normative sexual orientation that dominates nearly all social and institutional spaces (Kimball et al., 2018). *Crip theory* (Kafer, 2013; McRuer, 2006, 2011) extends arguments made by queer theorists, and centers the disability experience as a means of analyzing and understanding marginalized identities. Crip theory emphasizes that *able-bodiedness* and *able-mindedness* share similarities to compulsory heterosexuality (McRuer, 2006). If "able" bodies and minds are the social norm, then disabled bodies and minds become classified as outside the social norm. LGBTQ+ college students living with disabilities encounter stigma as a result of multiple interlocking oppressive social systems (e.g., heteronormativity, cissexism, ableism), which push them further into socially marginalized spaces. They are stigmatized as "the other," or "the problem," for not conforming to compulsory norms of heterosexuality, gender, able-bodiedness, and able-mindedness.

Given their intersecting identities, LGBTQ+ college students with disabilities encounter negative attitudes, multiple sources of stigma (Drummond & Brotman, 2014), minority stressors, and microaggressions (Conover & Israel, 2019; Miller, 2015). Minority stressors include interpersonal forms of discrimination and prejudice, as well as internalized forms of stigma (i.e., internalized heterosexism; Meyer, 2003). Microaggressions include subtle verbal and behavioral forms of communication that express negative or marginalizing beliefs about a particular group (Sue et al., 2007). For LGBTQ+ college students living with disabilities, microaggressions could be related to sexual orientation, gender identity and expression, or disability. LGBTQ+ students with disabilities also may encounter other forms of stigma in higher education, namely, ableism, disablism, and horizontal oppression (Dispenza & DeBlaere, 2017).

The terms *ableism* and *disablism* are often used interchangeably (Bogart & Dunn, 2019), but there are nuanced differences between the two terms (Dispenza & DeBlaere, 2017; Dispenza, Hunter, & Kumar, 2018). Ableism, a term popularly used in the United States by academics, practitioners, and media, is a social-level form of oppression that discriminates and devalues persons who are not able-bodied or of able-mind (Bogart & Dunn, 2019). Students with disabilities may experience ableist environments at their college or university (e.g., no ramp for mobility in certain parts of campus, no modified texts for students with visual-related disabilities). Disablism, a term used outside of U.S. contexts, emphasizes the individual level and focuses on the exclusionary, discriminatory, and violent experiences that persons encounter as a result of having a disability (Goodley & Runswick-Cole, 2011). Students with disabilities may encounter disablism if they are excluded from participating in certain courses or coursework because of the nature of their disability, or if they are physically assaulted because of their disability.

Furthermore, LGBTQ+ college students living with disabilities may encounter *horizontal oppression* (Dispenza & DeBlaere, 2017; Dispenza, Hunter, & Kumar, 2018), which is when individuals encounter stigma, prejudice, or stereotypes from their own respective communities. LGBTQ+ students with disabilities may be oppressed or discriminated by LGBTQ+ communities for having a disability, or they may be ostracized by members of the disability community for having a sexual or gender minority identity. These experiences could also impact their mental and psychosocial health. For instance, disability-related microaggressions within sexual minority communities corresponded negatively with ratings of social support satisfaction (Conover & Israel, 2019). Similarly, Conover and Israel (2019) found that both disability and sexual-orientation-related microaggressions were associated with higher ratings of depressive symptomology among sexual minority persons living with physical disabilities.

**Disclosure and Identity**

College students are not required to disclose their disability to faculty or staff, except when providing appropriate documentation to disability services and offices that arrange reasonable accommodations. College students also should never be required to disclose their sexual orientation or gender identity. Yet, LGBTQ+ persons living with disabilities still have to decide whether to conceal or disclose their disability, sexuality, and gender identities based on how safe they deem their environmental contexts (Dispenza et al., 2019). In one study, Miller (2018) explored how LGBTQ+ college students living with disabilities constructed their identities. He found that students utilized an array of different perspectives and strategies that allowed them opportunities to exercise creativity, build community, and construct resilience (see Miller, 2018, for further information on these perspectives and strategies).

In a different study, Miller et al. (2019) found that LGBTQ+ college students living with disabilities selectively disclosed their intersecting identities strategically, and did so based on whether or not it helped them better focus on schoolwork or nurture meaningful interpersonal relationships with classmates. In some other instances, students either disclosed their identities indirectly, disclosed only one identity, or "passed" for certain privileged identities (i.e., straight, cisgender, living without a disability) to avoid any instances of stigma, minority stress, or discrimination (Miller et al., 2019).

**Resilience**

*Resilience* is often defined as adapting to adversity, and scholars classify it as either a trait, a process, or an outcome (Southwick et al., 2014). An individual's experience of resilience can change over their lifespan, across contexts, and is connected to multiple determinants (e.g., biology, culture, ecological systems; Southwick et al., 2014). For persons with disabilities, resilience is associated with hope, self-esteem, life satisfaction, and optimistic career development planning (Chan et al., 2013; Fujikawa et al., 2013; Stewart & Yuen, 2011). For LGBTQ+ individuals, social support, emotional openness, hope, optimism, and lower reactivity to prejudice promote resilience (Kwon, 2013).

Research and scholarship on the resiliency of LGBTQ+ persons living with disabilities are still in their infancy (Hunter et al., 2020), and even more sparse among LGBTQ+ college students living with disabilities (Miller, 2018). However, there is some scholarship that attempts to elucidate the phenomenon of resilience among LGBTQ+ college students living with disabilities. In a qualitative study, Hunter and colleagues (2020) interviewed LGBTQ+ persons with disabilities regarding their lived experiences with resilience. They identified *resilience maximizers*, or experiences that nurtured and maintained resilience. Resilience maximizers included self-acceptance, advocacy, participating in affirming communities, and the desire to be viewed as worthy and capable human beings (Hunter et al., 2020). LGBTQ+ persons with disabilities in the study also identified *resilience minimizers*, or experiences that detracted or hindered their capacity to be resilient. Participants possessed a fear that their identities would not be accepted by their social supports (e.g., family, friends, coworkers) or that they might be punished (e.g., financial or emotional abuse) by loved ones and family members for having a sexual or gender minority identity while living with a disability (Hunter et al., 2020).

The study and implementation of resilience, however, are not without limitations or criticisms. The construct of resilience continues to lack an empirically operationalized definition, and the mechanisms in which contexts and determiners intersect are not well understood (Southwick et al., 2014)—especially not for LGBTQ+ persons living with disabilities. Societal expectations of resilience can further disenfranchise marginalized persons living in cultures that prize ideologies of individualism and meritocracy (Meyer, 2015). Meyer (2015) described that certain perspectives on resilience remove responsibility from the ecological system that may be contributing to the experiences of stress and hardship. Thus, LGBTQ+ persons living with disabilities may be victimized for not being "resilient enough" in higher education settings and may be held personally responsible for not overcoming adversities that are likely rooted in their ecological systems. However, it is important to consider the role of resilience because it can help mitigate some of deleterious effects of stigma and minority stress for this population (Hunter et al., 2020).

## PRACTICES, STRATEGIES, AND INTERVENTIONS

Professionals working in higher education could benefit from using conceptual frameworks and models to bolster support for LGBTQ+ college students living with disabilities. Further, higher education professionals need to understand how various ecological contexts (e.g., campus climate, legislative histories and mandates, lifespan development) influence the lives of LGBTQ+ college students with disabilities. Following are several considerations for practice, strategies, and interventions.

### Universal Design as a Conceptual Framework

Universal Design (UD) can function as a conceptual framework that ensures environments, services, products, and learning experiences are used by people with a wide range of characteristics and abilities (Lid, 2014). UD maximizes usability, learning, and environmental access without the need for major modifications, significant alterations, or specialized designs. UD has been historically employed with persons with disabilities, and applied in K–12/higher education settings. UD requires some amount of forethought by a user, which makes this an important conceptual practice and strategy in higher education. University and college administrators, staff, and faculty can rely on UD principles to approach campus policies, strategic planning, student success indicators, and pedagogical practices, especially if they are attempting to be inclusive of diverse sexual orientations, ability statuses, gender identities and expressions.

At a fundamental level is the understanding that persons with disabilities—just as those without disabilities—are diverse beings with sexual desires, needs, and identities. UD principles share some similarities with McRuer's (2006) crip theory, in which the intentionality is to create environments (broadly defined as physical, virtual, and social) that are accessible for all persons, including those with diverse sexual orientations, genders, and disabilities (Dispenza, Hunter, & Kumar, 2018). Examples of this include examining and reducing heteronormative and ableist language in higher education policies and regulations, advocating for curriculum and extracurricular activities that include representations of persons with disabilities who hold diverse sexual orientations and genders, or ensuring that physical, virtual, and social spaces are accessible to LGBTQ+ students with disabilities (e.g., open to same-gender partners or family members and free from stigmatizing attitudes).

For health care providers on college campuses this also includes ensuring that LGBTQ+ college students with disabilities have equal access to sexual and reproductive health care. Students with disabilities sometimes attend college with a history of being excluded from learning about their sexuality, and often receive negative messaging regarding LGBTQ+ identities. Additionally, LGBTQ+ students with disabilities may not have the same level of knowledge or awareness as their peers regarding sex or romantic relationships. Thus, LGBTQ+ college students with disabilities should not be excluded from having accessible sex education, access to condoms, birth control, screening access for sexually transmitted infections, and sexuality-related counseling services. UD guidelines for learning (e.g., multiple means of engagement, representation, action and expression; CAST [https://www.cast.org]) may be especially helpful when trying to help LGBTQ+ college student living with disabilities learn about their sexuality.

We further recommend that faculty, staff, and administrators assess the universality of physical, structural, and social spaces. Assessment can take the form of architectural surveys, campus climate surveys (e.g., administered via online or traditional paper questionnaires), or focus groups with various stakeholders. In particular, administrators may benefit from assessing social attitudes of personnel, and provide subsequent trainings (e.g., the use of universally inclusive language for LGBTQ+ students with disabilities) to improve campus conditions. We encourage university administrators, faculty, and staff to use CAST and UniversalDesign.com (https://www.universaldesign.com) to learn more about UD. Although these resources are not specific to LGBTQ+ students, administrators and faculty can critically reflect how UD can be inclusive of LGBTQ+ students with disabilities at their institutions. Further, by utilizing these resources, university administrators, staff, and faculty can develop specialized protocols and assessment tools that assess the feasibility and usability of UD in their respective institutions across diverse student populations. It may be particularly useful to incorporate UD in college and university strategic planning efforts, and as indicators of students' success (e.g., retention, graduation).

### Supporting the Transition to Adulthood

In the United States, students 18 to 25 years of age—regardless of disability status, sexual orientation, or gender identity and expression—experience a shift from adolescence to emerging adulthood. In emerging adulthood (Arnett, 2000), individuals move from family-centered values and roles toward an ambiguous period, free from parental or adult expectations and rich with identity exploration and uncertainty. In the following, we further elucidate how college students recenter their identities, engage with social and academic communities, and seek supports in and outside of the classroom.

### Recentering

Emerging adults "recenter" themselves through this process, developing an adult orientation along with a sense of self, independence, and agency (Tanner & Arnett, 2011). Hinton and Meyer (2014) identified factors tied to an effective transition to adulthood for adolescents with disabilities, including strong social support, adaptation between current resources and life situation, resilience, self-determination, and healthy coping skills.

Students with disabilities may find the process of recentering more difficult, especially if they also possess sexual or gender minority identities that are stigmatized by their interpersonal social supports or ecological environments. This is why it is crucial for university administrators, staff, and faculty to examine how LGBTQ+ college students living with disabilities perceive the safety of their campus environments. In a qualitative study, Miller (2015) found that LGBTQ+ college students living with disabilities struggled with creating an authentic self-presentation as they felt the pressure to disclose or conceal various oppressed or privileged identities. Students in Miller's (2015) study exerted large amounts of emotional effort to manage their intersecting identities, instead of focusing their energy on academic tasks. Because of this added effort, students with multiple marginalized identities may struggle to explore and develop an authentic sense of self. They may also struggle with their academics given the psychological energy they expend on managing their identities.

### Engagement

In the midst of recentering one's sense of self, students are actively engaging with their college or university institution. University engagement and campus involvement during the transition to college are crucial for student development and academic integration (Astin, 1985). Tinto's (1975, 1993) model of student persistence suggests that students need to connect emotionally and cognitively to their respective institutions. However, LGBTQ+ students with disabilities may endure certain struggles transitioning to campus (Harley et al., 2002; Miller et al., 2019), further inhibiting their capacity to connect with various facets of their college or university. Students with disabilities may have difficulty completing college (National Council on Disability, 2015), and the rate at which LGBTQ+ college students living with disabilities complete college is unknown. Lack of disability-related knowledge and understanding from faculty, staff, and administrators are often cited as the reasons why college students with disabilities do not complete higher education (Barnar-Brak et al., 2010). These same faculty, staff, and administrators also may fail to understand that their students with disabilities have diverse sexual orientations and gender identities.

University and college students are successful when they create connections to their academics, faculty, and academic support services (Chambliss & Takacs,

2014), despite the fact that students also experience uncertainty, unwillingness to engage faculty, and perceive that they do not need academic support. LGBTQ+ college students with disabilities may encounter some of these issues, or anticipate barriers when interacting with faculty, peers in the classroom, and academic support services. Universities and colleges could consider putting policies and procedures in place to effectively train and resource faculty and academic departments to meet the needs of students. In particular, college and university faculty, staff, and administrators should receive training on federal and state policies pertaining to the rights of students with disabilities (discussed further in the section titled Institutional and Legal Policies), as well as how academic institutions have historically excluded students with disabilities from accessing or engaging in higher education. Faculty, staff, and administrators also could benefit from training that seeks to enhance affirming attitudes toward students with disabilities and students who hold LGBTQ+ identities. Trainings and outcomes with faculty, staff, and administrators should be evaluated.

**Support in and out of the Classroom**
Faculty should create a safe and inclusive learning environment by affirming disability, sexual orientation, and gender diversity in their syllabi, course materials, and even during class lectures. From a UD perspective, faculty also could consider identifying various texts and media (e.g., movies, videos, podcasts) that showcase the voices or scholarship of LGBTQ+ persons with disabilities. This has the potential of increasing representation and relevance of course material to LGBTQ+ students with disabilities. Additionally, LGBTQ+ college students with disabilities may need direct confirmation that a classroom is safe (Miller, 2015), and faculty are encouraged to have actual conversations about how to foster, nurture, and address issues of emotional and physical safety in the classrooms for all students.

University and college administrators, faculty, and staff also could work to promote resilience and strengthen supports outside of the classroom. LGBTQ+ college students with disabilities may benefit from robust training and extracurricular opportunities that help them build social and academic support networks, while also helping them to enhance resilience and coping (Conover & Israel, 2019; Hinton & Meyer, 2014; Hunter et al., 2020; Miller, 2015, 2017, 2018). They may further benefit from programming and interventions that celebrate the diversity of intersecting identities. For example, colleges and universities that host sexuality health programming events should include disability, sexual orientation, and gender diversity into their programming, so that no one group is excluded. Similarly, faculty may want to infuse topics of intersectionality, sexuality, and disability into their curriculum, since Miller (2018) found that a significant number of students became knowledgeable and empowered by these topics from their classroom experiences. As always, trainings, programming, classroom experiences, and outcomes should be evaluated by faculty, staff, and administrators.

## Institutional and Legal Policies

In our experience, faculty, staff, and administrators often do not fully comprehend institutional, state, and federal legislation pertaining to college and university students living with disabilities. Persons living with disabilities on college campuses can seek services as mandated by Section 504 of the Rehabilitation Act of 1973 and the Americans With Disabilities Act (ADA) of 1990, which require educational institutions to provide reasonable accommodations to persons living with disabilities (Squires & Countermine, 2018). These laws, along with the Individuals With Disabilities Education Improvement Act of 2004, have helped to increase rightful services to college and university students with disabilities (Evans et al., 2005), which may enhance their academic and career prospects. However, as persons with disabilities are being acknowledged for possessing other intersecting cultural identities, such as gender diversity and sexual orientation, additional challenges for these college students are becoming more evident even when resources are available (e.g., comfortability of potential identity disclosure, access to buildings, knowledge of where to gain the resources; Miller, 2018; Smith et al., 2008). For example, students seeking on-campus housing may need certain accommodations based on their disability or gender identity and expression, such as a single room. But they may be hesitant to make such requests for fear of disclosing their identities to residential life staffers because of the possibility of being rejected, humiliated, or denied (Miller et al., 2019).

Differences in legal and procedural supports may make transition and access into college more challenging for LGBTQ+ students with disabilities. Student experiences in K–12 settings vary widely and their experience of support and parental involvement may differ. Students with disabilities may find themselves navigating the transition from a very formal support environment in secondary education, where counselors, social workers, schools, and often parents or other family members were responsible for providing support and mandated services (Knight et al., 2018), into one that is less so. They enter the college environment where students receive fewer accommodations and are required to be more proactive in seeking services and supplying faculty and staff with documentation (Morrison et al., 2009). The transition from high school individual educational planning and a team approach to student support shifts to a model where students are required to be proactive, agentic, and self-determined in order to academically succeed (Goode, 2007; Miller, 2017, 2018).

As students transition from high school, where parents and guardians may have been very involved in their academic and personal affairs, particularly for students with disabilities, some students may struggle to seek services on their own (Hadley et al., 2003). Students with LGBTQ+ identities may not be out to their friends and family, or they may navigate systems with caution in order to avoid disclosing aspects of their sexual orientation or gender identity to college and university staff for fear of their LGBTQ+ identity being inadvertently outed to parents or other family members. LGBTQ+ college students with disabilities may also be navigating these systems alone for the first time due to a lack of family or social support. We encourage administrators, faculty, and staff to be sensitive to family-related issues and to understand that family support may vary considerably between students holding the same identities.

In many cases, students and parents are often surprised to that the Federal Educational Rights and Privacy Act (FERPA) that ensures confidentiality for documents and communication related to students enrolled in colleges and universities. Students must take ownership and navigate what information they share, how to share it, and with whom. Similarly, parents and guardians are often shocked to find they are unable to access students' information. College personnel cannot assume all students are equally prepared to take ownership of their experience and may need to assess individual student's levels of autonomy and agency.

As part of their development into autonomy, LGBTQ+ college students with disabilities may face issues regarding medical care, mental health, psychological support, and accommodations that are above and beyond other students. The compartmentalization of services on many campuses forces students to disclose personal information to multiple personnel in order to receive adequate care. The intersection of sexual orientation, disability, and gender identities may require students to navigate the disclosure of more personal information than they are comfortable sharing to gain access to the range of support services they require (Goode, 2007; Harley et al., 2002). Research indicates that even when universities have a firm policy about disabilities, the implementation of process and service procedures may lag, creating a sense of disconnect between campus philosophy and accessibility for students (Goode, 2007).

Policies, procedures, and access to services should be clear to all students, faculty, and staff. Programming should proactively assume all students may need assistance and access, not just those who are preidentified in the application, orientation, or registration process. Administration and departments must continue to evaluate their actions and call upon student feedback to improve access and accommodation. Faculty, staff, and administrators should also examine their campus policies pertaining to identity disclosure and determine when and under which circumstances disclosure is necessary. They should also conduct a cost–benefit analysis and revise policies as necessary. We suggest this not as a way of ignoring identity disclosure but as a means of increasing sensitivity to intentional inquiry into student identities.

## Additional Considerations for Campus Personnel

University and college students are eager to take advantage of the many facets of student life while maintaining high academic achievement. For undergraduate and graduate students, student life encompasses student housing, dining, student organizations and extracurricular clubs, athletics, on- and off-campus job responsibilities, work study, Greek life, health and well-being, work, and of course academics. These aspects of student life have not always been historically or universally accessible to either students with disabilities or LGBTQ+ students. To help address some of these issues, we offer some additional considerations for university and college campus personnel, including recommendations for trainings, promoting resources and accommodations, online education, and housing.

**Trainings for Campus Personnel**
LGBTQ+ college students living with disabilities may encounter an unwelcoming or "cold" campus climate. Negative perceptions, attitudes, and the level of knowledge of staff, faculty, and even academic advisors can contribute negatively to the experiences of LGBTQ+ students living with disabilities (Abes & Wallace, 2018; Barnar-Brak et al., 2010; Hong, 2015). They need support from university personnel to help guide them in their overall college experience (Squires & Countermine, 2018), and we cannot stress enough that administrators, faculty, and staff should participate in trainings to better understand the identities and needs of LGBTQ+ students with disabilities in order to effectively contribute to their academic success (Miller, 2018). Trainings should include a focus on multicultural competence and cultural humility. Hopefully, this would help administrators, faculty, and staff gain a greater awareness of the complex nuances and developmental distresses LGBTQ+ students living with disabilities may experience during their college experience (Miller, 2018). Trainings should focus on dispelling monolithic assumptions about disability, sexual orientation, and gender diversity. For example, the level of support for a student who comes to campus as an openly pansexual cisgender female living with Type 1 diabetes may differ from the level needed for a student who has been living with cerebral palsy and is just beginning the discovery process of her sexual and gender identities (Miller, 2018). Such trainings could help those teaching and working with these individuals to understand how to provide greater support and resources so that they may succeed in all aspects of their college experience.

**Promoting Resources and Accommodations**
Many university and college campuses provide on-campus resources for support (e.g., Office of Disability Services, Multicultural Center, LGBTQIA+ Center, Housing Services) that could help LGBTQ+ college students with disabilities. However, these students may be unaware of these resources. Therefore, faculty, administrators, and staff should be knowledgeable about the needs of these individuals so they can guide them to resources and help them develop necessary skills for self-advocacy when appropriate and if desired (Abes & Wallace, 2018; Miller, 2018). Again—and we cannot stress this enough—faculty, staff, and administrators should consider assessing campus climate and the universal accessibility of academic and social life for LGBTQ+ students with disabilities. In doing so, they could conduct a needs analysis and look at strengths (e.g.,

affirming policies, sensitivity) and weaknesses (e.g., exclusion, physical barriers) that could be remedied or improved.

LGBTQ+ college students living with disabilities may encounter obstacles as they explore on-campus resources. As stated previously, they may want to seek an accommodation from an Office of Disability Services, but they may feel hesitant to pursue services due to fear of disclosure of their sexual or gender minority identity (Henry et al., 2010; Woodford & Kulick, 2015). Similarly, LGBTQ+ college students living with disabilities who use assistive technologies (e.g., wheelchairs, scooters, canes, walkers) may want to attend LGBTQ+ centered school-sponsored events, but the events may lack structural accommodations to assist them in accessing physical spaces. These examples may seem like minute challenges to the average college student, but for LGBTQ+ college students living with disabilities, these challenges can significantly impact their student life involvements and academic outcomes (Henry et al., 2010). Physical accommodations help remove structural barriers to access and improve the academic success of students with disabilities (Squires & Countermine, 2018). Therefore, college administrators need to consider increasing their understanding of the multiple intersecting identities students hold so that they can provide adequate resources to enhance their student life and academic experiences (Miller, 2018).

Although accommodations and supports are available to students who register their disability with their college or university, some students fear potential negative consequences of receiving accommodations. Deckoff-Jones and Duell (2018) found that students with a psychiatric disability were at higher risk of being negatively perceived by their peers for receiving accommodations. The same study found that these views of students with disabilities receiving accommodations can negatively affect their social connection on college campuses (Deckoff-Jones & Duell, 2018). Relatedly, in an analogue study pertaining to employment ratings of hypothetical lesbian and gay persons living with disabilities, Dispenza, Kumar, et al. (2018) found that college students were more likely to rate sexual minority women living with psychiatric disabilities least favorably among sexual minority and heterosexual persons. Thus, concerns by LGBTQ+ college students living with disabilities are warranted, which could limit their access to the necessary accommodations and supports available for them to successfully navigate the campus environment.

**Online Education**
Faculty, staff, and administrators also need to consider the experiences of online education for LGBTQ+ students living with disabilities. Miller (2017) found that students with intersecting identities described their online engagement as beneficial to their college experience. The same study found that LGBTQ+ college students with disabilities may view building community and connecting with others based on their identities more desirable and easier online than on a traditional brick-and-mortar campus (Miller, 2017). In addition,

students may find it easier to disclose their identities online and to connect with others with similar identities in local chat rooms and online groups. Therefore, physical college campuses may want to consider discovering ways to create online opportunities for LGBTQ+ students living with disabilities to connect with others and receive services (Miller, 2017).

**Housing**

Another important area of student life to examine for LGBTQ+ college students living with disabilities is accessibility of appropriate housing. Establishing housing arrangements on a college campus creates anxiety for any college student. While college housing administrators may want to meet the needs of all students, sexual minority persons living with a disability may present them with additional concerns. Vaccaro and Kimball (2019) suggested college students with disabilities benefit from quiet or isolated spaces in order to manage their disabilities and focus on their academics but are often denied a single-room housing assignment. Further, LGBTQ+ students often face housing discrimination and experiences of discrimination, harassment, bullying, and assault due to inappropriate housing placement (Seelman, 2016; Vaccaro & Kimball, 2019). To assist students in attaining appropriate student housing, campuses need to contemplate the various student identities and the potential challenges students may face in housing accommodations for their safety and well-being.

## CONCLUSION

This chapter provided a conceptual review of relevant scholarship that elucidated some of the contexts and nuances that inform the lives of LGBTQ+ college students living with disabilities. Although scholarship is limited, our hope is that this chapter has provided faculty, staff, and administrators with conceptual strategies for assessment and training interventions. For purposes of assessment, faculty, staff, and administrators should evaluate their campus climate for systemic oppression and stigma, UD implementation, as well as policies and practices related to identity disclosure. For purposes of training, faculty, staff, and administrators are encouraged to bolster resilience and self-determination, increase awareness of transition issues, and enhance multicultural competence and cultural humility.

## DISCUSSION QUESTIONS

1. To date, what types of experiences and interactions have you had with LGBTQ+ students living with disabilities on college campuses? If you suspect that you have not had many, take some time to reflect as to why you think this could be the case.

2. Take a moment to visit the campus library, student center, a dining hall, or even a classroom. How might LGBTQ+ students living with disabilities (including physical, sensory, medical, or psychological) experience these environments? To what degree are these spaces accessible to students with a variety of disabilities? To what degree are these spaces affirming and inclusive of LGBTQ+ students?

3. What policies targeting inclusion of LGBTQ+ students with disabilities does your campus have that are not actively implemented or clear to faculty, staff, and students? How might you address this discrepancy with the administration?

4. Observe the social interactions taking place among students, faculty, and staff when visiting the campus library, student center, dining hall, or classroom. To what degree are these spaces inclusive and/or oppressive to LGBTQ+ students with disabilities?

5. Based on the material presented in this chapter, reflect on the ways in which your campus is safe, affirming, and inclusive of LGBTQ+ students with disabilities.

6. Reflect on the ways in which your campus may seem or appear less safe, affirming, or inclusive of LGBTQ+ students with disabilities. What can you and your campus do to improve?

## RESOURCES

1. CAST (https://www.cast.org). A website that provides an overview of UD principles and designs for educators and community stakeholders.

2. UniversalDesign.com (https://www.universaldesign.com). A website that provides resources for training an education relation to universal design.

## REFERENCES

Abes, E. S., & Wallace, M. M. (2018). "People see me, but they don't see me": An intersectional study of college students with physical disabilities. *Journal of College Student Development*, 59(5), 545–562. https://doi.org/10.1353/csd.2018.0052

Americans With Disabilities Act of 1990, Pub. L. No. 101–336, 104 Stat. 328 (1990).

Arnett, J. J. (2000). Emerging adulthood: A theory of development from the late teens through the twenties. *American Psychologist*, 55(5), 469–480. https://doi.org/10.1037/0003-066X.55.5.469

Astin, A. W. (1985). Involvement: The cornerstone of excellence. *Change: The Magazine of Higher Education*, 17(4), 35–39. https://doi.org/10.1080/00091383.1985.9940532

Barnar-Brak, L., Lectenberger, D., & Lan, W. Y. (2010). Accommodation strategies of college students with disabilities. *The Qualitative Report*, 15(2), 411–429. https://doi.org/10.46743/2160-3715/2010.1158

Björkenstam, C., Tinghög, P., Cochran, S., Andersson, G., Alexanderson, K., & Branstrom, R. (2016). Is work disability more common among same-sex than different-sex married people? *Epidemiology (Cambridge, Mass.), 6,* 242. https://doi.org/10.4172/2161-1165.1000242

Bogart, K. R., & Dunn, D. S. (2019). Ableism special issue introduction. *Journal of Social Issues, 75*(3), 650–664. https://doi.org/10.1111/josi.12354

Chambliss, D. F., & Takacs, C. G. (2014). *How college works.* Harvard University Press. https://doi.org/10.4159/harvard.9780674726093

Chan, J. Y. C., Chan, F., Ditchman, N., Phillips, B., & Chou, C.-C. (2013). Evaluating Snyder's hope theory as a motivational model of participation and life satisfaction for individuals with spinal cord injury: A path analysis. *Rehabilitation Research, Policy, and Education, 27*(3), 171–185. https://doi.org/10.1891/2168-6653.27.3.171

Cochran, S. D., Björkenstam, C., & Mays, V. M. (2017). Sexual orientation differences in functional limitations, disability, and mental health services use: Results from the 2013–2014 National Health Interview Survey. *Journal of Consulting and Clinical Psychology, 85*(12), 1111–1121. https://doi.org/10.1037/ccp0000243

Conover, K. J., & Israel, T. (2019). Microaggressions and social support among sexual minorities with physical disabilities. *Rehabilitation Psychology, 64*(2), 167–178. https://doi.org/10.1037/rep0000250

Deckoff-Jones, A., & Duell, M. N. (2018). Perceptions of appropriateness of accommodations for university students: Does disability type matter? *Rehabilitation Psychology, 63*(1), 68–76. https://doi.org/10.1037/rep0000213

Dispenza, F., Brennaman, C., Harper, L., Harrigan, M., Chastain, T. E., & Procter, J. E. (2019). Career development of sexual and gender minority persons living with disabilities: A constructivist grounded theory study. *The Counseling Psychologist, 47*(1), 98–128. https://doi.org/10.1177/0011000018819425

Dispenza, F., & DeBlaere, C. (2017). Sexual orientation and ability status. In K. L. Nadal, S. L. Mazzula, & D. P. Rivera (Eds.), *The SAGE encyclopedia of psychology and gender.* SAGE.

Dispenza, F., Hunter, T., & Kumar, A. (2018). The needs of gender and sexual minority persons living with disabilities. In B. Smalley, J. Warren, & N. Barefoot (Eds.), *LGBT health: Meeting the health needs of gender and sexual minorities* (pp. 143–159). Springer Publishing Company. https://psycnet.apa.org/record/2017-36752-009

Dispenza, F., Kumar, A., Standish, J., Norris, S., & Procter, J. (2018). Disability and sexual orientation disclosure on Employment Interview Ratings: An analogue study. *Rehabilitation Counseling Bulletin, 61*(4), 244–255. https://doi.org/10.1177/0034355217725888

Drummond, J., & Brotman, S. (2014). Intersecting and embodied identities: A queer woman's experience of disability and sexuality. *Sexuality and Disability, 32*(4), 533–549. https://doi.org/10.1007/s11195-014-9382-4

Evans, N. J., Assadi, J. L., & Herriott, T. K. (2005). Encouraging the development of disability allies. *New Directions for Student Services, 2005*(110), 67–79. https://doi.org/10.1002/ss.166

Family Educational Rights and Privacy Act of 1974, 20 U.S.C. § 1232g (1974).

Fredriksen-Goldsen, K. I., Kim, H.-J., & Barkan, S. E. (2012). Disability among lesbian, gay, and bisexual adults: Disparities in prevalence and risk. *American Journal of Public Health, 102*(1), e16–e21. https://doi.org/10.2105/AJPH.2011.300379

Fujikawa, M., Lee, E.-J., Chan, F., Catalano, D., Hunter, C., Bengston, K., & Rahimi, M. (2013). The Connor-Davidson scale as a positive psychology measure for people with spinal cord injuries. *Rehabilitation Research, Policy, and Education, 27*(3), 213–222. https://doi.org/10.1891/2168-6653.27.3.213

Goode, J. (2007). Managing disability: Early experiences of university students with disabilities. *Disability & Society, 22*(1), 35–48. https://doi.org/10.1080/09687590601056204

Goodley, D., & Runswick-Cole, K. (2011). The violence of disablism. *Sociology of Health & Illness, 33*(4), 602–617. https://doi.org/10.1111/j.1467-9566.2010.01302.x

Hadley, W. M., Twale, D. J., & Evans, J. (2003). First-year students with specific learning disabilities: Transition and adjustment to academic expectations. *The Journal of College Orientation and Transition, 11*(1), 35–46. https://doi.org/10.24926/jcotr.v11i1.2583

Harley, D. A., Nowak, T. M., Gassaway, L. J., & Savage, T. A. (2002). Lesbian, gay, bisexual, and transgender college students with disabilities: A look at multiple cultural minorities. *Psychology in the Schools, 39*(5), 525–538. https://doi.org/10.1002/pits.10052

Henry, W. J., Fuerth, K., & Figliozzi, J. (2010). Gay with a disability: A college student's multiple cultural journey. *College Student Journal, 44*(2), 377–388. https://psycnet.apa.org/record/2010-11460-014

Hinton, V., & Meyer, J. (2014). Emerging adulthood: Resilience and support. *Rehabilitation Research, Policy, and Education, 28*(3), 143–157. https://doi.org/10.1891/2168-6653.28.3.143

Hong, B. S. S. (2015). Qualitative analysis of the barriers college students with disabilities experience in higher education. *Journal of College Student Development, 56*(3), 209–226. https://doi.org/10.1353/csd.2015.0032

Hunter, T., Dispenza, F., Huffstead, M., Suttles, M., & Bradley, Z. (2020). Queering disability: Exploring resilience of sexual and gender minority persons living with disabilities. *Rehabilitation Counseling Bulletin, 64*(1), 31–41. https://doi.org/10.1177/0034355219895813

Individuals With Disabilities Education Act, 20 U.S.C. § 1400 (2004).

Kafer, A. (2013). *Feminist, queer, crip*. Indiana University Press.

Kimball, E., Vaccaro, A., Tissi-Gassoway, N., Bobot, S. D., Newman, B. M., Moore, A., & Troiano, P. F. (2018). Gender, sexuality, & (dis)ability: Queer perspectives on the experiences of students with disabilities. *Disability Studies Quarterly, 38*(2). https://doi.org/10.18061/dsq.v38i2.5937

Knight, W., Wessel, R. D., & Markle, L. (2018). Persistence to graduation for students with disabilities: Implications for performance-based outcomes. *Journal of College Student Retention: Research, Theory & Practice, 19*(4), 362–380. https://doi.org/10.1177/1521025116632534

Kwon, P. (2013). Resilience in lesbian, gay, and bisexual individuals. *Personality and Social Psychology Review, 17*(4), 371–383. https://doi.org/10.1177/1088868313490248

Lid, I. M. (2014). Universal design and disability: An interdisciplinary perspective. *Disability and Rehabilitation, 36*(16), 1344–1349. https://doi.org/10.3109/09638288.2014.931472

McRuer, R. (2006). *Crip theory: Cultural signs of queerness and disability*. NYU Press.

McRuer, R. (2011). Disabling sex: Notes for a crip theory of sexuality. *GLQ, 17*(1), 107–117. https://doi.org/10.1215/10642684-2010-021

Meyer, I. H. (2003). Prejudice, social stress, and mental health in lesbian, gay, and bisexual populations: Conceptual issues and research evidence. *Psychological Bulletin, 129*(5), 674–697. https://doi.org/10.1037/0033-2909.129.5.674

Meyer, I. H. (2015). Resilience in the study of minority stress and health of sexual and gender minority persons. *Psychology of Sexual Orientation and Gender Diversity, 2*(3), 209–213. https://doi.org/10.1037/sgd0000132

Miller, R. A. (2015). "Sometimes you feel invisible": Performing queer/disabled in the university classroom. *The Educational Forum, 79*(4), 377–393. https://doi.org/10.1080/00131725.2015.1068417

Miller, R. A. (2017). "My voice is definitely strongest in online communities": Students using social media for queer and disability identity-making. *Journal of College Student Development, 58*(4), 509–525. https://doi.org/10.1353/csd.2017.0040

Miller, R. A. (2018). Toward intersectional identity perspectives on disability and LGBTQ identities in higher education. *Journal of College Student Development, 59*(3), 327–346. https://doi.org/10.1353/csd.2018.0030

Miller, R. A., Wynn, R. D., & Webb, K. W. (2019). "This really interesting juggling act": How university students manage disability/queer identity disclosure and visibility. *Journal of Diversity in Higher Education, 12*(4), 307–318. https://doi.org/10.1037/dhe0000083

Morrison, J. Q., Sansosti, F. J., & Hadley, W. M. (2009). Parent perceptions of the anticipated needs and expectations for support for their college-bound students with Asperger's syndrome. *Journal of Postsecondary Education and Disability, 22*(2), 78–87.

National Council on Disability. (2015, May 19). *Reauthorization of the Higher Education Act (HEA): The implications for increasing the employment of people with disabilities* [Policy brief]. https://ncd.gov/publications/2015/05192015

Raue, K., & Lewis, L. (2011). *Students with disabilities at degree-granting postsecondary institutions* (NCES 2011–018). U.S. Department of Education, National Center for Education Statistics, U.S. Government Printing Office. https://nces.ed.gov/pubs2011/2011018.pdf

Section 504 of the Rehabilitation Act of 1973, 34 C.F.R., Dept. of Health, Education, and Welfare, Part 104.

Seelman, K. L. (2016). Transgender adults' access to college bathrooms and housing and the relationship to suicidality. *Journal of Homosexuality, 63*(10), 1378–1399. https://doi.org/10.1080/00918369.2016.1157998

Smith, L., Foley, P. F., & Chaney, M. P. (2008). Addressing classism, ableism, and heterosexism in counselor education. *Journal of Counseling and Development, 86*(3), 303–309. https://doi.org/10.1002/j.1556-6678.2008.tb00513.x

Southwick, S. M., Bonanno, G. A., Masten, A. S., Panter-Brick, C., & Yehuda, R. (2014). Resilience definitions, theory, and challenges: Interdisciplinary perspectives. *European Journal of Psychotraumatology, 5*(1), Article 25338. https://doi.org/10.3402/ejpt.v5.25338

Squires, M. E., & Countermine, B. (2018). College students with disabilities explain challenges encountered in professional preparation programs. *Exceptionality Education International, 28*(1), 22–44. https://doi.org/10.5206/eei.v28i1.7757

Stewart, D. E., & Yuen, T. (2011). A systematic review of resilience in the physically ill. *Psychosomatics, 52*(3), 199–209. https://doi.org/10.1016/j.psym.2011.01.036

Sue, D. W., Capodilupo, C. M., Torino, G. C., Bucceri, J. M., Holder, A. M. B., Nadal, K. L., & Esquilin, M. (2007). Racial microaggressions in everyday life: Implications for clinical practice. *American Psychologist, 62*(4), 271–286. https://doi.org/10.1037/0003-066X.62.4.271

Tanner, J. L., & Arnett, J. J. (2011). Presenting "emerging adulthood": What makes it developmentally distinctive? In J. J. Arnett, M. Kloep, L. B. Hendry, & J. L. Tanner (Eds.), *Debating emerging adulthood: Stage or process?* (pp. 13–30). Oxford University Press. https://doi.org/10.1093/acprof:oso/9780199757176.003.0002

Tinto, V. (1975). Dropout from higher education: A theoretical synthesis of recent research. *Review of Educational Research, 45*(1), 89–125. https://doi.org/10.3102/00346543045001089

Tinto, V. (1993). *Leaving college: Rethinking the causes and cures of student attrition* (2nd ed.). University of Chicago Press.

Vaccaro, A., & Kimball, E. (2019). Navigating disability in campus housing: An ecological analysis of student affairs work. *Journal of Student Affairs Research and Practice, 56*(2), 168–180. https://doi.org/10.1080/19496591.2018.1490307

Witten, T. M. (2014). End of life, chronic illness, and trans-identities. *Journal of Social Work in End-of-Life & Palliative Care, 10*(1), 34–58. https://doi.org/10.1080/15524256.2013.877864

Woodford, M. R., & Kulick, A. (2015). Academic and social integration on campus among sexual minority students: The impacts of psychological and experiential campus climate. *American Journal of Community Psychology, 55*(1–2), 13–24. https://doi.org/10.1007/s10464-014-9683-x

# Creating Safe Spaces for Lesbian, Gay, Bisexual, Transgender, and Queer (LGBTQ+) Student–Athletes

Taylor M. McCavanagh and Michael C. Cadaret

### KEY KNOWLEDGE AREAS

- Sexual prejudice and cisgenderism are woven through athletic domains, historically creating challenges for LGBTQ+ athletes.

- LGBTQ+ student–athletes face diverse identities across sexual orientation, gender identity, race, culture, and socioeconomic status that make enhanced campus-based LGBTQ+ resources more crucial.

- A proposed Safe Zone programming specific to college athletic departments explores the complexity of being an LGBTQ+ student–athlete and identifies the specific needs of LGBTQ+ student–athletes.

College students who identify as lesbian, gay, bisexual, transgender, or queer (LGBTQ+) experience victimization, fear of rejection, and the stress associated with managing a stigmatized identity (Stroup et al., 2014). LGBTQ+ students, compared with non-LGBTQ+ students, report higher stress, greater impairment due to serious mental health concerns, including academic concerns, and face high rates of discrimination on their campuses (Dunbar et al., 2017; Rankin et al., 2010; Seelman et al., 2017). More specifically, transgender students who do not conform to stereotypical gender expectations are frequently subjected to harassment and bullying, often leading to feelings of hopelessness, isolation, depression, and low self-esteem (Buzuvis, 2012; Carroll, 2014;

---

https://doi.org/10.1037/0000281-009
*Affirming LGBTQ+ Students in Higher Education*, D. P. Rivera, R. L. Abreu, and K. A. Gonzalez (Editors)
Copyright © 2022 by the American Psychological Association. All rights reserved.

Greytak et al., 2009). Minority stress theory (Meyer, 2003) maintains that these experiences can lead to greater distress and psychological impairment (see the Introduction to this volume). For LGBTQ+ student–athletes, the athletic environment poses an even more acute setting for facing stigmatization and marginalization (Cashmore & Cleland, 2012). The adverse influence of dominant, cisgender, and heteronormative culture is embedded within the social and institutional systems of athletics, thereby increasing identity-related distress for student–athletes with LGBTQ+ identities (Atteberry-Ash et al., 2018; Meyer, 2003; Rankin & Merson, 2012; Seelman et al., 2017). Thus, practitioners who interact with student–athletes and athletic departments should have increased concern for LGBTQ+ student–athletes. As a response, the present chapter examines the unique challenges faced by LGBTQ+ student–athletes and the challenges posed by the social and institutional environments of collegiate athletics. In the process, we highlight the key knowledge areas outlined above. The chapter proposes a case example of a safe space program specific to athletic departments called Brave Space (McCavanagh & Cadaret, 2019). We conclude the chapter with discussion questions and practical strategies for creating inclusive spaces in collegiate athletics.

## LGBTQ+ STUDENT–ATHLETE EXPERIENCES

To understand the experience of student–athletes who identify as LGBTQ+, one must acknowledge factors related to identity development. The identity of a student, an athlete, an LGBTQ+ individual, and an LGBTQ+ individual of color are all factored into this experience and impact the way student-athletes negotiate to this process.

### Competing Identities

Student involvement in the campus community is theorized to be a strong predictor of retention and persistence in higher education (Astin, 1999; Strayhorn, 2018). For the college athlete, involvement in sports can be facilitative of college entrance and attendance. While involvement in athletics has many positive benefits for college students, other factors can complicate student–athlete experiences. For the present discussion, we focus on the following aspects of identity: athletic identity, diverse sexual and gender identities, and racial identity. We highlight these due to their complexity when considering LGBTQ+ student–athletes intersecting, and often, competing identities.

Brewer et al. (1993) conceptualized athletic identity as the degree to which an athlete identifies with their athletic role. Athletic identity can be influenced by friends, family members, and coaches within their athletic dimension (Heird & Steinfeldt, 2013). Furthermore, the strength of athletic identity in regard to a person's self-concept is influenced by previous athletic experiences and success or failure in the athletic domain (Horton & Mack, 2000). A collegiate student–athlete who identifies as LGBTQ+ may feel a tension between their athletic identity and their sexuality, gender, or race. Research suggests that such tension would be present, resulting in LGBTQ+ student–athletes privileging their athletic identity to their own detriment (Ali & Barden, 2015; Anderson, 2002; Cashmore & Cleland, 2012). As an example, for student–athletes who identify as LGBTQ+, the decision to disclose their sexual or gender minority identity is dependent upon the level of comfort or discomfort they experience within their team, sport, and athletic environment (Anderson, 2002). Due to college and university athletic departments endorsing greater hostility toward LGBTQ+ individuals (Cashmore & Cleland, 2012), LGBTQ+ student–athletes are thereby more likely to report hiding their diverse sexual or gender identity in order to represent their university's athletic department in what they perceive to be a positive way. Additionally, these student–athletes often do not participate in LGBTQ+ clubs or events on their college campus due to the fear of others identifying them as part of the queer community (McCavanagh, 2019).

In terms of athletic performance, heterosexist (i.e., discrimination against gay people on the assumption that heterosexuality is the "normal" sexual orientation) and cissexist (i.e., discrimination against transgender individuals) environments disrupt performance levels and add an additional layer of stress (Anderson, 2002; Demers, 2006). In fact, research has shown that 33% of LGBTQ+ student–athletes experienced a negative change in their participation in sports after disclosing their LGBTQ+ identity, reporting that heterosexist and cissexist environments filled with derogatory language created safety concerns and lowered well-being and mental health (Greytak et al., 2009; McCavanagh, 2019).

In sum, student–athletes who have internalized the dominant heteronormative messages of sport, who belong to unwelcoming teams and environments, and who view their athletic identity as primary face unique challenges to integrating and incorporating all aspects of their self-concepts. As a result, disclosure of one's LGBTQ+ identity can be hidden from teammates and coaches, and delayed to the larger social support system (Cox et al., 2010; Klein et al., 2015; Legate et al., 2012). Thus, when LGBTQ+ student–athletes feel they must conceal their identities, they are alienated from social and institutional supports that could promote positive sexual and gender identity development (Ali & Barden, 2015). Such an exclusion can lead to greater difficulties in disclosing their sexual or gender identity and their integration of self (Meyer, 2003).

**Coming Out in College**

Research suggests that colleges and universities remain largely hostile environments for LGBTQ+ students due to heterosexism and cisgenderism (i.e., cultural and systemic ideology that denies self-identified gender identities that do not align with sex assigned at birth; Garvey et al., 2015). These environments promote sexual prejudice and heterosexist behaviors (Fassinger, 1991; Strayhorn, 2018), perpetuating an unwelcoming and unsupportive climate towards LGBTQ+ students (Evans & Broido, 1999; Garvey et al., 2015; Rankin et al., 2010; Vaccaro, 2012; Woodford et al., 2013). Often, the fear of negative responses and rejection from others pressures LGBTQ+ individuals to remain closeted as protection from prejudice (Ali & Barden, 2015; Coker et al., 2010; Evans & Broido, 1999; Rasmussen, 2004; Rosario et al., 2006). This self-protective action is not without consequences. Indeed, when LGBTQ+ individuals remain closeted, their mental health is significantly impacted by feelings of guilt, anxiety, depression, loneliness, isolation, and lower levels of life satisfaction (Ali & Barden, 2015; Comeaux, 2012; Gearity & Metzger, 2017; Griffith & Hebl, 2002; Rosario et al., 2006; Waldron, 2016). The decision to disclose one's sexual identity is often an attempt to create a sense of relief and to increase life satisfaction (Legate et al., 2012). Positively, individuals may experience feelings of personal growth, increased self-esteem, improved emotional and mental health, and decreased levels of anxiety and depression after disclosure (Ali & Barden, 2015; Bonet et al., 2007; Corrigan et al., 2013). However, disclosure can also be met with social disapproval, a loss of relationships, familial rejection, negative judgments, and physical, emotional, or verbal harassment (Bonet et al., 2007; Corrigan et al., 2013; Legate et al., 2012).

### Issues for LGBTQ+ Students of Color

Collegiate students who identify as LGBTQ+ experience discrimination and harassment on many college campuses (Evans, 2002; Henry et al., 2011). This discrimination is particularly challenging for LGBTQ+ students with intersecting identities, such as being a Person of Color. LGBTQ+ students may face antigay harassment and violence (Leider, 2000), while Black students may experience racial stereotypes and oppression (Fries-Britt & Turner, 2001). Black LGBTQ+ college students therefore face multiple stigmas, creating a complex set of unique stressors that could negatively impact collegiate success (Harris, 2003; Henry et al., 2011). Black LGBTQ+ students experience physiological and psychological issues that are unique to being Black and LGBTQ+. For example, this population is more likely to have poorer health, be overweight, have higher rates of tobacco and alcohol use, have higher incidences of negative mental health outcomes, and report greater concurrent discrimination based on gender, race, and sexual orientation (Balsam et al., 2011; Follins et al., 2014; Fredriksen-Goldsen et al., 2010; Green, 2007; Henry et al., 2011; Mays et al., 2002). Additionally, Black LGBTQ+ students could encounter decreased ability to come to terms with diverse sexual or gender identities due to the levels of heterosexism and cissexism within the Black community (Lewis, 2003), hampering positive experiences and identity development (Henry et al., 2011). These experiences often intensify within college settings and especially within collegiate athletic domains.

### Issues Within Collegiate Athletics

As LGBTQ+ student–athletes are preparing to share their authentic selves within their athletic community, issues related to marginalization as well as supportive resources are considered. These individuals brace themselves for the possibility of discrimination, while also seeking for visibility and support in their community.

**LGBTQ+ Collegiate Student–Athletes**
Given the established implicit and explicit hostility toward members of the LGBTQ+ community, student–athletes and athletic staff should be able to respond promptly and effectively to the presence of student–athletes who identify as LGBTQ+. Collegiate student–athletes who are supported after disclosing their sexual or gender minority identity report less stress, less anxiety, and higher self-esteem (Anderson, 2002; Demers, 2006). On the other hand, college teams that provide little tolerance for LGBTQ+ teammates perpetuate an unwelcoming and unsafe environment (Bush et al., 2012; Cashmore & Cleland, 2012). This environment includes engaging in microaggressions—subtle forms of bias and discrimination—toward LGBTQ+ student–athletes (Ong et al., 2013; Sue, 2010; Sue et al., 2007). Common microaggressions experienced by LGBTQ+ student–athletes include derogatory name calling and rude and insensitive behavior such as hostile language and avoidance (Anderson, 2002; Demers, 2006; McCavanagh & Cadaret, 2019; Norman, 2012). Student–athletes also have the added fear of rejection from the athletic system as a whole, including by teammates, opponents, coaches, staff, and fans of the athletic community. Additionally, Black LGBTQ+ student–athletes may find themselves rejected from not only this racist and heterosexist environment, but also from their own racial and sexual communities (Anderson, 2005). Hostile language and physical violence can take place in nonathletic settings as well as during competitions or practices, potentially diminishing the performance level of LGBTQ+ student–athletes due to an increased fear for their safety. Even worse, research shows that when discriminatory acts occur toward LGBTQ+ student–athletes, teammates and coaches disregard the behavior and do not hold others accountable (McCavanagh & Cadaret, 2019). Thus, athletic departments, and colleges and universities in general, would be failing to support LGBTQ+ student–athletes in their athletic environment.

However, despite the seemingly bleak findings just presented, Cashmore and Cleland (2012) noted there seems to be a positive shift in attitudes toward acceptance of LGBTQ+ student–athletes. Examples of this cultural shift include: (a) the Out to Play project launched by Campus Pride in 2011, designed to address anti-LGBTQ+ slurs and conduct within college sports to create a safer and more LGBTQ+-friendly athletic community (Griffin et al., 2012); (b) Athlete Ally, a nonprofit resource founded by Hudson Taylor in 2011 to encourage all individuals involved in sports to respect every member of their communities, regardless of perceived or actual sexual orientation, gender identity, or gender expression (Griffin et al., 2012); (c) the You Can Play Project created in 2013 by Patrick Burke of the National Hockey League and dedicated to ensuring equality, respect, and safety for athletes regardless of sexual orientation or gender identity (Stefanilo, 2013); (d) the U.S. men's and women's national soccer teams wearing rainbow pride jerseys in honor of LGBTQ+ Pride month (Jarvis, 2015); and (e) the New York Mets hosting New York City's Lesbian and

Gay Big Apple Corps marching band to perform the national anthem (Witz, 2017). With increased advocacy and public displays of acceptance toward the LGBTQ+ community, the presence of LGBTQ+ student–athletes is beginning to be normalized within sports, encouraging collegiate student–athletes and professional athletes to be their authentic selves. While these gains are important, there needs to be an intentional and continued push forward to create safer environments for athletic departments in higher education.

**Collegiate Student–Athletes of Color**
The experience of college athletes of color greatly reflects the place of People of Color within the United States (Simiyu, 2012). As cultural and ethnic diversity increases in the United States, the number of college applications from students of color also increases (Henry et al., 2011). This trend is echoed in collegiate sports, with the increase of athletes of color, specifically Black athletes. Even though the number of athletes of color continues to rise, racial discrimination is sustained. Historically, racism serves to advance White supremacy by helping maintain a status quo that, while inequitable to other racial and ethnic groups, allows White people to preserve their position of power (Bell, 1980; Delgado & Stefancic, 2011). Sports are at the center of this racial ideology, supporting the people with the most power and influence (Coakley, 2009; Simiyu, 2012; Walton & Butryn, 2006). Research has shown that Black athletes continue to experience racism, but in more subtle or covert forms (Agyemang et al., 2010). In Eitzen's (2000) study, Black student–athletes reported experiencing a lack of preparation for college courses, a lack of Black people in leadership positions in the athletic department, and stereotypes from professors and members of the athletic department (Eitzen, 2000). These participants also reported segregation among teammates, contributing to very little meaningful interaction outside of what was required as teammates (Eitzen, 2000).

The sport realm has presented an imagined perception of sameness in regard to BIPOC athletes. However, this false perception masks the persistent reproductions of inequality between racial groups (Bimper, 2015; Bonilla-Silva, 2001; Feagin, 2006; Hylton, 2010). For example, Black student–athletes make up less than 4% of students at Division I universities, whereas 61% of men's basketball players and 46% of football players are Black (Beamon, 2014; Harper et al., 2013; Lapchick, 2012). This overrepresentation of Black men participating in collegiate sports makes it appear that the athletic domain is free from racial discrimination. Even with this overrepresentation of Black student–athletes, the leadership positions within the athletic system, including athletic directors and faculty athletic representatives, remains overwhelmingly White (Bimper, 2015; Lapchick, 2012).

## PRACTICES, STRATEGIES, AND INTERVENTIONS

Understanding the difficult challenges that LGBTQ+ student–athletes encounter, interventions for supportive and affirming action must be put into place to ameliorate their experience. This section discusses the implementation and effects of educational interventions for athletic environments.

## Safe Spaces in Higher Education

In an effort to provide support and education concerning LGBTQ+ students, colleges and universities have begun to implement Safe Zone programs (Ballard et al., 2008; Poynter & Tubbs, 2008). Sometimes known as "safe space" programs or by other names, these programs share similar goals: to provide (a) opportunities to have conversations regarding LGBTQ+ issues, (b) accurate information about the LGBTQ+ community, and (c) skill-building strategies to confront sexual prejudice within college campuses (Poynter & Tubbs, 2008). Safe Zone trainings also provide staff and faculty with ally stickers to demonstrate support and awareness of the LGBTQ+ community and provide space for LGBTQ+ students to disclose their identity (Evans, 2002).

Although Safe Zone programming has demonstrated improvement on campus climates towards LGBTQ+ individuals, there is a disconnect from the Safe Zone programming occurring within the larger college campus compared with trainings offered specifically within athletic departments. While sport organizations have incorporated changes toward diversity and inclusion (Adams & Anderson, 2012), such as the National Collegiate Athletic Association's (NCAA) initiative to include sexual orientation, gender identity, and gender expression in their nondiscrimination polices (Barbour et al., 2014), institutional prejudice is still seen within collegiate athletic systems. As an example, Barbour et al. (2014) found that coaches have requested that student–athletes who identified as lesbian, gay, or bisexual keep their sexual orientation a secret to avoid perceived negative representation of the team. Also, heterosexual student–athletes have reported a fear of having LGBTQ+ teammates in the same locker room or hotel room as themselves (Barbour et al., 2014). Additionally, in a study conducted by McCavanagh (2019), lesbian, gay, and bisexual student–athletes reported wanting to come out sooner in their athletic collegiate experience but lacking comfort in their process due to the absence of visible support from others in the athletic department. These student–athlete participants also reported that their own athletic team never experienced a Safe Zone training, and, to their knowledge, neither did any coaches or staff of the athletic department (McCavanagh, 2019). Thus, the need for Safe Zone programming is evident for LGBTQ+ student–athlete support. As long as coaches and student–athletes do not challenge their own bias toward LGBTQ+ student–athletes, these athletes will continue to encounter hostile athletic environments. The lack of appropriate knowledge and education about the LGBTQ+ community could contribute to ongoing negative treatment of LGBTQ+ student–athletes. Acceptance of LGBTQ+ student–athletes can be fostered by individuals learning more about the LGBTQ+ community.

Broadly addressing these concerns, the NCAA has offered guidelines for increasing inclusion of LGBTQ+ student–athletes and staff, including codes of conduct, policies, resources, and programing as part of their *Champions of Respect* publication (Griffin & Hudson, 2012). Additionally, the NCAA has published a "best practices" guide for inclusion of transgender student–athletes (NCAA Office of Inclusion, 2011). University and college athletics departments are encouraged to familiarize themselves with these resources as a guide for increasing, at the organizational level, knowledge and awareness of LGBTQ+ student–athlete needs. Despite these initiatives, among others, the climate within sports has remained discriminatory towards LGBTQ+ student–athletes, especially with concern to transgender and gender nonconforming athletes. At the time of this writing, state legislative bodies have introduced approximately 20 bills to ban transgender athletes from competition (American Civil Liberties Union [ACLU], 2021). These discriminatory laws are being introduced regardless of evidence that transgender athletes do not have an athletic advantage and in most cases are at increased personal risk when competing or participating in sport due to discrimination and other negative experiences (Jones et al., 2017). Thus, as the rights of LGBTQ+ student–athletes and staff are consistently under attack, we suggest college and university athletic departments engage in activities that will continually increase their knowledge, skills, and awareness of LGBTQ+ rights. As such, training can engage athletic staff and students to foster inclusion and promote activism and advocacy on behalf of LGBTQ+ student–athletes.

**Case Example: Brave Space Initiative**

Since Safe Zone programming has been shown to be effective within college campuses (Poynter & Tubbs, 2008), McCavanagh and Cadaret (2019) developed the Brave Space Initiative, a case study involving an LGBTQ+ educational intervention for athletic environments. The purpose of this initiative was to create a safer, more accepting, affirming, supportive, and inclusive environment for LGBTQ+ individuals within an athletic department. The mission of this initiative was accomplished via educational workshops designed to generate greater awareness, knowledge, empathy, and commitment to actions regarding issues, concerns, and inequality related to sexual orientation, gender identity, and gender expression among student–athletes, coaches, staff, and administrators (McCavanagh & Cadaret, 2019). Additionally, the training provided an opportunity to facilitate open and uncomfortable conversations. The intention of this intervention was to increase awareness of personal bias, enhance comfort with using appropriate language, and improve one's ability to have a dialogue about LGBTQ+ community issues. Two workshops were implemented at a Division II college: (a) a group of randomized student–athletes involved in the Student–Athlete Advisory Committee (SAAC) and (b) the coaches and athletic staff.

**Training One: Student–Athletes**

The student–athletes workshop involved social education and an experiential learning component. The social education section focused on providing the student–athletes information about the discrimination and prejudice experienced by LGBTQ+ college students, LGBTQ+ college student–athletes, and LGBTQ+ college athletic staff to demonstrate the need for this intervention. This section continued by providing information about NCAA definitions and terminology, inequalities faced by LGBTQ+ student–athletes, and microaggressions targeting LGBTQ+ student–athletes. We then facilitated a discussion of the ways to show support as an ally. The workshop concluded with a start–stop–continue activity; the student–athletes reflected on what they can *start* doing to support LGBTQ+ student–athletes, what they have done in the past that may have perpetuated sexual and gender-based prejudice that they want to *stop* doing, and what they have done that has demonstrated support for the LGBTQ+ community that they want to *continue* doing.

### Outcome of Case Example

To test the effectiveness of the workshop, pre- and postintervention surveys were administered to all participants. Student–athletes received a six-item questionnaire (see Table 8.1) developed by the first author to evaluate comfort, ability, awareness, and confidence about addressing several issues faced by the LGBTQ+ community. Results of a paired samples t-test for the student–athletes showed a statistically significant increase on group mean scores assessing

**TABLE 8.1. Items for Student-Athlete Pre/Post Evaluation and Descriptive Statistics**

| Item | N | Range | M (Time 1) | SD (Time 1) | M (Time 2) | SD (Time 2) |
| --- | --- | --- | --- | --- | --- | --- |
| 1. Please rate your comfort in using appropriate language when discussing LGBTQ topics. | 23 | 1–5 | 3.65 | .775 | 4.09 | .792 |
| 2. Please rate your awareness of personal biases towards the LGBTQ community. | 23 | 1–5 | 3.43 | .895 | 4.04 | .928 |
| 3. Please rate your ability to distinguish between sexual orientation and gender identity. | 23 | 1–5 | 3.65 | .714 | 4.17 | .650 |
| 4. Please rate your awareness of issues pertaining to LGBTQ-identified individuals. | 23 | 1–5 | 3.45 | .884 | 4.09 | .792 |
| 5. Please rate your ability to have a dialogue around issues in the LGBTQ community. | 23 | 1–5 | 3.30 | .926 | 4.00 | .852 |
| 6. Please rate your confidence in being an ally for the LGBTQ community. | 23 | 1–5 | 3.91 | .848 | 4.22 | .671 |

confidence, knowledge, and ability in addressing issues faced by LGBTQ+ student–athletes from pre- to post-intervention survey, $t(22) = -3.77, p < .001$ (two-tailed); see Table 8.1. The mean increase across items assessed at pre- and post-test was .146 with a 95% confidence interval of $-.853$ to $-.248$. The eta statistic ($\eta^2 = .39$) indicated a large effect size.

**Training Two: Athletic Staff**

The coaches and athletic staff workshop began with an empathy-building activity to induce the feelings of being an LGBTQ+ student–athlete. This group then received the same social education that the student–athletes group received. Lastly, case scenarios were provided to spark discussion about how the coaches and athletic staff would respond in each situation. This discussion provided a space for vulnerability, critical thinking, and constructive feedback.

**Outcome of Case Example**

To test the effectiveness of the athletic staff workshop, pre- and postintervention and 1-month follow up surveys were administered to all participants. The pre- and postintervention surveys were developed by the second author and consisted of eight items designed to rate participant confidence level about addressing LGBTQ+ community issues within their athletic community (see Table 8.2). Additionally, these participants received the same survey measure at a 1-month follow-up, in which they additionally identified how they had addressed sexual and gender-based prejudice within their athletic environment. For the athletic staff, a paired samples t-test found no significant difference from pre- to post-survey, $t(25) = -.899, p = .37$, with the exception of one item (i.e., I am confident I could educate and create dialogue about LGBTQ+ issues), $t(25) = -1.99, p < .05$ (two-tailed); see Table 8.2. The eta squared statistic ($\eta^2 = .14$) indicated a large effect size. Scores at the 1-month follow-up showed no significant increase from pre- to 1-month survey, $t(8) = -.120, p = .27$, and post- to 1-month survey, $t(25) = -.135, p = .89$. In sum, athletic staff endorsed an increase in their confidence, albeit minor, on the items administered. The statistically nonsignificant results could be a result of measurement or ceiling effects. At baseline, athletic staff rated their confidence to address issues facing LGBTQ+ student–athletes as 84.74 out of a possible 100 as an average across the eight items. Thus, athletic staff came to the intervention with high confidence to address issues facing LGBTQ+ student–athletes. Encouragingly, the results showed consistent increase across items as a result of the workshop. Further information will need to be collected in the future, such as qualitative program review to greater contextualize effectiveness.

In conclusion, the results for student–athletes demonstrated a significant increase in awareness, confidence, and comfort toward issues surrounding LGBTQ+ individuals and situations that could arise within athletic teams and departments (McCavanagh & Cadaret, 2019).

Thus, the program demonstrated encouraging effectiveness as a pilot intervention. We suggest several areas for improvement for future implementation.

Creating Safe Spaces for LGBTQ+ Student–Athletes 151

TABLE 8.2. Items for Ally Self-Efficacy Scale Administered to Coaches and Descriptive Statistics

| Item | N | Range | M (Time 1) | SD (Time 1) | M (Time 2) | SD (Time 2) | N | M (Time 3) | SD (Time 3) |
|---|---|---|---|---|---|---|---|---|---|
| I am confident I could: | | | | | | | | | |
| 1. Support a student-athlete who discloses to me their LGBTQ+ identity | 26 | 1–100 | 86.15 | 16.98 | 90.37 | 13.72 | 9 | 92.33 | 8.39 |
| 2. Confront a colleague or student who tells demeaning jokes toward the LGBTQ+ community | 26 | 1–100 | 87.50 | 16.08 | 89.26 | 15.91 | 9 | 86.78 | 16.54 |
| 3. Support a colleague who discloses to me their LGBTQ+ identity | 26 | 1–100 | 89.62 | 14.55 | 92.59 | 10.95 | 9 | 95.89 | 6.09 |
| 4. Challenge or confront individuals that use derogatory language (e.g., "that's so gay"; "no homo"; etc.) | 26 | 1–100 | 85.00 | 17.49 | 87.78 | 17.17 | 9 | 86.67 | 16.86 |
| 5. Advocate on behalf of LGBTQ+ colleagues and athletes in my athletic department | 26 | 1–100 | 88.85 | 17.49 | 88.33 | 13.52 | 9 | 95.00 | 7.39 |
| 6. Mediate conflict between athletes surrounding discriminatory behaviors towards an LGBTQ+ identified student-athlete(s) | 26 | 1–100 | 87.31 | 12.75 | 87.04 | 13.25 | 9 | 87.00 | 14.18 |
| 7. Educate and create dialogue about LGBTQ+ issues | 26 | 1–100 | 71.92 | 15.11 | 81.11 | 20.82 | 9 | 82.89 | 22.42 |
| 8. Participate and encourage dialogue/events that educate others about LGBTQ+ issues | 26 | 1–100 | 81.54 | 12.73 | 85.93 | 16.47 | 9 | 87.33 | 18.86 |

First, we offer strategies and resources for both facilitators and athletic departments. Becoming familiar with these aims as well as incorporating the strategies into continued training and department goals would be a monumental first step towards LGBTQ+ inclusivity. Next, the current sessions were delivered in a brief format (a single 60-minute session). Future administration of the Brave Space intervention would be improved by offering two 1-hour sessions with the first session covering LGBTQ+ ally education (i.e., terminology, examining own biases, and learning how to respond effectively to situations) and the second session focusing on discussion and case scenarios and expanding training beyond sexuality to include gender-identity and expression. Finally, to measure effectiveness of the intervention, we suggest using established scales to measure changes in awareness and beliefs among students and staff along with intervention and campus specific evaluation. Measures such as the Sexual Orientation Counselor Competency Scale (Bidell, 2005) and the Privilege and Oppression Inventory (Hays et al., 2007) have previously been used to evaluate a Safe Zone training (Byrd & Hays, 2013). Utilizing these or similar scales would add to determining the efficacy of Brave Space trainings among student–athletes and athletic department staff.

## CONCLUSION

The present chapter outlined the importance of focused attention on the experiences of LGBTQ+ student–athletes. As collegiate athletic departments remain largely hostile environments for LGBTQ+ students due to issues of heterosexism, cissexism, and cisgenderism (Garvey et al., 2015), the need for supportive interventions that increase inclusivity while promoting student retention and persistence are evident. Safe space programs have shown efficacy for larger college environments to attenuate the impact of negative environments for LGBTQ+ students (Poynter & Tubbs, 2008). Taking into consideration the unique culture of collegiate athletics, the Brave Space Initiative was proposed. Results showed encouraging shifts in awareness and confidence toward being effective allies for LGBTQ+ student–athletes. Continued efforts to support LGBTQ+ student–athletes will be important to create a larger cultural shift within collegiate athletics.

### Practical Strategies and Resources for Inclusive Spaces in Athletics

- Follow NCAA LGBTQ+-inclusive guidelines of nondiscrimination policies, codes of conduct, communication, and trainings:
  - *NCAA Inclusion of Transgender Student–Athletes* (https://ncaaorg.s3.amazonaws.com/inclusion/lgbtq/INC_TransgenderHandbook.pdf)
  - *Five Ways to Have an LGBTQ-Inclusive Athletics Department* (https://www.ncaa.org/about/resources/inclusion/five-ways-have-lgbtq-inclusive-athletics-department)

- Allow transgender athletes to participate based on the gender category they declare for themselves, rather than whether those athletes have undergone medical transition
    - ACLU "Four Myths About Trans Athletes, Debunked" (https://www.aclu.org/news/lgbt-rights/four-myths-about-trans-athletes-debunked)
    - TransAthlete (https://www.transathlete.com)
- Learn about discrimination against LGBTQ+ people in sports
    - Institute for Sport and Social Justice (ISSJ; https://sportandsocialjustice.org)
    - You Can Play Project (https://www.youcanplayproject.org/about/mission)
    - The GLSEN Sports Project: "Changing the Game" (https://www.glsen.org/programs/changing-game)
    - Out Sports (https://www.outsports.com)
- Be an Ally
    - Visit Athlete Ally (https://www.athleteally.org)
    - Monitor own beliefs/assumptions about LGBTQ+ people
    - Use inclusive language of the LGBTQ+ community
    - Make clear expectations of respect for diversity within the team at the beginning of each season
    - Intervene to stop the use of anti-LGBTQ+ slurs, racial discrimination, and other disrespectful behavior
- Know available LGBTQ+ resources at your university or college
    - Campus Pride (https://www.campuspride.org/topics/athletics)
    - Encourage your athletic department to schedule workshops on LGBTQ+ issues in sports
    - Seek specific trainings that address challenges of transgender student–athletes, including medical transitioning, gender identities, and pronouns
    - Seek programming that specifically addresses issues and needs of student–athletes of color

## DISCUSSION QUESTIONS

1. You are a collegiate student–athlete who identifies as heterosexual. You start to recognize that one of your teammates has begun to isolate themselves in social settings, isn't able to perform up to their capabilities, and is starting to demonstrate signs of depression and anxiety. You notice that your teammate also tends to get very quiet when the team is discussing significant others, contributing very little input to conversations. What are some ways that you can support your teammate if they do identify as lesbian, gay, bisexual, transgender, or queer?

2. You are a coach of a collegiate soccer team. An athlete of yours is openly out as gay. For an away game, you pair up this athlete with another individual on your team who identifies as heterosexual to share a hotel room. The heterosexual athlete asks to speak to you about changing room assignments once you get to the hotel. How do you respond?

3. As a staff psychologist at your university, you have had several clients with marginalized sexual identities who have expressed their difficulty managing their sexual orientation as a student–athlete. What are some ways you can respond to the needs of LGBTQ+ student–athletes on your campus?

4. You are a faculty liaison to the women's lacrosse team. A student–athlete on the team has disclosed to a select number of teammates that she is gay. Without her consent, some of the teammates share this information with others on the team. This has created tension for the players, and the student appears to be isolating herself and depressed. So far, the coach has not responded to this incident. How would you address the issue with the coach, the player, and the team as a whole?

5. You are a graduate assistant manager for the football team. After a recent game, you overhear players using derogatory and demeaning language toward LGBTQ+ individuals in the locker room. You identify as part of the LGBTQ+ community but have not disclosed this to the team. You address your concerns with the coaching staff. They brush the behavior off as "locker room talk." How do you proceed, managing both your own feelings of safety and belonging along with the need to address inclusion and safety with the team?

## RESOURCES

### Mental Health Resources for Student–Athlete Support

- Anxiety and Depression Association of America (ADAA; https://adaa.org)
- Association for Lesbian, Gay, Bisexual, & Transgender Issues in Counseling (https://www.counseling.org/about-us/governance-bylaws/candidate-profiles/divisions-and-regions/association-for-lesbian-gay-bisexual-and-transgender-issues-in-counseling)
- Athlete Ally (https://www.athleteally.org)
- Black Mental Health Alliance (BMHA; https://blackmentalhealth.com/)
- Human Rights Campaign (https://www.hrc.org)
- LGBT National Help Center (https://www.glbthotline.org)
- LGBT National Hotline (888-843-4564)
- National Alliance on Mental Illness (https://nami.org)

- National Queer and Trans Therapists of Color Network (NQTTCN; https://nqttcn.com)

- The SIWE Project (https://thesiweproject.org)

- The Steve Fund (College Student of Color Mental Health Organization; https://www.stevefund.org)

- The Trevor Project (https://www.thetrevorproject.org)

- Trevor Lifeline (866-488-7386)

**REFERENCES**

Adams, A., & Anderson, E. (2012). Exploring the relationship between homosexuality and sport among the teammates of a small, Midwestern Catholic college soccer team. *Sport Education and Society, 17*(3), 347–363. https://doi.org/10.1080/13573322.2011.608938

Agyemang, K., Singer, J. N., & DeLorme, J. (2010). An exploratory study of Black male college athletes' perceptions on race and athlete activism. *International Review for the Sociology of Sport, 45*(4), 419–435. https://doi.org/10.1177/1012690210374691

Ali, S., & Barden, S. (2015). Considering the cycle of coming out: Sexual minority identity development. *The Professional Counselor, 5*(4), 501–515. https://doi.org/10.15241/sa.5.4.501

American Civil Liberties Union. (2021). *Legislation affecting LGBT rights across the country.* https://www.aclu.org/legislation-affecting-lgbt-rights-across-country

Anderson, E. (2002). Openly gay athletes contesting hegemonic masculinity in a homophobic environment. *Gender & Society, 16*(6), 860–877. https://doi.org/10.1177/089124302237892

Anderson, E. (2005). *In the game: Gay athletes and the cult of masculinity.* SUNY Press.

Astin, A. W. (1999). Student involvement: A developmental theory for higher education. *Journal of College Student Development, 40*(5), 518–529.

Atteberry-Ash, B., Woodford, M. R., & Spectrum Center. (2018). Support for policy protecting LGBT student athletes among heterosexual students participating in club and intercollegiate sports. *Sexuality Research & Social Policy, 15*(2), 151–162. https://doi.org/10.1007/s13178-017-0283-z

Ballard, S. L., Bartle, E., & Masequesmay, G. (2008). *Finding queer allies: The impact of ally training and safe zone stickers on campus climate* (ED517219). Education Resources Information Center (ERIC).

Balsam, K. F., Molina, Y., Beadnell, B., Simoni, J., & Walters, K. (2011). Measuring multiple minority stress: The LGBT People of Color Microaggressions Scale. *Cultural Diversity & Ethnic Minority Psychology, 17*(2), 163–174. https://doi.org/10.1037/a0023244

Barbour, C. L., Roberts, G., & Windover, R. (2014, October). *Recruiting and retaining LGBT athletes lessons from the population* [Paper presentation]. Diversity Research Symposium 2014: From Research to Action conference, Ball State University, Muncie, IN, United States. https://cardinalscholar.bsu.edu/handle/123456789/200534

Beamon, K. (2014). Racism and stereotyping on campus: Experiences of African American male student–athletes. *The Journal of Negro Education, 83*(2), 121–134. https://doi.org/10.7709/jnegroeducation.83.2.0121

Bell, D. (1980). Brown vs Board of Education and the interest convergence dilemma. *Harvard Law Review, 93*(3), 518–533. https://doi.org/10.2307/1340546

Bidell, M. P. (2005). The sexual orientation counselor competency scale: Assessing attitudes, skills, and knowledge of counselors working with lesbian, gay, and bisexual clients. *Counselor Education and Supervision, 44*(4), 267–279. https://doi.org/10.1002/j.1556-6978.2005.tb01755.x

Bimper, A. Y., Jr. (2015). Lifting the veil: Exploring colorblind racism in Black student athlete experiences. *Journal of Sport and Social Issues, 39*(3), 225–243. https://doi.org/10.1177/0193723513520013

Bonet, L., Wells, B. E., & Parsons, J. T. (2007). A positive look at a difficult time: A strength based examination of coming out for lesbian and bisexual women. *Journal of LGBT Health Research, 3*(1), 7–14. https://doi.org/10.1300/J463v03n01_02

Bonilla-Silva, E. (2001). *White supremacy and racism in the post-civil rights era.* Lynne Rienner.

Brewer, B. W., Van Raalte, J., & Linder, D. E. (1993). Athletic identity: Hercules' muscle or Achilles' heel? *International Journal of Sport Psychology, 24*(2), 237–254.

Bush, A., Anderson, E., & Carr, S. (2012). The declining existence of men's homophobia in British sport. *Journal for the Study of Sports and Athletes in Education, 6*(1), 107–120. https://doi.org/10.1179/ssa.2012.6.1.107

Buzuvis, E. (2012). Including transgender athletes in sex-segregated sport. In G. B. Cunningham (Ed.), *Sexual orientation and gender identity in sport: Essays from activists, coaches, and scholars* (pp. 23–34). Center for Sport Management Research and Education. https://digitalcommons.law.wne.edu/cgi/viewcontent.cgi?article=1248&context=facschol

Byrd, R. J., & Hays, D. (2013). Evaluating a Safe Space training for professional school counselors and trainees using a randomized control group design. *Professional School Counseling, 17*(1), 20–31. https://doi.org/10.1177/2156759X0001700103

Carroll, H. J. (2014). Joining the team: The inclusion of transgender students in the United States school-based athletics. In J. Hargreaves & E. Anderson (Eds.), *Routledge handbook of sport, gender and sexuality* (pp. 367–375). Taylor & Francis Group.

Cashmore, E., & Cleland, J. (2012). Fans, homophobia and masculinities in association football: Evidence of a more inclusive environment. *The British Journal of Sociology, 63*(2), 370–387. https://doi.org/10.1111/j.1468-4446.2012.01414.x

Coakley, J. (2009). *Sports in society: Issues and controversies* (10th ed.). McGraw Hill Higher Education.

Coker, T. R., Austin, S. B., & Schuster, M. A. (2010). The health and health care of lesbian, gay, and bisexual adolescents. *Annual Review of Public Health, 31*(1), 457–477. https://doi.org/10.1146/annurev.publhealth.012809.103636

Comeaux, E. (2012). Unmasking athlete microaggressions: Division I student–athletes' engagement with members of the campus community. *Journal of Intercollegiate Sport, 5*(2), 189–198. https://doi.org/10.1123/jis.5.2.189

Corrigan, P. W., Kosyluk, K. A., & Rüsch, N. (2013). Reducing self-stigma by coming out proud. *American Journal of Public Health, 103*(5), 794–800. https://doi.org/10.2105/AJPH.2012.301037

Cox, N., Dewaele, A., van Houtte, M., & Vincke, J. (2010). Stress-related growth, coming out, and internalized homonegativity in lesbian, gay, and bisexual youth. An examination of stress-related growth within the minority stress model. *Journal of Homosexuality, 58*(1), 117–137. https://doi.org/10.1080/00918369.2011.533631

Delgado, R., & Stefancic, J. (2011). *Critical race theory: An introduction.* NYU Press.

Demers, G. (2006). Homophobia in sport: Fact of life, taboo subject. *Canadian Journal for Women in Coaching, 6,* 1–12.

Dunbar, M. S., Sontag-Padilla, L., Ramchand, R., Seelam, R., & Stein, B. D. (2017). Mental health service utilization among lesbian, gay, bisexual, and questioning or queer college students. *The Journal of Adolescent Health, 61*(3), 294–301. https://doi.org/10.1016/j.jadohealth.2017.03.008

Eitzen, D. S. (2000). Racism in big-time college sport: Prospects for the year 2020 and proposal for change. In D. Brooks & R. Althouse (Eds.), *Racism in college athletics: The African American athlete's experience* (pp. 293–306). Fitness Information Technology, Inc.

Evans, N. J. (2002). The impact of an LGBT Safe Zone project on campus climate. *Journal of College Student Development, 43*(4), 522–539.

Evans, N. J., & Broido, E. M. (1999). Coming out in college residence halls: Negotiation, making means, challenges, supports. *Journal of College Student Development, 40*(6), 658–668.

Fassinger, R. E. (1991). The hidden minority: Issues and challenges in working with lesbian women and gay men. *The Counseling Psychologist, 19*(2), 157–176. https://doi.org/10.1177/0011000091192003

Feagin, J. R. (2006). *Systemic racism: A theory of oppression.* Routledge.

Follins, L. D., Walker, J. J., & Lewis, M. K. (2014). Resilience in Black lesbian, gay, bisexual, and transgender individuals: A critical review of the literature. *Journal of Gay & Lesbian Mental Health, 18*(2), 190–212. https://doi.org/10.1080/19359705.2013.828343

Fredriksen-Goldsen, K. I., Kim, H. J., Barkan, S. E., Balsam, K. F., & Mincer, S. L. (2010). Disparities in health-related quality of life: A comparison of lesbians and bisexual women. *American Journal of Public Health, 100*(11), 2255–2261. https://doi.org/10.2105/AJPH.2009.177329

Fries-Britt, S. L., & Turner, B. (2001). Facing stereotypes: A case study of Black students on a White campus. *Journal of College Student Development, 42*(5), 420–429.

Garvey, J. C., Taylor, J. L., & Rankin, S. (2015). An examination of campus climate for LGBTQ community college students. *Community College Journal of Research and Practice, 39*(6), 527–541. https://doi.org/10.1080/10668926.2013.861374

Gearity, B. T., & Metzger, L. H. (2017). Intersectionality, microaggressions and microaffirmations: Toward a cultural praxis of sport coaching. *Sociology of Sport Journal, 34*(2), 160–175. https://doi.org/10.1123/ssj.2016-0113

Green, A. I. (2007). On the horns of a dilemma: Institutional dimensions of the sexual career in a sample of middle-class, urban, Black, gay men. *Journal of Black Studies, 37*(5), 753–774. https://doi.org/10.1177/0021934705280305

Greytak, E., Kosciw, J., & Diaz, E. (2009). *Harsh realities: The experiences of transgender youth in our nation's schools.* GLSEN.

Griffin, P., Carroll, H., & Ziegler, C. (2012, October 24). *LGBTQ sports history timeline.* Campus Pride. https://www.campuspride.org/resources/lgbt-sports-history-timeline

Griffin, P., & Hudson, T. (2012). *Champions of respect: Inclusion of LGBTQ student–athletes and staff in NCAA programs.* NCAA Office of Inclusion. https://www.ncaapublications.com/productdownloads/CRLGBTQ.pdf

Griffith, K. H., & Hebl, M. R. (2002). The disclosure dilemma for gay men and lesbians: "Coming out" at work. *Journal of Applied Psychology, 87*(6), 1191–1199. https://doi.org/10.1037/0021-9010.87.6.1191

Harper, S., Williams, C., & Blackman, H. W. (2013). *Black male student–athletes and racial inequalities in NCAA Division I college sports.* University of Pennsylvania, Center for the Study of Race and Equity in Education.

Harris, W. G. (2003). African American homosexual males on predominately White college and university campuses. *Journal of African American Studies, 7*(1), 47–56. https://doi.org/10.1007/s12111-003-1002-9

Hays, D. G., Chang, C. Y., & Decker, S. L. (2007). Initial development and psychometric data for the Privilege and Oppression Inventory. *Measurement & Evaluation in Counseling & Development, 40*(2), 66–79. https://doi.org/10.1080/07481756.2007.11909806

Heird, E. B., & Steinfeldt, J. A. (2013). An interpersonal psychotherapy approach to counseling student athletes: Clinical implications of athletic identity. *Journal of College Counseling, 16*(2), 143–157. https://doi.org/10.1002/j.2161-1882.2013.00033.x

Henry, W. J., Fuerth, K. M., & Richards, E. M. (2011). Black and gay in college: A review of the experiences of students in double jeopardy. *College Student Affairs Journal, 30*(1), 63–96.

Horton, R. S., & Mack, D. E. (2000). Athletic identity in marathon runners: Functional focus or dysfunctional commitment? *Journal of Sport Behavior, 8*, 307–325.

Hylton, K. (2010). How a turn to critical race theory can contribute to our understanding of 'race', racism and anti-racism in sport. *International Review for the Sociology of Sport, 45*(3), 335–354. https://doi.org/10.1177/1012690210371045

Jarvis, N. (2015). The inclusive masculinities of heterosexual men within UK gay sports clubs. *International Review for the Sociology of Sport, 50*(3), 283–300. https://doi.org/10.1177/1012690213482481

Jones, B. A., Arcelus, J., Bouman, W. P., & Haycraft, E. (2017). Sport and transgender people: A systematic review of the literature relating to sport participation and competitive sport policies. *Sports Medicine, 47*(4), 701–716. https://doi.org/10.1007/s40279-016-0621-y

Klein, K., Holtby, A., Cook, K., & Travers, R. (2015). Complicating the coming out narrative: Becoming oneself in a heterosexist and cissexist world. *Journal of Homosexuality, 62*(3), 297–326. https://doi.org/10.1080/00918369.2014.970829

Lapchick, R. L. (2012). *Mixed progress throughout collegiate athletic leadership: Assessing diversity among campus and conference leaders for football bowl subdivision (FBS) schools in the 2012–13 academic year* [Report]. The Institute for Diversity and Ethics in Sport (TIDES), University of Central Florida.

Legate, N., Ryan, R. M., & Weinstein, N. (2012). Is coming out always a "good thing"? Exploring the relations of autonomy support, outness, and wellness for lesbian, gay, and bisexual individuals. *Social Psychological and Personality Science, 3*(2), 145–152. https://doi.org/10.1177/1948550611411929

Leider, S. (2000). *Sexual minorities on community college campuses* (ED447841). ERIC Digest.

Lewis, G. (2003). Black–White differences in attitudes toward homosexuality and gay rights. *Public Opinion Quarterly, 67*(1), 59–78. https://doi.org/10.1086/346009

Mays, V. M., Yancey, A. K., Cochran, S. D., Weber, M., & Fielding, J. E. (2002). Heterogeneity of health disparities among African American, Hispanic, and Asian American women: Unrecognized influences of sexual orientation. *American Journal of Public Health, 92*(4), 632–639. https://doi.org/10.2105/AJPH.92.4.632

McCavanagh, T. (2019). *The coming out experience of collegiate student–athletes who identify as lesbian, gay, and bisexual* [Unpublished doctoral dissertation]. Springfield College.

McCavanagh, T., & Cadaret, M. (2019). *Creating brave spaces in athletic environments: Testing the effects of a sexual orientation and gender diversity workshop* [Poster presentation]. 2019 American Psychological Association (APA) Annual Convention, Chicago, IL, United States.

Meyer, I. H. (2003). Prejudice, social stress, and mental health in lesbian, gay, and bisexual populations: Conceptual issues and research evidence. *Psychological Bulletin, 129*(5), 674–697. https://doi.org/10.1037/0033-2909.129.5.674

NCAA Office of Inclusion. (2011, August). *NCAA inclusion of transgender student–athletes* (Adopted April 2010). https://ncaaorg.s3.amazonaws.com/inclusion/lgbtq/INC_TransgenderHandbook.pdf

Norman, L. (2012). Gendered homophobia in sport and coaching: Understanding the everyday experiences of lesbian coaches. *International Review for the Sociology of Sport, 47*(6), 705–723. https://doi.org/10.1177/1012690211420487

Ong, A. D., Burrow, A. L., Fuller-Rowell, T. E., Ja, N. M., & Sue, D. W. (2013). Racial microaggressions and daily well-being among Asian Americans. *Journal of Counseling Psychology, 60*(2), 188–199. https://doi.org/10.1037/a0031736

Poynter, K. J., & Tubbs, N. J. (2008). Safe zones: Creating LGBT Safe Space ally programs. *Journal of LGBT Youth, 5*(1), 121–132.

Rankin, S., & Merson, D. (2012). *2012 LGBTQ national college athlete report*. Campus Pride.

Rankin, S., Weber, G., Blumenfeld, W., & Frazer, S. (2010). *2010 state of higher education for lesbian, gay, bisexual & transgender people*. Campus Pride.

Rasmussen, M. L. (2004). The problem of coming out. *Theory Into Practice, 43*(2), 144–150. https://doi.org/10.1207/s15430421tip4302_8

Rosario, M., Schrimshaw, E. W., Hunter, J., & Braun, L. (2006). Sexual identity development among gay, lesbian, and bisexual youths: Consistency and change over time. *Journal of Sex Research, 43*(1), 46–58. https://doi.org/10.1080/00224490609552298

Seelman, K. L., Woodford, M. R., & Nicolazzo, Z. (2017). Victimization and microaggressions targeting LGBTQ college students: Gender identity as a moderator of psychological distress. *Journal of Ethnic & Cultural Diversity in Social Work, 26*(1–2), 112–125. https://doi.org/10.1080/15313204.2016.1263816

Simiyu, W. W. N. (2012). Challenges of being a Black student athlete on U.S. college campuses. *Journal of Issues in Intercollegiate Athletics, 5*, 40–63.

Stefanilo, M., Jr. (2013). If you can play, you can play: An exploration of the current culture surrounding gay athletes in professional sports with a particular focus on Apilado v. NAGAAA. *Sports Lawyers Journal, 20*(1), 21–41.

Strayhorn, T. L. (2018). *College students' sense of belonging: A key to educational success for all students*. Routledge. https://doi.org/10.4324/9781315297293

Stroup, J., Glass, J., & Cohn, T. J. (2014). The adjustment to U.S. rural college campuses for bisexual students in comparison to gay and lesbian students: An exploratory study. *Journal of Bisexuality, 14*(1), 94–109. https://doi.org/10.1080/15299716.2014.872482

Sue, D. W. (Ed.). (2010). *Microaggressions and marginality: Manifestation, dynamics, and impact*. John Wiley & Sons.

Sue, D. W., Capodilupo, C. M., Torino, G. C., Bucceri, J. M., Holder, A. M. B., Nadal, K. L., & Esquilin, M. (2007). Racial microaggressions in everyday life: Implications for clinical practice. *American Psychologist, 62*(4), 271–286. https://doi.org/10.1037/0003-066X.62.4.271

Vaccaro, A. (2012). Campus microclimates for LGBT faculty, staff, and students: An exploration of the intersections of social identity and campus roles. *Journal of Student Affairs Research and Practice, 49*(4), 429–446. https://doi.org/10.1515/jsarp-2012-6473

Waldron, J. (2016). It's complicated: Negotiations and complexities of being a lesbian in sport. *Sex Roles, 74*(7–8), 335–346. https://doi.org/10.1007/s11199-015-0521-x

Walton, T. A., & Butryn, T. M. (2006). Policing the race: U.S. men's distance running and the crisis of Whiteness. *Sociology of Sport Journal, 23*(1), 1–28. https://doi.org/10.1123/ssj.23.1.1

Witz, B. (2017, July 7). As more teams host gay pride events, Yankees remain a holdout. *The New York Times*. https://www.nytimes.com/2017/07/07/sports/baseball/gay-pride-nights-baseball-yankees.html

Woodford, M. R., Howell, M. L., Kulick, A., & Silverschanz, P. (2013). "That's so gay": Heterosexual male undergraduates and the perpetuation of sexual orientation microaggressions on campus. *Journal of Interpersonal Violence, 28*(2), 416–435. https://doi.org/10.1177/0886260512454719

# 9

# Navigating New Terrain

*Sexual and Gender Diverse College Students Who Are the First in Their Families to Attend College*

Alison Cerezo and Amaranta Ramirez

**KEY KNOWLEDGE AREAS**

- The largest study of sexual and gender diverse college students found that about one quarter were the first in their families to attend college.

- College graduates earn approximately $1 million more than high school graduates over the course of their lifetime.

- A 2017 study found that only 23% of first-generation college students completed a bachelor's degree or higher.

Higher education in the United States is regarded as the great economic equalizer given the access it affords via career opportunities. The power of higher education to propel financial security is especially true for first-generation ("first-gen") college students because the great majority come from poor and working-class families where wealth accumulation is limited (Stephens et al., 2012). College graduates earn approximately $1 million more than high school graduates over the course of their lifetime, making clear the financial benefits of attaining a college degree (Carnevale et al., 2015). Furthermore, attainment of a college degree results in financial security beyond the degree attainer to include the larger familial system (e.g., one's partner, family of choice), underpinning the importance of college completion for the economic well-being of one's community.

---

https://doi.org/10.1037/0000281-010
*Affirming LGBTQ+ Students in Higher Education*, D. P. Rivera, R. L. Abreu, and K. A. Gonzalez (Editors)
Copyright © 2022 by the American Psychological Association. All rights reserved.

First-gen students account for nearly a third of all entering college students in the United States (Gist-Mackey et al., 2018). Thus, the representation of first-gen students is strong across all subpopulations of college students, including sexual and gender diverse (SGD) students. In fact, Rankin et al.'s (2010) survey of 5,129 SGD college students found that about one quarter were the first in their families to attend college. Despite the prevalence of first-gen students across all cultural groups, studies on the unique experiences and needs of SGD first-gen students are severely lacking in the higher education literature.

## ACADEMIC TRENDS ACROSS SGD AND FIRST-GEN STUDENTS

In the next section of the chapter, we cover important findings on the academic outcomes of first-gen students, followed by a focus on SGD students. There is a dearth of available data related to SGD first-gen students for reasons that include (a) a focus on first-gen students with a lens that primarily (and often solely) considers economic factors related to family of origin and community or neighborhood and (b) severe underrepresentation of SGD students in higher education research. Thus, data on first-gen and SGD students have been collected separately across the higher education literature. Our review describes similarities across these data that contribute to a better understanding of the unique needs of SGD first-gen students, namely, that

- first-gen students take longer to complete postsecondary education than their continuing-generation peers,
- 54% of first-gen students reported not being able to complete their bachelor's degree due to financial struggles, and
- one third of SGD students reported that they have considered leaving their respective campuses due to the harassment they face in relation to sexual orientation and gender identity.

### Attrition and Retention Trends Among First-Gen Students

First-gen students in the United States have consistently experienced higher attrition than continuing-generation (non-first generation in college) students. Data from the National Center for Education Statistics (NCES), spanning 1992–2000, revealed that nearly a quarter (24%) of first-gen students leave college without a degree (Chen, 2005). Attrition continues to grow at an alarming rate. Of first-gen students who enrolled in postsecondary education in 2004, 33% left college without receiving a degree. In 2012, 54% of first-gen students reported not being able to complete their bachelor's degree due to financial struggles (Redford & Hoyer, 2017). These findings demonstrate the gap in support and resources available to first-gen students. However, this steady rise in attrition can also be attributed to an increase in first-gen students pursuing college (Gist-Mackey et al., 2018). These outcomes indicate that more first-gen students are pursuing higher education than in years past, requiring higher education professionals to (a) identify better mechanisms to support them; (b) consider how first-gen status intersects with other student group memberships, as in the case of SGD students; and (c) identify salient issues that impact student attrition.

A careful read of higher education research reveals several high-risk periods when first-gen students are the most vulnerable to attrition. The first and second years in college see a sharp rise in dropouts (Ishitani, 2006, 2016; Woosley & Shepler, 2011), and the fourth year is a critical point, with attrition increasing by 40% in the fourth year if graduation was not attained (Ishitani, 2016). Attrition during these critical points is often related to financial stress, with students emerging from families making less than $23,000 seeing a 49% higher risk of dropping out than their higher income peers (Ishitani, 2003). This finding is confirmed by NCES, who reported that many first-gen students dropped out of college because they could no longer afford tuition (Redford & Hoyer, 2017). One study found that when income, gender, and race were controlled, dropout rates remained 71% higher for students whose parents did not have a college education compared with continuing-generation students (Ishitani, 2003). Differences in region also matter. First-gen students that arrive at college from small to midsize towns experience higher dropout rates than those from bigger cities (Ishitani, 2003). The process of acculturating to the college environment is especially important to consider for rural SGD students (see Chapter 10, this volume). Overall, data suggest that there is no simple solution to prevent dropout among first-gen students. Rather, many students are affected by a combination of challenging factors that include financial stress, norms within their home communities, and a lack of capital to navigate the stressors of college. Capital in the form of academic and social support that helps illuminate college expectations and culture is especially critical for SGD first-gen students.

Recent findings show that about a quarter (23%) of first-gen students in college completed a bachelor's degree or higher (Redford & Hoyer, 2017). A deeper analysis of the data reveals that first-gen students take longer to complete postsecondary education than their continuing-generation peers (Ishitani, 2006; Redford & Hoyer, 2017) and that persistence in this student community is not always straightforward. Federal data from the 2011–2012 academic year demonstrate that when compared with their continuing-generation peers, first-gen students were more likely to attend community college, go to college part time, use distance learning, be enrolled in a for-profit university, and be older (average 24 years old) while also being responsible for children (Aud et al., 2013). Further, first-gen students are more diverse with respect to race and ethnicity. Almost half (48%) of Latinx students are first gen, followed by 42% of Black/African American students, 39% of Asian students, and 28% of White students (U.S. Department of Education, 2014). Because first-gen students are a complex, multifaced student community, it may therefore be the case that promoting a traditional 4-year college trajectory is not a good fit for many SGD first-gen students. Higher education professionals should consider the intersectional challenges facing this community in their pursuit of an undergraduate degree.

### Attrition and Retention Trends Among SGD Students

Across the board, universities and colleges—in addition to federal and state bodies—do not collect data related to sexual orientation and gender identity, making it extremely difficult to understand the experiences and needs of SGD students (Sanlo, 2004). Research studies dating back to the early 1990s demonstrate that SGD college students regularly experience harassment related to sexual orientation and gender identity that has detrimental effects on their persistence in college (Rankin, 2003; Rankin & Reason, 2009; Rotheram-Borus et al., 1991). Compared with their heterosexual and cisgender peers, SGD college students are more likely to experience harassment (23% vs. 12%) and be targets of derogatory remarks (61% vs. 37%). Harassment is especially pronounced among gender-diverse students; 39% of transmasculine, 38% of transfeminine, and 31% of gender-nonconforming respondents reported experiencing harassment at nearly double the rate of cisgender men (20%) and cisgender women (19%; Rankin et al., 2010). Though the social climates of universities have shifted in recent years, SGD students continue to report unfavorable conditions, with one third of SGD students reporting that they have considered leaving their respective campuses due to the harassment they face in relation to sexual orientation and gender identity (McKinley et al., 2015; Rankin et al., 2010).

## CONCEPTUAL FRAMEWORK

In this chapter, we approached the topic of SGD first-gen students from an intersectional lens, recognizing that students' experiences are shaped by the ways they face marginalization and exclusion in several key domains, including institutions of higher education. The recommendations in this section also reflect our lived experiences as former SGD first-gen students pursuing an undergraduate degree, highlighting supports that were key to our success, as well as barriers that continue to persist on many college campuses.

### Intersectionality

Applied to the experiences of SGD first-gen students, intersectionality holds that the social and academic contexts that students occupy are impacted by their positionality across sexual orientation, gender identity, and social class, among other cultural domains. As a result, SGD first-gen students face unique barriers that occur at the intersection of these historically marginalized group memberships. For example, most college students' access to parental support, via experiential knowledge and/or financial assistance, is paramount to their academic persistence and success (McCarron & Inkelas, 2006). This often includes inherited social capital wherein the pursuit of a college degree is assumed at an earlier age given one's parents' social class background; a college academic mindset is thus inherited from one's family of origin. However, both SGD and first-gen students face critical barriers in their access to parental support. Many first-gen students lack basic, vital knowledge about financial aid and other academic factors that directly affect their success in college (Terenzini et al., 1996). In a similar vein, many SGD college students face barriers in their access to parental support related to sexual orientation and gender identity. Thus, for those students that are both SGD and first gen, access to parental support may be especially challenging, amplifying extant barriers related to both social class and SGD identity.

**Community Cultural Wealth**

Related to the concept of intersectionality is Yosso's (2005) community cultural wealth model, developed to counter the long-standing history of deficit-framed language and policies used to describe and respond to the needs of college students of color. *Community cultural wealth* is defined as "an array of knowledge, skills, and abilities and contacts possessed and utilized by Communities of Color to survive and resist macro and micro forms of oppression" (Yosso, 2005, p. 77). Yosso argued that the cultural wealth students of color arrive at campus with should be translated into the academic skills needed to navigate and succeed in higher education.

The essence of community cultural wealth is highly applicable to SGD students, many of whom possess knowledge, skills, and abilities rooted in their daily experiences of having to traverse stigma and discrimination—at both micro and macro levels—in relation to sexual orientation and gender diversity. By building on the skills SGD students already possess, higher education professionals can better help them respond to the social and academic demands of college. SGD first-gen students possess unique skills tied to the ways intersectional barriers have played out in their lives. For many, navigating social and academic spaces related to SGD and first-gen status means that students have a strong sense of many of the barriers in front of them, as well as insight into the types of resources needed to overcome them. The challenge is not about awareness of barriers as much as it is about how institutions of higher education do not tap into the unique knowledge of this community, resulting in a lack of resources and supports needed for them to survive in college. Community cultural wealth can be used to challenge common approaches to working with SGD students that are heavily reliant on protection and safety and instead encourage campus services to be rooted in the leadership potential of this student community.

A review of the SGD education research literature, both K–12 and higher education, demonstrates a heavy focus on issues of campus climate. This research shows that when SGD students perceive the campus environment as hostile, they are more likely to drop out (Rankin & Reason, 2009). We encourage researchers to go a step further to also consider SGD students' cultural wealth as a means to build leadership and academic excellence. Grounded in Yosso's

(2005) model, SGD-focused researchers and academic support staff should extend their work beyond ensuring basic protections on campus to also focus on fostering resilience and thriving that is rooted in SGD students' inherent strengths (see Cerezo & Bergfeld, 2013). Framing SGD first-gen students' academic experiences in both an intersectional and community cultural wealth lens shifts the narrative toward building the next generation of SGD leaders—individuals who have the skills to make a positive impact in their academic and cultural communities and whose work is driven by a more just social class awareness.

On the basis of the studies mentioned earlier, when considering how to harness SGD first-gen students' community cultural wealth, we recommend that colleges develop work and internship opportunities for SGD first-gen students to provide academic mentorship to K–12 students that promote college-going behaviors. We also recommend developing a campus leadership academy for SGD first-gen students to partner with local community leaders that serve income-restricted and/or SGD communities.

## RECOMMENDATIONS FOR SUPPORTING SGD FIRST-GEN STUDENTS

In this section, we offer recommendations for supporting SGD first-gen students that fall into two major domains: (a) fostering social adjustment to college and (b) creating opportunities for financial stability. Our approach to the recommendations section was first to review important relevant research and, second, suggest recommendations based on trends and gaps in the literature.

### Social Adjustment to College

Social adjustment to college has been well-established as a key ingredient in the academic success of college students. *Social integration*, also termed social adjustment to college, describes the ways students become socially integrated into college life, including the formation of social networks (Tinto, 1975). Social adjustment to college has been identified as an especially important factor in the academic success of underrepresented college students. It is through peer social networks that many students, and first-gen students, in particular, are able to build the social capital needed to access critical information and resources tied to persistence and completion of an undergraduate degree (Gerdes & Mallinckrodt, 1994; Toews & Yazedjian, 2007; Wintre & Bowers, 2007).

As many researchers have suggested, first-gen students often struggle with building social capital. In particular, differences in cultural expectations between one's home community and the university make relaying one's college needs to parents especially difficult (Gloria et al., 2005). Many of these students engage in code-switching, which can create a barrier between their lived experiences on campus and their community-of-origin life. This can be viewed as a survival skill; however, it can create a barrier to being able to convey one's college needs and experiences to parents. In fact, many first-gen students report low parental expectation for obtaining an undergraduate degree (Gist-Mackey et al., 2018; Lee et al., 2004), as well as low support for their academic endeavors from both family and home community (i.e., neighborhood peers; Garriott & Nisle, 2018; Jenkins et al., 2013). Further, first-gen students report ongoing misunderstandings from family members about college life that make prioritizing school over earning money or helping one's family especially difficult (Longwell-Grice et al., 2016; Sy et al., 2011).

For SGD students, finding sources of support within the university setting may be especially difficult because of the uncertainty involved in disclosing their sexual orientation and/or gender identity, potentially exposing themselves to harassment and bullying (Sanlo, 2004). Locating a supportive community of college peers and key adults is paramount to positive mental health and academic success. This is especially true given that many SGD students lack family support in relation to their sexual orientation and gender identity (Graham, 2019; Mulcahy et al., 2016; Muñoz-Plaza et al., 2002; Sheets & Mohr, 2009). It is quite common for SGD students to rely more heavily on social relationships formed outside of their family of origin, often referred to as *family of choice* (Goldfried & Goldfried, 2001), that are affirming of their wholes selves as SGD individuals. This may also be the case for first-gen students who do not have family support for college. In the case of SGD first-gen students, building a support network in college is imperative on multiple fronts—students are able to secure social support while also accessing critical information and resources that support their higher education aspirations. In Exhibit 9.1, we have synthesized these pieces of knowledge into concrete recommendations for action.

**Building Financial Security**

One of the greatest predictors for retention among first-gen students is financial stability. Ishitani (2016) found that first-gen students who have multiple financial aid packages are the most likely to persist in this community, demonstrating the steadfast financial resilience needed to remain in college. It is important to note that as first-gen students balance school with work and home responsibilities, they often have limited time to apply for competitive grants and scholarships—factors needed to develop "multiple financial aid packages" (see Ishitani, 2016). Findings reveal that first-gen students take longer to complete postsecondary education, which includes attending multiple universities before the conferment of their degree (Redford & Hoyer, 2017). It is therefore imperative that universities make every attempt possible to connect first-gen students with important financial aid information and opportunities to better support their retention in college.

Family support for education is an especially important factor to consider among SGD college students. It is estimated that more than 700,000 SGD youth in the United States face homelessness as a result of family rejection due to sexual orientation and gender identity (Morton et al., 2017). As described by Quintana et al. (2010), family rejection is severely harmful to SGD youth,

**EXHIBIT 9.1**

**Recommendations for Fostering Social Adjustment to College**

Many colleges and universities organize Summer Bridge and other orientation programs for low-income and first-gen students. We recommend course content on SGD student experiences and resources on campus.

Given the issue of campus climate for sexual and gender diverse (SGD) college students, as well as the importance of social capital for first-gen students, universities should take intentional steps to help students build social community. This may involve offering SGD-specific campus housing, sponsoring SGD affinity groups in campus housing and other campus areas, and periodically notifying the general student body about SGD and first-gen resources.

Develop a peer-mentoring program for SGD students. Data reveal that first-gen students are especially vulnerable to attrition during the first, second, and fourth years in college and that many students are older and have children. Staff should be intentional to consider nontraditional students in the SGD peer-mentoring program, including recruiting students that have transferred from a community college or other institution.

Provide social support that includes dinners and social gatherings during times of the year when most students are with their families of origin. Consider that many SGD first-gen students are unable to return home due to family rejection and/or the high cost of travel.

Form a campus PFLAG or other family support group. Many parents and family members struggle with learning how to support their SGD child in isolation. A family support group can provide parents with important information about the links between support and mental health, as well as connect struggling parents with accepting parents as a way to provide peer mentoring and support.

Offer campus orientations for parents, as well as ongoing information sessions. Higher education professionals should intentionally connect with and educate parents about the campus realities of their children and how they can practically support their children.

---

contributing to "catastrophic consequences on their economic stability, educational attainment . . . [and] economic future" (para. 1). Higher education research would be remiss not to consider the immense barrier family rejection poses in the lives of many SGD college students. It is likely that many SGD students face severe financial stress as a result of family rejection that is not being discussed or addressed in the larger SGD higher education literature. For these reasons, we present the practice recommendations in Exhibit 9.2.

## CONCLUSION

Although SGD first-gen students face numerous complex barriers in their pursuit of higher education, they also possess a wealth of knowledge rooted in their experiences of regularly navigating oppressive systems. These experiences lead to significant resilience potential; when adequately supported by higher education professionals, SGD first-gen college students have the power to transform their cultural wealth into academic success. Adopting both an intersectional and community cultural wealth lens provides professionals with the skills needed to help grow the next generation of SGD first-gen leaders.

**EXHIBIT 9.2**

**Recommendations for Building Financial Security**

Intentionally place financial aid counselors in cultural student spaces, including regular visits to sexual and gender diverse (SGD) student communities (via Associated Students). Placement of counselors in these spaces will provide direct access and will likely remove worries SGD students have about discriminatory treatment in relation to their sexual orientation and gender identity.

Ensure that financial aid staff is knowledgeable about family rejection and how it impacts SGD students' financial resources. It may be the case that an SGD first-gen student is independent of their parents but does not have the knowledge of how to make their financial aid package reflective of their unique needs.

Partner federal work–study opportunities with SGD community organizations—both small, grassroots organizations as well as large civil rights organizations. Such partnerships allow SGD first-gen students to work with mentors and to imagine career possibilities that might otherwise be unavailable to them. Further, students can gain leadership skills while also earning money to pay for college.

Partner with foster care programs and community-based organizations regularly frequented by SGD youth and young adults. Given the relation between family rejection and youth homelessness, SGD youth are overrepresented in foster care settings, where they often lack the knowledge and resources needed to pursue higher education.

## MENTAL HEALTH RESOURCES FOR SGD FIRST-GEN STUDENTS

- Financial stress contributes to mental health concerns. Alert students to funding opportunities such as the Point Foundation (https://pointfoundation.org/), which offers financial support to SGD students pursuing higher education.

- Organizations such as Beyond12 (https://beyond12.org/) offer peer-networking support for first-gen students. These kinds of services reduce loneliness, improve students' social capital, and help students build community.

- I'm First! (https://imfirst.org/) is an organization devoted to building first-gen students' social capital to succeed in college. This includes demystifying certain college tasks that might be elusive to students (e.g., letters of recommendation, office hours).

## DISCUSSION QUESTIONS

1. Are SGD students' voices represented in key campus efforts? In other words, how often are SGD students provided with opportunities to share insight on housing, financial aid, and other resources integral to persistence and graduation?

2. Does your financial aid office have an established mechanism for asking about sexual orientation and gender identity? In other words, are staff trained in how to discuss whether students have parental support for education, including the ability to live at home safely?

3. Does your campus offer safe, financially accessible housing options for SGD students? Are students able to turn to your campus for housing options when they are not safe to live at home?

4. Do SGD campus resources (i.e., staff and programs) outreach to nontraditional and transfer students? National data suggest that first-gen students are more likely to be older and have attended multiple institutions of higher education. Given that Rankin et al.'s (2010) study revealed that about one in four SGD students is first gen, it is imperative that SGD campus resources be responsive to the economic realities of their students.

**REFERENCES**

Aud, S., Wilkinson-Flicker, S., Kristapovich, P., Rathbun, A., Wang, X., & Zhang, J. (2013). *The condition of education 2013* (NCES 2013-037). U.S. Department of Education, National Center for Education Statistics. https://nces.ed.gov/pubs2013/2013037.pdf

Carnevale, A. P., Chea, B., & Hanson, A. R. (2015). *The economic value of college majors*. https://cew.georgetown.edu/wp-content/uploads/Exec-Summary-web-B.pdf

Cerezo, A., & Bergfeld, J. (2013). Meaningful inclusion of LGBTQ voices: The importance of diversity representation and counterspaces. *Journal of LGBT Issues in Counseling, 7*(4), 355–371. https://doi.org/10.1080/15538605.2013.839341

Chen, X. (2005). *First generation students in postsecondary education: A look at their college transcripts* (NCES 2005–171). U.S. Department of Education, National Center for Education Statistics. https://nces.ed.gov/pubs2005/2005171.pdf

Garriott, P. O., & Nisle, S. (2018). Stress, coping, and perceived academic goal progress in first-generation college students: The role of institutional supports. *Journal of Diversity in Higher Education, 11*(4), 436–450. https://doi.org/10.1037/dhe0000068

Gerdes, H., & Mallinckrodt, B. (1994). Emotional, social, and academic adjustment of college students: A longitudinal study of retention. *Journal of Counseling and Development, 72*(3), 281–288. https://doi.org/10.1002/j.1556-6676.1994.tb00935.x

Gist-Mackey, A. N., Wiley, M. L., & Erba, J. (2018). "You're doing great. Keep doing what you're doing": Socially supportive communication during first-generation college students' socialization. *Communication Education, 67*(1), 52–72. https://doi.org/10.1080/03634523.2017.1390590

Gloria, A. M., Castellanos, J., & Orozco, V. (2005). Perceived educational barriers, cultural congruity, coping responses, and psychological well-being of Latina undergraduates. *Hispanic Journal of Behavioral Sciences, 27*(2), 161–183. https://doi.org/10.1177/0739986305275097

Goldfried, M. R., & Goldfried, A. P. (2001). The importance of parental support in the lives of gay, lesbian, and bisexual individuals. *Journal of Clinical Psychology, 57*(5), 681–693. https://doi.org/10.1002/jclp.1037

Graham, B. E. (2019). Queerly unequal: LGBT+ students and mentoring in higher education. *Social Sciences, 8*(6), 171. https://doi.org/10.3390/socsci8060171

Ishitani, T. T. (2003). A longitudinal approach to assessing attrition behaviors among first-generation students: Time varying effects of pre-college characteristics. *Research in Higher Education, 44*(4), 433–449. https://doi.org/10.1023/A:1024284932709

Ishitani, T. T. (2006). Studying attrition and degree completion behavior among first-generation college students in the United States. *The Journal of Higher Education, 77*(5), 861–885. https://doi.org/10.1353/jhe.2006.0042

Ishitani, T. T. (2016). First-generation student's persistence at four-year institutions. *College and University, 91*(3), 22–34.

Jenkins, S. R., Belanger, A., Connally, M. L., Boals, A., & Duron, K. M. (2013). First-generation undergraduate students' social support, depression and life satisfaction. *Journal of College Counseling, 16*(2), 129–142. https://doi.org/10.1002/j.2161-1882.2013.00032.x

Lee, J. J., Sax, L. J., Kim, K. A., & Hagedorn, L. S. (2004). Understanding students' parental education beyond first-generation status. *Community College Review, 32*(1), 1–20. https://doi.org/10.1177/009155210403200101

Longwell-Grice, R., Adsitt, N. Z., Mullins, K., & Serrata, W. (2016). The first ones: Three studies on first-generation college students. *NACADA Journal, 36*(2), 34–46. https://doi.org/10.12930/NACADA-13-028

McCarron, G. P., & Inkelas, K. K. (2006). The gap between educational aspirations and attainment for first-generation college students and the role of parental involvement. *Journal of College Student Development, 47*(5), 534–549. https://doi.org/10.1353/csd.2006.0059

McKinley, C. J., Luo, Y., Wright, P. J., & Kraus, A. (2015). Re-examining LGBT resources on college counseling center websites: An over-time and cross-country analysis. *Journal of Applied Communication Research, 43*(1), 112–129. https://doi.org/10.1080/00909882.2014.982681

Morton, M. H., Dworsky, A., & Samuels, G. M. (2017). *Missed opportunities: Youth homelessness in America.* http://voicesofyouthcount.org/wp-content/uploads/2017/11/VoYC-National-Estimates-Brief-Chapin-Hall-2017.pdf

Mulcahy, M., Dalton, S., Kolbert, J., & Crothers, L. (2016). Informal mentoring for lesbian, gay, bisexual and transgender students. *The Journal of Educational Research, 109*(4), 405–412. https://doi.org/10.1080/00220671.2014.979907

Muñoz-Plaza, C., Quinn, S. C., & Rounds, K. A. (2002). Lesbian, gay, bisexual and transgender students: Perceived social support in the high school environment. *High School Journal, 85*(4), 52–63. https://doi.org/10.1353/hsj.2002.0011

Quintana, N. S., Rosenthal, J., & Krehely, J. (2010). *On the streets: The federal response to gay and transgender homeless youth.* https://cdn.americanprogress.org/wp-content/uploads/issues/2010/06/pdf/lgbtyouthhomelessness.pdf

Rankin, S. (2003). *Campus climate for gay, lesbian, bisexual and transgender people: A national perspective.* https://www.whoi.edu/cms/files/CampusClimate_23425.pdf

Rankin, S., & Reason, R. (2009). *Campus climate assessment and planning.* ACPA Books and Media.

Rankin, S., Weber, G. N., Blumenfeld, W. J., & Frazer, S. (2010). *State of higher education for LGBT people.* https://www.campuspride.org/wp-content/uploads/campuspride2010lgbtreportssummary.pdf

Redford, J., & Hoyer, K. M. (2017). *First-generation and continuing-generation college students: A comparison of high school and postsecondary experiences* (NCES 2018–009). U.S. Department of Education, National Center for Education Statistics. https://nces.ed.gov/pubs2018/2018009.pdf

Rotheram-Borus, M. J., Rosario, M., & Koopman, C. (1991). Minority youths at high risk: Gay males and runaways. In M. E. Colten & S. Gore (Eds.), *Social institutions and social change. Adolescent stress: Causes and consequences* (pp. 181–200). Aldine de Gruyter.

Sanlo, R. (2004). Lesbian, gay, and bisexual college students: Risk, resiliency, and retention. *Journal of College Student Retention, 6*(1), 97–110. https://doi.org/10.2190/FH61-VE7V-HHCX-0PUR

Sheets, R. L., & Mohr, J. J. (2009). Perceived social support from friends and family and psychosocial functioning in bisexual young adult college students. *Journal of Counseling Psychology, 56*(1), 152–163. https://doi.org/10.1037/0022-0167.56.1.152

Stephens, N. M., Fryberg, S. A., Markus, H. R., Johnson, C. S., & Covarrubias, R. (2012). Unseen disadvantage: How American universities' focus on independence undermines the academic performance of first-generation college students. *Journal* of *Personality and Social Psychology, 102*(6), 1178–1197. https://doi.org/10.1037/a0027143

Sy, S. R., Fong, K., Carter, B., Boehme, J., & Alpert, A. (2011). Parent support and stress among first-generation and continuing-generation female students during the transition to college. *Journal of College Student Retention, 13*(3), 383–398. https://doi.org/10.2190/CS.13.3.g

Terenzini, P. T., Springer, L., Yaeger, P. M., Pascarella, E. T., & Nora, A. (1996). First-generation college students: Characteristics, experiences, and cognitive development. *Research in Higher Education, 37*(1), 1–22. https://doi.org/10.1007/BF01680039

Tinto, V. (1975). Dropout from higher education: A theoretical synthesis of recent research. *Review of Educational Research, 45*(1), 89–125. https://doi.org/10.3102/00346543045001089

Toews, M. L., & Yazedjian, A. (2007). College adjustment among freshmen: Predictors for White and Hispanic males and females. *College Student Journal, 41*(4), 891–900.

U.S. Department of Education. (2014). *Profile of undergraduate students: 2011–12* (NCES 2015–167). https://nces.ed.gov/pubs2015/2015167.pdf

Wintre, M. G., & Bowers, C. D. (2007). Predictors of persistence to graduation: Extending a model and data on the transition to university model. *Canadian Journal of Behavioural Science, 39*(3), 220–234. https://doi.org/10.1037/cjbs2007017

Woosley, S. A., & Shepler, D. K. (2011). Understanding the early integration experiences of first-generation college students. *College Student Journal, 45*(4), 700–714.

Yosso, T. J. (2005). Whose culture has capital? A critical race theory discussion of community cultural wealth. *Race, Ethnicity and Education, 8*(1), 69–91. https://doi.org/10.1080/1361332052000341006

# 10

# Supporting Rural LGBTQ+ Communities in Higher Education

Joel D. Goodrich and Michael James McClellan

**KEY KNOWLEDGE AREAS**

- Rural LGBTQ+ emerging adults have unique strengths and methods of adapting to their environment; these include independence, creativity, self-initiative, open-mindedness, and skills in navigating social situations.

- Due to maintaining multiple marginalized social identities, rural LGBTQ+ emerging adults are likely to experience external and internal stressors, and be at an increased risk for psychological distress and mental health disparities; acculturative stress may further compound these concerns.

- By helping rural LGBTQ+ students build resilience, universities can help them build resistance to life stressors and acculturation stress, and aid in bouncing back when problems occur.

- Universities can help rural LGBTQ+ students by implementing policies and programs that are affirmative, providing culturally tailored education to staff and students and connecting students to social supports and appropriate resources.

- Student affairs professionals can also assist by engaging in outreach, considering programming focused on interpersonal connection, emotional well-being, sex and sexuality, suicide prevention, and helping to connect students with other relevant campus services and supports.

---

https://doi.org/10.1037/0000281-011
*Affirming LGBTQ+ Students in Higher Education*, D. P. Rivera, R. L. Abreu, and K. A. Gonzalez (Editors)
Copyright © 2022 by the American Psychological Association. All rights reserved.

Rural lesbian, gay, bisexual, transgender, queer, and questioning (LGBTQ+) students are more likely to experience social isolation from supportive others, and they may attempt to hide their relationships with other queer community members (Barefoot et al., 2015; Cody & Welch, 1997; Oswald & Culton, 2003; Wienke & Hill, 2013; Yarbrough, 2004). They may be more likely to face oppression from local society and government, have fewer community and economic resources, and fear harassment and violence (Barefoot et al., 2015; Oswald & Culton, 2003; Palmer et al., 2012; Wienke & Hill, 2013). Extrapolating from studies of college students moving from rural areas (Dees, 2006; Xiulan, 2015), it is likely that rural LGBTQ+ students may experience acculturative stress, especially when navigating urban university settings. They may also be less likely to experience unique factors related to resilience and positive health outcomes (e.g., a strong sense of self-efficacy and independence, the potential for a close familial bond with LGBTQ+ individuals in their home environment, greater work satisfaction, etc.). Conversely, when drawing from available research about both rural and LGBTQ+ populations, it is apparent that rural LGBTQ+ students may also display hardy resilience, greater happiness and satisfaction in their work, a strong sense of self-efficacy and independence, close-knit relationships with other queer folks, creativity, and other unique strengths (Singh et al., 2011; Smalley & Warren, 2012; Vaughan & Rodriguez, 2014). This chapter explores the unique challenges of rural LGBTQ+ individuals in higher education, their strengths, and the role of educational and mental health staff in promoting resilience, connection to resources, and positive outcomes for rural LGBTQ+ students.

## OVERVIEW OF RESEARCH AND THEORETICAL FRAMEWORKS

In finding ways to support LGBTQ+ students, it is essential for university officials to understand important concepts such as the intersection of rurality and the LGBTQ+ culture and how minority stress and the rural LGBTQ+ experience shapes students, the acculturation process, and help-seeking behaviors.

### The Intersection of Rural and LGBTQ+ Cultures

Existing definitions of "rurality" vary widely based on the specific economic or research-related purpose at hand (Cromartie & Bucholtz, 2008; Ratcliffe et al., 2016). For example, studies have used factors such as population density or population thresholds, distance from urban development, and differing types of land use within a community (e.g., amount of paved areas or farms, among others) as ways to define "rural" (Ratcliffe et al., 2016). The United States Census Bureau (Ratcliffe et al., 2016) defines rural as the nonurban areas of the country that can, for example, include either areas with fewer than 50,000 residents or towns with fewer than 2,500 inhabitants. Rural population estimates range from 17% to 49% of the U.S. population based on the definition used in calculations (Cromartie & Bucholtz, 2008).

Demographic information regarding LGBTQ+ individuals in rural areas is quite limited (Whitehead et al., 2016). The Movement Advancement Project (2019) estimates that there are somewhere between 2.9 million and 3.8 million rural LGBT-identified individuals in the United States. Unfortunately, very little information exists about transgender or gender nonconforming populations living in rural areas (Horvath et al., 2014). LGBTQ+ people who live in rural areas are racially diverse (Movement Advancement Project, 2019). Within the rural population as a whole, an estimated 22% are People of Color: approximately 9% identify as Hispanic or Latinx, 8% identify as Black, over 2% are Native American or Pacific Islander, and 1% are of Asian heritage (Housing Assistance Council, 2012). Rural regions in the United States are becoming more racially diverse: most incoming residents in rural areas between the turn of the millennium and 2010 were People of Color (K. Johnson, 2012). It is also important to note that collecting statistics on ethnic diversity in rural areas may be challenging, such as how or whether migrant farming communities are counted, problems with documentation, and so on.

Rural culture is not monolithic, and specific rural cultural practices vary widely from region to region across the United States (Smalley & Warren, 2012). Smalley and Warren (2012) identified five common factors that may affect rural LGBTQ+ individuals' mental health or help-seeking behaviors: (a) remoteness and isolation, (b) poverty, (c) religion, (d) behavioral norms, and (e) mental health stigma. The remoteness and social isolation of living in rural areas encourages "rugged individualism," discourages help seeking, and allows these individuals to be more prone to working through problems on their own when confronted with challenges. Higher poverty rates in this population makes accessing resources that could help with mental health challenges more difficult. Conservative religious practices, or familiarity with these practices, can cause rural LGBTQ+ individuals to internalize negative attitudes toward themselves and other members of their communities. Behavioral norms that are permissive toward substance use, for example, make it difficult to address these issues when they become problematic, and negative stigma often associated with help-seeking or mental health services often serves as an additional barrier to rural LGBTQ+ college students seeking support when it is needed (Smalley & Warren, 2012).

### Minority Stress and Rural LGBTQ+ Experiences

Meyer's (2003) minority stress theory informs us that minority group membership interacts with external stigma and negative environmental events to influence the development of internal stress and negative health outcomes. We can postulate from this theory that rural LGBTQ+ college students will be more likely to experience environmental stressors and disparities, and less likely to access beneficial resources, than their straight, cisgender, urban peers. For rural LGBTQ+ college students of color, these disparities may be even more pronounced.

Given minority stress theory, one might assume that the projected experience of rural queer college students would be quite dismal, but this may not be the case. Rural communities often produce individuals who value both fierce independence and close-knit relationships with families and communities. They are also often self-starters and creative problem solvers (Smalley & Warren, 2012). When asked to describe the positive aspects of their identity, LGBTQ+ people have identified qualities including authenticity/congruency, open-mindedness, creativity, social savviness, connection with families of choice, a strong social justice focus, and resilience (Riggle et al., 2008, 2011; Rostosky et al., 2010; Singh et al., 2011; Vaughan & Rodriguez, 2014). It is, therefore, quite possible that strengths associated with the intersecting identities of queerness and rurality may produce an individual who is resilient to internal and external stressors.

## Common Experiences Among Rural LGBTQ+ People

One of the most commonly recorded experiences of rural LGBTQ+ people is social isolation, and it is seen as a significant stressor in the daily lives of rural queer persons (Barefoot et al., 2015; Oswald & Culton, 2003; Wienke & Hill, 2013). If one is to form a relationship with an LGBTQ+ community member, that relationship is often closely guarded (Cody & Welch, 1997). It may thus be difficult to find other members of the LGBTQ+ community, especially outside of a bar setting (Barefoot et al., 2015; Oswald & Culton, 2003; Wienke & Hill, 2013).

Many LGBTQ+ individuals in rural areas face significant systemic oppression, but not all are unhappy. Rural LGBTQ+ folks often fear being out in their communities because of an increased risk of facing hostile attitudes, heterosexism, discrimination, less political power, and fewer established local legal protections (Oswald & Culton, 2003). Hiding one's sexuality in rural locations thus becomes the norm (Annes & Redlin, 2012; Oswald & Culton, 2003). In illustration, gay men in both the rural United States and France reported focusing significant time and energy attempting to pass as heterosexual by maintaining an outward appearance of stereotypically masculine traits (Annes & Redlin, 2012). Yet lesbian and gay people living in rural areas have also been found to be generally happier and more satisfied with their work than those in either very large or very small urban locales; this happiness may depend on a sense that they have exercised a choice in their living situation, rather than allowing themselves to simply be pigeonholed into residing in an urban environment (Wienke & Hill, 2013).

In comparison with urban LGBTQ+ youth, LGBTQ+ adolescents living in rural areas may feel more socially isolated and have fewer available supports (Yarbrough, 2004). They tend to report hearing more heterosexist and homophobic remarks and be at greater risk of experiencing violence (Barefoot et al., 2015; Palmer et al., 2012). Rural gay and lesbian individuals are more likely to experience low socioeconomic status than urban comparisons (Wienke & Hill, 2013). In contrast to urban gay men and rural/urban lesbians, rural gay men are more likely to report experiencing depression and anxiety (Kauth et al., 2017). This adds to research on both LGBTQ+ students and rural college students suggesting that both groups are at an increased risk of depression, social isolation, and suicidality (R. Johnson et al., 2013; Lipson et al., 2019; Meng et al., 2013).

**Rural to Urban Environmental Acculturation**

Across sexual and gender identities, rural college students do appear to go through an acculturation process as they navigate college environments. When navigating urban college settings, rural students tend to use three main strategies: (a) attempting acculturation through completely assimilating into urban culture, (b) keeping themselves separate from urban culture, and (c) attempting to find an integrative balance between the two (Dees, 2006; Xiulan, 2015). They are likely to underestimate their ability to adapt to urban culture, especially if they are of low socioeconomic status (Xiulan, 2015). They may feel lost in the city and university, moving comparatively slowly in a fast-paced environment, and feeling undervalued and looked down upon due to their "rustic" background (Xiulan, 2015). For example, other students may ask them to repeat speech content because they want to "want to hear your accent again." They may be frustrated and confused with conflicting cultural views regarding sex, sexuality, gender, and religious beliefs (Dees, 2006). Components that do tend to be maintained from rural students' culture of origin include their religious faith, connectedness with family and community, and conservative views of sexuality and gender (Dees, 2006).

Although rural LGBTQ+ students who attend rural universities have fewer community-oriented environmental stressors than might be experienced in more urban settings, the degree to which they experience relief from acculturative stress can still be shaped by the social identities of their fellow students and university officials. For example, exposure to a student population that is largely made up of other rural students or administrators could serve to make rural LGBTQ+ students feel more "at home" versus a rural campus that was largely made up of students and/or administrators from urban areas who have simply moved to or commute to the rural campus for school or work. For rural LGBTQ+ students, this acculturation process would presumably be more complex. In an attempt to fit in with urban queer communities, rural students may feel pulled to completely reject their heritage, family of origin, and prior values. Conversely, students may find that they are drawn back to their own home and community of origin, and values that better align with their personal or religious beliefs. For those that have not felt affirmed in religious communities, religion might be shunned as a whole or new connections might be formed with supportive faith communities in the urban college environment. More expansive urban views on sex, sexuality, and gender might be taken on in favor of more conservative views, or the rural LGBTQ+ student might feel caught in conflict and oscillate between the two viewpoints. As noted at the beginning of this paragraph, whether rural LGBTQ+

students face those same conflicts on rural campuses largely depends on the make-up of other students and university officials and whether they are from rural or urban areas.

**Help-Seeking Behaviors**

In a national online survey of the experiences of the general populace of college students, individuals identifying as gay, lesbian, or bisexual were found to be more likely to utilize mental health services than their heterosexual peers (Baams et al., 2018). They, along with individuals identifying as queer, were more likely to have experienced mental health concerns including suicidality than heterosexual participants (Baams et al., 2018). No clear interaction effects were discovered between race/ethnicity and sexual orientation on mental health help-seeking behaviors (Baams et al., 2018).

In comparison with the general population, help-seeking behavior may be more curtailed among rural queer people (Willging et al., 2006). In a series of semistructured interviews with rural LGBTQ+ residents of New Mexico to determine barriers to utilization of local mental health care resources, participants endorsed (a) mental health stigma and a desire to alleviate symptoms independently, (b) a lack of visible and cohesive LGBTQ+ social networks, (c) a lack of financial or transportation resources, and (d) a distrust of providers perceived as uneducated or openly hostile toward LGBTQ+ people (Willging et al., 2006). Some participants chose to remain silent about their sexual orientation or gender identity in order to navigate spaces perceived as hostile. Participants of color in particular were likely to rely more on families, faith-based mental health services, and alternative healing practices rather than finding support with LGBTQ+ community members or nonreligious mental health providers (Willging et al., 2006).

## PRACTICES, STRATEGIES, AND INTERVENTIONS

Fostering resiliency, improving program offerings, and proactively engaging the rural LGBTQ+ population through outreach are important to student success.

**Resilience Factors**

The more resilient a queer person is, the greater their chance of making it through internal or external stressors and protecting themselves from suicidality (Fenway Institute, 2018; Moody & Smith, 2013; Singh et al., 2011). Resilience is often thought of as the ability for a person to resist and rebound from stresses and traumatic events (Bonanno, 2004; Chang et al., 2018). We know that a gay, bisexual, lesbian, or transgender college student is resilient when they have hope for the future, and can identify and talk about their emotions with others in their life (Kwon, 2013; Lyons, 2015; Singh et al., 2011; Snyder et al., 1991). Transgender and gender nonconforming (TGNC) individuals able to bounce back from stressors generally accept and have pride in themselves, their gender identity, and its expression; they are also connected to their heritage (Chang et al., 2018; Singh et al., 2011). A transgender student who is resilient likely has a working knowledge of the way in which stigma and discrimination impact their lives, and the systemic nature of that oppression (Chang et al., 2018; Singh et al., 2011). They are self-advocates who can assert their needs and ways in which they are oppressed (Chang et al., 2018; Singh et al., 2011).

Coming out is commonly seen as a steppingstone in developing a healthy LGBTQ+ identity, but this perspective lacks needed nuance. Coming out may help to improve an LGBTQ+ person's resilience to stressors, and reduce the chance of experiencing self-stigma and related mental health disorders, but this depends on personal comfort, safety, and choice (American Psychological Association [APA], 2012; Ford, 2004; Kwon, 2013). Coming out can be an emotionally exhausting process (APA, 2012; Ford, 2004); it is also a process without a designated end point (APA, 2012). Coming out may also increase one's risk of external stressors such as rejection from family members or friends, being targeted for violence, and social isolation (APA, 2012; Balsam et al., 2005; Chang et al., 2018). This may especially be the case for rural LGB individuals, who are more likely to experience heterosexist discrimination then their urban counterparts when out in their communities (Swank et al., 2013). University staff should be cautious, then, in encouraging students to come out to the campus, their friends, and their families, but of course be supportive if a student makes that choice for themselves; not all LGBTQ+ individuals will find it important or necessary to come out (APA, 2012; Yarbrough, 2004).

Queer students are likely to be resilient if they are connected to and active in a broader community of LGBTQ+ people, and with supportive loved ones who may or may not identify as LGBTQ+ themselves (Chang et al., 2018; Kwon, 2013; Lyons, 2015; Singh et al., 2011). Connection to community may be especially important for those from rural areas, who may be more likely to feel isolated from others. Connection to the broader LGBTQ+ community offers a further protective layer, a form of collective resistance known as *community resilience* (Chang et al., 2018; Masten, 2015; Singh et al., 2011). It may similarly be helpful to connect queer students from rural areas to support groups or student organizations focused on the experiences of people with rural heritages. Such groups should consider including storytelling or art, an opportunity to share food or be in nature together, even bringing in rural elders as guest speakers, as these activities have been associated with resilience (DeCou et al., 2013).

It is important to highlight that while the term resilience is relatively new in dialogues within the social sciences, it has its roots in a politico–economic philosophy that espouses the idea of a free-market economy largely devoid of regulatory oversight, focused on actively reducing government responsibility, which arguably rests on systemic inequality at the expense of those with marginalized identities (Chandler, 2016; Gill & Orgad, 2018; Kaufmann, 2016; Krüger, 2019). Within this framework, resilience is a concept championed by those in power to remove their responsibility for the conditions of socially marginalized individuals (Derickson, 2016; Krüger, 2019). To be resilient, you must have certain access to several material resources and services, those most available to individuals with White, middle class, and able-bodied identities (Derickson, 2016; Gill & Orgad, 2018; Krüger, 2019). Likewise, by highlighting resilience as a positive characteristic, we may begin to assume that those with marginalized identities (e.g., queer and rural students) hold responsibility for upholding this quality, and if they are not resilient, they are abnormal and worthy of social disapprobation (Kaufmann, 2016; Krüger, 2019). In ignoring these features underlying the concept, we may act in an ableist, racist, and classist manner and overlook real responsibilities that governments, societies, and, for our purposes, academic institutions have to provide the necessary materials and environmental conditions which foster its qualities. Furthermore, systems of governance, education, etc. truly bear responsibility for eliminating systems and environmental conditions that require resilience strategies from those with marginalized identities in the first place.

**LGBTQ+ Programming Review**

Rural culture is often associated with patriarchy, conservatism, religiosity, traditional gender roles, and heterocentric family structures—all of which may impact the well-being of LGBTQ+ individuals who grew up in rural locations (Barefoot et al., 2015). The LGBTQ+ literature provides a number of recommendations that can be helpful to student affairs professionals. Ottenritter's (2012) article on creating inclusive environments for LGBTQ+ college students, faculty, and staff provides three general assumptions that are helpful to consider. First, Ottenritter purports that supportive campus environments are an essential component for LGBTQ+ student success. Student, faculty, and staff attitudes, beliefs, and behaviors are impacted by the campus climate, so creating an environment that is conducive to rural LGBTQ+ student success is important. Second, Ottenritter posits that people are complex and are made up of many intersecting social identities. It is important for campus community members to understand, value, and respect that diversity. Universities can and must play an important role in providing training to students, faculty, and staff members who need help understanding these important diversity issues in order to build a more inclusive environment. Ottenritter also assumes that universities understand that student retention is vital to overall institutional and student success. So, creating environments where rural LGBTQ+ students feel supported has a direct impact on these students' ability to be successful.

The literature provides a number of recommendations for creating supportive campus environments for rural LGBTQ+ students (Black et al., 2012; Ottenritter, 2012; Pitcher et al., 2018; Seelman, 2014; Smith et al., 2018). Those recommendations can be grouped into the following four categories that broadly span the university environment: (a) policies and procedures, (b) services, (c) education, and (d) social. First, affirming university policies that support rural LGBTQ+

students can have a significant impact on creating supportive university environments (Black et al., 2012; Ottenritter, 2012; Pitcher et al., 2018; Smith et al., 2018). Those policies or procedures include nondiscrimination policies (Smith et al., 2018), as well as university-wide policies that support student, faculty, and staff diversity training; use of affirming language and pronouns (Singh et al., 2013); expanding demographic options on forms to be more inclusive of TGNC community member's lived experience (American Psychological Association of Graduate Students Subcommittee on Sexual Orientation and Gender Diversity [APAGS], 2019); allowing students to easily change their names without requiring legal documentation to support those changes; and creating gender neutral restrooms, locker rooms, and living spaces that are accepting and consistent with these students' needs (Seelman, 2014). Pitcher et al. (2018) and Smith et al. (2018) both viewed supportive, affirming nondiscrimination policies as positive and pointed out that a university's failure to include such policies is viewed by the TGNC community as negative. Seelman (2014), however, pointed out that nondiscrimination policies are only positive and helpful to TGNC students if universities follow through and use those policies to hold university community members accountable for following those policies.

A second pillar of creating a supportive university environment for rural LGBTQ+ students involves student services (Ottenritter, 2012; Pitcher et al., 2018; Seelman, 2014). Student services broadly impact college students, and these services are a valuable component of the overall university experience (Ottenritter, 2012; Pitcher et al., 2018). Student services broadly include university programs or activities that promote student learning and/or engagement (Pitcher et al., 2018), as well as university admissions and student success initiatives (Seelman, 2014), student organizations (Pitcher et al., 2018), counseling centers (Smith et al., 2018; Swanbrow Becker et al., 2017), university health services (Singh et al., 2013), and university housing (APAGS, 2019). Campus community members who are affiliated with these services should be well-trained to work with rural LGBTQ+ students, so that they understand, are supportive of, and attentive to the needs of these students (Barefoot et al., 2015; Oswald & Culton, 2003; Ottenritter, 2012; Pitcher et al., 2018). Student services representatives should also be familiar with the wide range of university, local, and national resources that are available to support rural LGBTQ+ students (Barefoot et al., 2015; Oswald & Culton, 2003; Ottenritter, 2012; Pitcher et al., 2018) and actively work together to meet student needs.

For example, it would be invaluable for a resident assistant who learns that a transgender student is feeling homesick and depressed to be familiar with and able to get the student quickly connected to other campus resources, including student organizations that were trans-affirming and could offer needed social support or to therapists in the counseling center who were sensitive to these students' needs. The office of institutional technology could work to normalize and simplify the process of making name or gender changes within university databases or email. Facilities management officials could play an important role in consulting on or enacting structural changes to university spaces, such as restrooms and residence halls. Further, administrators could play an important role in shaping organizational structures that promote interdepartmental collaborations that better support rural LGBTQ+ students, such as creating meeting opportunities for facilities services, an LGBTQ+ campus organization, and the university housing office to discuss restroom designs in the residence halls.

A third key to creating supportive campus environments is academic affairs (Ottenritter, 2012; Seelman, 2014). Rural LGBTQ+ students should expect to engage with faculty who are trained to meet their needs as well as other students in learning spaces that are open and accepting (Ottenritter, 2012). Recommendations presented in the literature suggest that course syllabi should include language that specifically identifies the learning environment as a safe space, sets an expectation of openness and acceptance, and disavows intolerance (Katz et al., 2016). Course syllabi should include LGBTQ+ authors (APAGS, 2019). Other ideas include developing speaker panels that include LGBTQ+ panelists (Kwon & Hugelshofer, 2012), as well as developing learning communities that allow LGBTQ+ students and/or allies to work together in safe learning spaces around a shared curriculum.

A fourth pillar of creating supportive campus environments for rural LGBTQ+ community members is the individual student's social environment (Smith et al., 2018). Ideally, rural LGBTQ+ students would show up to campus with solid social support from friends and family (Smith et al., 2018), but this is not always the case. It is important for these students to have access to a community of allies across campus who understand rural LGBTQ+ students and their needs and who have been empowered to serve these students (Smith et al., 2018). These allies can be other students, faculty, or staff members who have been trained to work with and better understand the needs of these students as well as equipped with the knowledge of important campus resources and are willing to help (Smith et al., 2018). These allies can also help shape university culture by working to promote and advocate for rural LGBTQ+ students (Smith et al., 2018). For example, allies could help by challenging binary assumptions of gender and sexuality (APAGS, 2019).

Two helpful resources were noted in the literature to help student affairs professionals who are seeking to evaluate the needs of their campuses or who are considering appropriate assessment outcomes for LGBTQ+ students. Ottenritter (2012) provided a checklist for conducting an environmental scan to help university officials assess their level of preparedness to serve LGBTQ+ students across campus educational, services, and policy/procedural domains. This tool provides helpful questions, such as "Are LGBTQ+ people appropriately included in textbooks and materials used in class, including credit, noncredit, and workforce development classes?" (Ottenritter, 2012, p. 537). In addition, Black et al. (2012) recommended three broad outcome assessment areas: social (e.g., peer acceptance, school connectedness, and homonegative language), psychological (e.g., self-acceptance, mental health issues, and internalized homophobia), and physical outcomes (e.g., harassment, victimization, and suicidality) for sexual minority students. Although these two resources do not specifically reference rurality, they could be adapted to include questions or outcomes related to rurality. For example, Ottenritter's checklist could simply add this question to their preparedness planning: "Do our campus educational, services, and policy/procedural domains address the unique needs of rural and/or rural LGBTQ+ students, such as tendency toward isolation, economic disadvantage, engagement with religion, behavioral norms, and mental health stigma?"

**The Importance of Outreach**

Since rural students may be less likely to reach out for help, campus/community outreach could be an effective prevention and intervention tool for student service providers to consider. When considering outreach programming for LGBTQ+ students from rural areas, it is particularly important to address some aforementioned factors, such as isolation, enhanced risk of suicide, self-stigma, lack of access to care, and reduced help-seeking. Programming that emphasizes assertive communication, interpersonal relationship building, and interpersonal skill development may be especially important for queer clients who feel isolated from peers and family members (Pachankis, 2014). Having frank, positive discussions about emotions and sex and sexuality, as well as providing a space encouraging of gender exploration, can help ameliorate self-stigma (Pachankis, 2014). Suicide prevention trainings on campus are very much needed to help with the increased risk of suicidal ideation and attempts faced by rural and LGBTQ+ students (Johnson et al., 2013; Lipson et al., 2019; Meng et al., 2013). Peer mentor programs could be useful in connecting rural queer students to care and in decreasing help-seeking stigma (Centers for Disease Control and Prevention [CDC], 2019). For rural students who commute from home, or for those who participate in distance learning classes, the use of online support groups or teletherapy may be useful in helping reduce social isolation and transportation concerns (Barefoot et al., 2015; CDC, 2019). Finally, hosting events that celebrate the histories and heritages of rural and LGBTQ+ individuals may help students feel more connected, and tap into community resilience factors.

## CONCLUSION

This chapter focused on the unique needs of rural LGBTQ+ college students and offered recommendations on how to support these students. Rural LGBTQ+ college students face a number of challenges, and rural LGBTQ People of Color can experience a compounding effect of their multiple, oppressed, social identities. It is important that these students attend universities that provide affirming and supportive learning and social environments. In order for a university to determine whether it is serving the needs of rural LGBTQ+ students, administrators should conduct an environmental scan of campus preparedness and of social, psychological, and physical student outcomes. Forms and policies should be evaluated for their inclusiveness of rural LGBTQ+ experiences and identities. Faculty and staff should be trained to provide culturally competent care and education. Student affairs professionals can better support rural LGBTQ+ students by emphasizing interventions focused on building resilience, interpersonal skills, social support, emotional well-being, psychoeducation regarding sex and sexuality, suicide prevention trainings, and by connecting to networks of other local and national support systems for rural and LGBTQ+ populations.

## DISCUSSION QUESTIONS

1. What resources does your institution or local community provide that can support rural LGBTQ+ students who may have fewer connections with family and social supports at home?
2. How can your department better connect rural LGBTQ+ students with supportive and affirming campus and community resources?
3. How can departmental and/or institutional policies be improved to enhance the experience of LGBTQ+ students at your university?
4. In what ways can safe spaces be created for students, faculty, and staff within your unit to help enhance and improve feelings of safety for both rural LGBTQ+ and nonrural LGBTQ+ students?
5. How might rural LGBTQ+ students serve in planning, creating, and maintaining LGBTQ+ spaces that are supportive of people from rural backgrounds?

## RESOURCES

1. Movement Advancement Project *Rural* page: https://www.lgbtmap.org/rural
2. Colorbloq Red Collection for queer and trans People of Color living in rural, southern, and "red" states: https://www.colorbloq.org/red-collection
3. QORRN—The Queer-Oriented Rural Resource Network: https://www.qorrn.com
4. Queer Appalachia (The Electric Dirt Collective): https://www.queerappalachia.com
5. SONG—Southerners on New Ground, a social justice movement in the Southern United States: https://southernersonnewground.org
6. Out in the Open: https://www.weareoutintheopen.org

## REFERENCES

American Psychological Association. (2012). Guidelines for psychological practice with lesbian, gay, and bisexual clients. *American Psychologist*, 67(1), 10–42. https://doi.org/10.1037/a0024659

American Psychological Association Graduate Students Subcommittee on Sexual Orientation and Gender Diversity. (2019). *A guide for supporting trans and gender diverse students*. https://www.apa.org/apags/governance/subcommittees/supporting-diverse-students.pdf

Annes, A., & Redlin, M. (2012). The careful balance of gender and sexuality: Rural gay men, the heterosexual matrix, and "effeminophobia." *Journal of Homosexuality, 59*(2), 256–288. https://doi.org/10.1080/00918369.2012.648881

Baams, L., De Luca, S. M., & Brownson, C. (2018). Use of mental health services among college students by sexual orientation. *LGBT Health, 5*(7), 421–430. https://doi.org/10.1089/lgbt.2017.0225

Balsam, K. F., Rothblum, E. D., & Beauchaine, T. P. (2005). Victimization over the life span: A comparison of lesbian, gay, bisexual, and heterosexual siblings. *Journal of Consulting and Clinical Psychology, 73*(3), 477–487. https://doi.org/10.1037/0022-006X.73.3.477

Barefoot, K., Rickard, A., Smalley, K., & Warren, J. (2015). Rural lesbians: Unique challenges and implications for mental health providers. *Rural Mental Health, 39*(1), 22–33. https://doi.org/10.1037/rmh0000014

Black, W. W., Fedewa, A. L., & Gonzalez, K. A. (2012). Effects of "Safe School" programs and policies on the social climate for sexual-minority youth: A review of the literature. *Journal of LGBT Youth, 9*(4), 321–339. https://doi.org/10.1080/19361653.2012.714343

Bonanno, G. A. (2004). Loss, trauma, and human resilience: Have we underestimated the human capacity to thrive after extremely aversive events? *American Psychologist, 59*(1), 20–28. https://doi.org/10.1037/0003-066X.59.1.20

Centers for Disease Control and Prevention. (2019). *Preventing suicide in rural America* [Policy brief]. https://www.cdc.gov/ruralhealth/suicide/policybrief.html

Chandler, D. (2016). Debating neoliberalism: The exhaustion of the liberal problematic. In D. Chandler & J. Reid (Eds.), *The neoliberal subject: Resilience, adaptation, and vulnerability* (pp. 9–16). Rowman & Littlefield International.

Chang, S. C., Singh, A. A., & dickey, l. m. (2018). *A clinician's guide to gender-affirming care: Working with transgender and gender nonconforming clients*. Context Press.

Cody, P. J., & Welch, P. L. (1997). Rural gay men in northern New England: Life experiences and coping styles. *Journal of Homosexuality, 33*(1), 51–67. https://doi.org/10.1300/J082v33n01_04

Cromartie, J., & Bucholtz, S. (2008). *Defining the "rural" in rural America*. U.S. Department of Agriculture Economic Research Service. https://www.ers.usda.gov/amber-waves/2008/june/defining-the-rural-in-rural-america/

DeCou, C. R., Skewes, M. C., & López, E. D. (2013). Traditional living and cultural ways as protective factors against suicide: Perceptions of Alaska Native university students. *International Journal of Circumpolar Health, 72*(1), 20968. https://doi.org/10.3402/ijch.v72i0.20968

Dees, D. M. (2006). "How do I deal with these new ideas?": The psychological acculturation of rural students (ERIC No. EJ740129). *Journal of Research in Rural Education, 21*(6), 1–11. ERIC Number: EJ740129.

Derickson, K. D. (2016). Resilience is not enough. *City, 20*(1), 161–166. https://doi.org/10.1080/13604813.2015.1125713

Fenway Institute. (2018). *Suicide risk and prevention for LGBTQ+ people*. https://www.lgbthealtheducation.org/wp-content/uploads/2018/10/Suicide-Risk-and-Prevention-for-LGBTQ-Patients-Brief.pdf

Ford, V. E. (2004). Coming out as lesbian or gay: A potential precipitant of crisis in adolescence. *Journal of Human Behavior in the Social Environment, 8*(2–3), 93–110. https://doi.org/10.1300/J137v08n02_06

Gill, R., & Orgad, S. (2018). The amazing bounce-backable woman: Resilience and the psychological turn in neoliberalism. *Sociological Research Online, 23*(2), 477–495. https://doi.org/10.1177/1360780418769673

Horvath, K. J., Iantaffi, A., Swinburne-Romine, R., & Bockting, W. (2014). A comparison of mental health, substance use, and sexual risk behaviors between rural and non-rural transgender persons. *Journal of Homosexuality, 61*(8), 1117–1130. https://doi.org/10.1080/00918369.2014.872502

Housing Assistance Council. (2012, April). *Race and ethnicity in rural America* [Rural Research Briefs]. https://ruralhome.org/rrn-race-and-ethnicity/

Johnson, K. M. (2012). *Rural demographic change in the new century: Slower growth, increased diversity* (Issue Brief No. 44). The Carsey School of Public Policy, University of New Hampshire Scholars Repository. https://scholars.unh.edu/carsey/159

Johnson, R. B., Oxendine, S., Taub, D. J., & Robertson, J. (2013). Suicide prevention for LGBT students. *New Directions for Student Services, 2013*(141), 55–69. https://doi.org/10.1002/ss.20040

Katz, J., Federici, D., Ciovacco, M., & Cropsey, A. (2016). Effect of exposure to a safe zone symbol on perceptions of campus climate for sexual minority students. *Psychology of Sexual Orientation and Gender Diversity, 3*(3), 367–373. https://doi.org/10.1037/sgd0000186

Kaufmann, M. (2016). Exercising emergencies: Resilience, affect and acting out security. *Security Dialogue, 47*(2), 99–116. https://doi.org/10.1177/0967010615613209

Kauth, M. R., Barrera, T. L., Denton, F. N., & Latini, D. M. (2017). Health differences among lesbian, gay, and transgender veterans by rural/small town and suburban/urban setting. *LGBT Health, 4*(3), 194–201. https://doi.org/10.1089/lgbt.2016.0213

Krüger, M. (2019). Building instead of imposing resilience: Revisiting the relationship between resilience and the state. *International Political Sociology, 13*(1), 53–67. https://doi.org/10.1093/ips/oly025

Kwon, P. (2013). Resilience in lesbian, gay, and bisexual individuals. *Personality and Social Psychology Review, 17*(4), 371–383. https://doi.org/10.1177/1088868313490248

Kwon, P., & Hugelshofer, D. S. (2012). Lesbian, gay, and bisexual speaker panels lead to attitude change among heterosexual college students. *Journal of Gay & Lesbian Social Services, 24*(1), 62–79. https://doi.org/10.1080/10538720.2012.643285

Lipson, S. K., Raifman, J., Abelson, S., & Reisner, S. L. (2019). Gender minority mental health in the U.S.: Results of a national survey on college campuses. *American Journal of Preventive Medicine, 57*(3), 293–301. https://doi.org/10.1016/j.amepre.2019.04.025

Lyons, A. (2015). Resilience in lesbians and gay men: A review and key findings from a nationwide Australian survey. *International Review of Psychiatry, 27*(5), 435–443. https://doi.org/10.3109/09540261.2015.1051517

Masten, A. S. (2015). *Ordinary magic: Resilience in development.* Guilford Press.

Meng, H., Li, J., Loerbroks, A., Wu, J., & Chen, H. (2013). Rural/urban background, depression and suicidal ideation in Chinese college students: A cross-sectional study. *PLOS ONE, 8*(8), e71313. https://doi.org/10.1371/journal.pone.0071313

Meyer, I. H. (2003). Prejudice, social stress, and mental health in lesbian, gay, and bisexual populations: Conceptual issues and research evidence. *Psychological Bulletin, 129*(5), 674–697. https://doi.org/10.1037/0033-2909.129.5.674

Moody, C., & Smith, N. G. (2013). Suicide protective factors among trans adults. *Archives of Sexual Behavior, 42*(5), 739–752. https://doi.org/10.1007/s10508-013-0099-8

Movement Advancement Project. (2019). *Where we call home: LGBT people in rural America.* http://www.lgbtmap.org/rural-lgbt

Oswald, R., & Culton, L. (2003). Under the rainbow: Rural gay life and its relevance for family providers. *Family Relations, 52*(1), 72–81. https://doi.org/10.1111/j.1741-3729.2003.00072.x

Ottenritter, N. (2012). Crafting a caring and inclusive environment for LGBTQ+ community college students, faculty, and staff. *Community College Journal of Research and Practice, 36*(7), 531–538. https://doi.org/10.1080/10668926.2012.664094

Pachankis, J. E. (2014). Uncovering clinical principles and techniques to address minority stress, mental health, and related health risks among gay and bisexual men. *Clinical Psychology: Science and Practice, 21*(4), 313–330. https://doi.org/10.1111/cpsp.12078

Palmer, N., Kosciw, J., & Bartkiewicz, M. (2012). *Strengths and silences: The experiences of lesbian, gay, bisexual, and transgender students in rural and small town schools*. GLSEN. https://www.glsen.org/sites/default/files/2019-11/Strengths_and_Silences_2012.pdf

Pitcher, E. J., Camacho, T. P., Renn, K. A., & Woodford, M. R. (2018). Affirming policies, programs, and supportive services: Using an organizational perspective to understand LGBTQ+ college student success. *Journal of Diversity in Higher Education, 11*(2), 117–132. https://doi.org/10.1037/dhe0000048

Ratcliffe, M., Burd, C., Holder, K., & Fields, A. (2016). *Defining rural at the U.S. Census Bureau*. United States Census Bureau. https://www.census.gov/content/dam/Census/library/publications/2016/acs/acsgeo-1.pdf

Riggle, E. D., Rostosky, S. S., McCants, L. E., & Pascale-Hague, D. (2011). The positive aspects of a transgender self-identification. *Psychology & Sexuality, 2*(2), 147–158. https://doi.org/10.1080/19419899.2010.534490

Riggle, E. D., Whitman, J. S., Olson, A., Rostosky, S. S., & Strong, S. (2008). The positive aspects of being a lesbian or gay man. *Professional Psychology: Research and Practice, 39*(2), 210–217. https://doi.org/10.1037/0735-7028.39.2.210

Rostosky, S. S., Riggle, E. D., Pascale-Hague, D., & McCants, L.E. (2010). The positive aspects of a bisexual self-identification. *Psychology & Sexuality, 1*(2), 131–144. https://doi.org/10.1080/19419899.2010.484595

Seelman, K. L. (2014). Recommendations of transgender students, staff, and faculty in the USA for improving college campuses. *Gender and Education, 26*(6), 618–635. https://doi.org/10.1080/09540253.2014.935300

Singh, A. A., Hays, D. G., & Watson, L. S. (2011). Strength in the face of adversity: Resilience strategies of transgender individuals. *Journal of Counseling and Development, 89*(1), 20–27. https://doi.org/10.1002/j.1556-6678.2011.tb00057.x

Singh, A. A., Meng, S., & Hansen, A. (2013). "It's already hard enough being a student": Developing affirming college environments for trans youth. *Journal of LGBT Youth, 10*(3), 208–223. https://doi.org/10.1080/19361653.2013.800770

Smalley, K. B., & Warren, J. C. (2012). Rurality as a diversity issue. In K. B. Smalley, J. C. Warren, & J. P. Rainer (Eds.), *Rural mental health: Issues, policies, and best practices* (pp. 37–47). Springer Publishing. https://www.springerpub.com/rural-mental-health-9780826107992.html

Smith, A. J., Hallum-Montes, R., Nevin, K., Zenker, R., Sutherland, B., Reagor, S., Ortiz, M. E., Woods, C., Frost, M., Cochran, B., Oost, K., Gleason, H., & Brennan, J. M. (2018). Determinants of transgender individuals' well-being, mental health, and suicidality in a rural state. *Rural Mental Health, 42*(2), 116–132. https://doi.org/10.1037/rmh0000089

Snyder, C. R., Harris, C., Anderson, J. R., Holleran, S. A., Irving, L. M., Sigmon, S. T., Yoshinobu, L., Gibb, J., Langelle, C., & Harney, P. (1991). The will and the ways: Development and validation of an individual-differences measure of hope. *Journal of Personality and Social Psychology, 60*(4), 570–585. https://doi.org/10.1037/0022-3514.60.4.570

Swanbrow Becker, M. A., Nemeth Roberts, S. F., Ritts, S., Branagan, W. T., Warner, A. R., & Clark, S. L. (2017). Supporting transgender college students: Implications for clinical interventions and campus prevention. *Journal of College Student Psychotherapy, 31*(2), 155–176. https://doi.org/10.1080/87568225.2016.1253441

Swank, E., Fahs, B., & Frost, D. (2013). Region, social identities, and disclosure practices as predictors of heterosexist discrimination against sexual minorities in the United States. *Sociological Inquiry, 83*(2), 238–258. https://doi.org/10.1111/soin.12004

Vaughan, M. D., & Rodriguez, E. M. (2014). LGBT strengths: Incorporating positive psychology into theory, research, training, and practice. *Psychology of Sexual Orientation and Gender Diversity, 1*(4), 325–334. https://doi.org/10.1037/sgd0000053

Whitehead, J., Shaver, J., & Stephenson, R. (2016). Outness, stigma, and primary health care utilization among rural LGBT populations. *PLOS ONE, 11*(1), e0146139. https://doi.org/10.1371/journal.pone.0146139

Wienke, C., & Hill, G. J. (2013). Does place of residence matter? Rural–urban differences and the wellbeing of gay men and lesbians. *Journal of Homosexuality, 60*(9), 1256–1279. https://doi.org/10.1080/00918369.2013.806166

Willging, C. E., Salvador, M., & Kano, M. (2006). Pragmatic help seeking: How sexual and gender minority groups access mental health care in a rural state. *Psychiatric Services, 57*(6), 871–874. https://doi.org/10.1176/ps.2006.57.6.871

Xiulan, Y. (2015). From passive assimilation to active integration: The adaptation of rural college students to cities. *Chinese Education & Society, 48*(2), 92–104. https://doi.org/10.1080/10611932.2015.1014714

Yarbrough, D. G. (2004). Gay adolescents in rural areas: Experiences and coping strategies. *Journal of Human Behavior in the Social Environment, 8*(2–3), 129–144. https://doi.org/10.1300/J137v08n02_08

# 11

# Supporting LGBTQ International Students in Higher Education

Nadine Nakamura, Jan E. Estrellado, and Saeromi Kim

**KEY KNOWLEDGE AREAS**

- LGBTQ international students experience many of the same challenges that heterosexual, cisgender international students and LGBTQ domestic students do but often are invisible in international student and LGBTQ student spaces in institutions of higher education.
- LGBTQ international students may need varying levels of support regarding their international student status, sexual orientation, and gender identity.
- The needs of LGBTQ international students are underaddressed by current college student identity development models and theoretical frameworks.
- LGBTQ international student experiences vary widely and therefore require careful assessment of specific barriers and needs.
- LGBTQ international students may have concerns about returning to their home countries and may need support with making this transition.

There were over a million international students in higher education studying in the United States in the 2018–2019 academic year, representing approximately 5% of the total population enrolled in higher education in the United States (Open Doors, 2019). Almost 50% of these students were in the science, technology, engineering, and math fields (Zong & Batalova, 2018). Undergraduate international students outnumber those who are graduate students

(Open Doors, 2019). China and India represent more than half of all international students, with South Korea, Saudi Arabia, Canada, Vietnam, Taiwan, Japan, Brazil, and Mexico composing the rest of the top 10 sending countries (Open Doors, 2019). Universities often recruit international students because they pay higher rates for tuition and because of the diversity that they bring to campus.

When we think of diversity among international students, we often focus on their country of origin. However, just like domestic students, international students represent many other aspects of human diversity, including sexual orientation and gender identity. Some LGBTQ international students come from countries that persecute LGBTQ people, and others come from countries that have LGBTQ-affirming laws (Nguyen et al., 2017). Thus, motivations to study abroad for these students may vary depending on what the social climate is like back home. For example, some LGBTQ international students may seek to study abroad in an environment where they hope to feel safer exploring their LGBTQ identity. Others may be less aware of their LGBTQ identity at the time of moving abroad for their studies and may begin to question their sexual orientation or gender identity in a foreign environment. In some cases, LGBTQ international students may decide to seek asylum and should be made aware that asylum law requires them to file an asylum petition within 1 year of arrival. If they are outside the time limit, they should consult with an immigration attorney because there can be extraordinary and changed circumstance exceptions to the 1-year bar (Shaw et al., 2021).

International students, regardless of sexual orientation and gender identity, may be viewed as a monolith on their campuses, especially if they are on a campus with a large number of international students from the same country of origin. Assumptions may be made that international students are heterosexual and cisgender rather than being open to the possibility that, like domestic students, they likely represent a range of sexual orientations and gender identities. Such assumptions mean that international students might be seen as unidimensional (Malcolm & Mendoza, 2014), whereby their identity as a foreign national overshadows their other identities in the eyes of student service providers. Heterosexist and cissexist assumptions can send the message to LGBTQ international students that their sexual and/or gender minority identities are not accepted. These experiences can also reinforce ideas that people from their country of origin are heterosexual and cisgender and that being LGBTQ is a Western phenomenon.

It is important to view LGBTQ international students through a lens of intersectionality (Crenshaw, 1989), recognizing how both privileged and marginalized identities interact and impact their experiences in higher education in the United States. LGBTQ international students may experience heterosexism and cissexism as domestic American students do. They may also experience other forms of discrimination that they may not have encountered before coming to the United States, including racism and xenophobia. In these cases, they may be adjusting to being an ethnic or racial minority for the first time (Fries-Britt et al., 2014). Some may also experience religious discrimination and may have to adjust to being part of the religious minority rather than the religious majority. In addition to the age-related, traditional identity developmental issues often associated with the college student experience (Chickering & Reisser, 1993; Evans et al., 2010), many LGBTQ international students may experience additional challenges related to multiple forms of identity development.

## INTERNATIONAL STUDENT LITERATURE

Research on international college students in the United States focuses primarily on identity development, sociocultural adjustment, psychological well-being, and coping strategies. These factors are important to consider because they can contribute to an international college student's ability to successfully navigate college life socially, emotionally, and academically.

E. Kim (2012) offered a theoretical framework, the international student identity (ISI) model, to understand the developmental stages an international student might experience. The ISI model consists of six phases: (a) preexposure (the student prepares to leave the home country), (b) exposure (the student is in the host country), (c) enclosure (the student anchors themselves with people from their own ethnic or national group), (d) emergence (the student begins to engage with other groups and activities), (e) integration (the student develops new identities based on their previous and current relationships), and (f) internationalization (the student embraces the multicultural aspects of their experience). The ISI model offers a helpful framework for understanding the unique experiences of international students that may not be reflected in traditional student identity development literature. However, as is the case with most identity development models, this model does not account for intersectionality and the simultaneous identity development that may be occurring for international students in other areas of their identities.

International students are likely to experience loneliness during their transition to a new country and college. Isolation may be especially pronounced for those who lack support in their home country when coupled with not knowing the customs and/or language of the host country. In addition, international students may face multiple types of discrimination that might further contribute to loneliness and a poorer quality of life. Liu et al. (2016) found that female Asian international students experienced discrimination due to their gender, race, and nationality. All three types of discrimination predicted decreased levels of life satisfaction, which were mediated by levels of loneliness.

Social support, both before and while living in the host country, can help students manage feelings of loneliness and homesickness. While Liu et al. (2016) predicted levels of life satisfaction among female Asian international students, they also found that connections to other female students served as a protective factor against the effects of discrimination on life satisfaction. Preexisting social support can also help buffer the effects of stress and isolation. The social identity model of social change (SIMSC; Haslam et al., 2008) suggests that attachments to old groups and social identities before significant life changes help anchor people through the challenges of the adjustment but can also help the person form attachments to new identities and groups. Ng et al. (2018) examined the experiences of international students in Australia through the SIMSC lens, concluding that the students' previous social group memberships not only helped protect them from the stress of transitioning to the host country but also helped them form new relationships to their host families or college peers.

Several factors likely influence the psychosocial adjustment of international students in the United States. In a systematic review of the literature, Zhang and Goodson (2011) found that the ability to navigate life in the United States (e.g., English-language proficiency, duration of time living in the United States, levels of social support, acculturation, social interactions with Americans) and individual factors (e.g., personality, gender, stress levels, self-efficacy) were predictors of psychosocial adjustment. Their analysis of 64 studies suggests that campus environments most effectively support international students' mental health and well-being when they address both "macrolevel" factors (i.e., college type, ethnicities of students at the college, levels of perceived discrimination), as well as "microlevel" issues (i.e., coping skills, social inclusion, and exposure to stress; p. 149). While the majority of the international student literature has focused on intrapersonal and interpersonal factors, systemic and environmental issues also likely contribute to their adjustment to the new educational setting.

## Literature on LGBTQ International Students

The literature on LGBTQ international students is limited. Nguyen et al. (2017) conducted a systematic review of the literature on LGBQ international students published up until 2016. In all, they included 10 studies, with only two peer-reviewed articles among these. They identified a theme related to identity formation and migration. In particular, they highlighted that while sexual identity development models take more of an individualistic approach, for Asian sexual minority individuals, collectivism and filial piety often play a role. Coming out can impact the social position of one's family within their community, which can be a deterrent to coming out. Another theme was the double barrier experience whereby sexual minority international students experience pressures and not fitting into multiple communities. They may feel excluded in LGBTQ spaces both on campus and in the surrounding community. They may also feel unwelcome by their ethnic communities or that they have to conceal their sexual orientation to get support and acceptance. The final theme relates to discrimination and heteronormativity, whereby sexual minority international students experience racism and heterosexism. The literature at the time of the review lacked a specific focus on transgender and gender-diverse international students, which is reflected in the themes.

Oba and Pope (2013) wrote broadly about the needs of LGBTQ international students. They identified four challenges: issues related to sexual identity, relationship challenges, health issues, and returning to home countries. Some international students may begin their sexual identity development when they begin college in the United States and have to grapple with identity disclosure. Coming out, particularly in the age of social media, can have long-lasting consequences with regard to who will have access to information in the future, even back home. However, not disclosing one's sexual orientation or gender identity can mean isolation. Depending on what country the international student is coming from, they may not have received much information about sexual health (although this is also true for LGBTQ young people in the United States). There may be additional barriers to receiving such information once in the United States, including language barriers, lack of culturally sensitive service providers, and discomfort disclosing sexual health and history information to a stranger. Oba and Pope stated that an additional challenge relevant to LGBTQ international students is returning to their home country, particularly if that country is less affirming of their sexual orientation and/or gender identity than the United States. There may be real safety and legal ramifications to being "out" on returning. Identity management may be an issue with which such students need help anticipating and preparing for.

Quach and colleagues (2013) examined sexual identity development among sexual minority international students from China. The authors addressed how an important developmental task for college students is identity development. They reviewed models of general identity development, sexual identity models, collectivistic ideals and identity development, and Asian Pacific Islander sexual identity models. They discussed limitations to these models for this population and suggested the need to account for the role of societal norms and family dynamics when creating new frameworks. The framework described by Quach et al. suggests that students returning to China may need to grapple with repercussions if they embrace the type of sexual minority identity that may be accepted in the United States. As college students in the United States, they will likely be encouraged to explore and embrace their individual needs, which will be at odds with cultural expectations to prioritize filial responsibilities and avoid bringing shame to one's family. However, this topic has not been the subject of empirical inquiry, and there is a need for such research to be conducted.

More research is needed on LGBTQ international students from different countries because they are likely to have unique experiences and face different challenges related to their other identities. Quach and colleagues (2013) provided us with an overview of issues relevant to LGBTQ international students from China, but we were unable to identify any studies that focused on LGBTQ international students from the other top sending countries, India and Korea. LGBTQ international students on campuses with many other international students from their countries of origin likely have very different experiences from those represented in smaller numbers. Being on a campus that has a higher concentration of students who share your country of origin has both potential benefits and drawbacks. There is more potential for social support from others who speak the same language and share similar customs, which could help with feelings of isolation and homesickness, as suggested by the broader international student literature (Liu et al., 2016). However, LGBTQ international students may feel more pressure to conceal their LGBTQ identities in such environments. In this way, LGBTQ international students who have fewer peers from their country of origin on campus may feel more open to exploring their LGBTQ identities but may struggle with not having peers who speak their native language. Another area that warrants research attention is the experiences of LGBTQ international students who are transgender or gender diverse. In addition, it would be useful to conduct research on how LGBTQ international students adjust to returning to their countries of origin once they have completed their education abroad. Such empirical findings could inform college staff, including mental health providers, on how to help prepare these students for their return home.

**Political Climate**

The current sociopolitical climate in the United States may directly affect LGBTQ international students and is an important area for conceptualization, assessment, and treatment. The Institute of International Education (2019) indicated that for the first time in 3 years, undergraduate and graduate enrollment of international students has decreased. While there are more international students overall, the rate of increase has slowed from 10% in 2014–2015 to 0.5% in 2018–2019. Among the factors contributing to the decrease in enrollment are "feeling unwelcome in the U.S.," "physical safety in the U.S.," and "social and political environment in the U.S." (Institute of International Education, 2019).

At the time of this writing, LGBTQ international students were studying in the United States when both anti-immigrant and anti-LGBTQ legislation was being passed. The Trump administration had proposed and/or enacted legislation that threatened the visas of international students, separated and detained asylum-seeking families, refused to resettle refugees from select Muslim-majority countries, denied foster care to children in houses headed by same-sex couples, and allowed doctors to refuse health care to transgender people based on providers' religious beliefs. Hamann and Morgenson (2017) described the impact of the Trump administration's policies on their immigrant and Muslim communities, primarily in Lincoln, Nebraska. The ripple effect of anti-immigrant and anti-Muslim sentiment is far reaching, affecting not only individuals and families but also particularly schools and places of employment.

The sociopolitical climate of xenophobia, particularly during times of global health concerns, is also likely to affect LGBTQ international students. Migrants and refugees tend to be blamed for spreading diseases, and as a result, acts of bias, harassment, and discrimination against them increase during global pandemics, such as COVID-19 (United Nations, 2020). Trump's references to COVID-19 as the "Chinese virus" and "kung flu" correlated with an increase in racially biased incidents against Asians and Asian Americans (Asian Pacific Policy and

Planning Council, 2020). Anti-immigrant sentiments, reinforced at both systemic and interpersonal levels, likely create a painfully unpredictable environment for LGBTQ international students.

The impact of these political and legislative efforts and the subsequent social ramifications are only beginning to be understood in the research literature. Albright and Hurd (2020) found that marginalized students, identified by the authors as Black, Latinx, Muslim, LGBTQ+, and women students, reported higher levels of stress related specifically to Trump than nonmarginalized students. In addition, students with multiple marginalized identities were associated with higher levels of Trump-related stress. The aftereffects of the stress created by Trump-era policies will likely continue for some time.

Racism is another aspect of the U.S. political climate that affects the well-being of LGBTQ international students. This is certainly true for Black international students who are likely to encounter anti-Black racism in their daily lives while also potentially feeling invisible in the discourse regarding immigration. Non-Black international students are likely to have been exposed to U.S. anti-Blackness through the presence of U.S. media in their home countries but may lack knowledge about the history of anti-Black racism in the United States. As a result, they may inadvertently collude with anti-Black racism. For example, Asian international students may be cast as "model minorities" by others who view them in a more positive light than other racial minorities. Without a critical understanding of how the model minority myth has been used in the United States to uphold White supremacy, Asian international students may unwittingly accept it (Tran et al., 2018). At the same time, due to the political xenophobic and racist rhetoric surrounding COVID-19, Asian international students are also experiencing heightened vulnerability (G. S. Kim & Shah, 2020).

Service providers will want to explore how the current political climate in the United States affects LGBTQ international students with whom they work. Does the student feel safe on and off campus? Are there student organizations that might provide support for the student? Does the area and community surrounding the campus have visible, diverse populations, or is it a homogenous environment? Providers who understand these contexts will be able to apply support strategies for LGBTQ international students more effectively.

It is also important to be mindful of political climates internationally when working with LGBTQ international students. In many countries, persecution, imprisonment, and execution based on perceived LGBTQ identity or behavior is a constant threat (Itaborahy & Zhu, 2014). LGBTQ people in such contexts often face violence at the hands of people within their families and communities, as well as by the state (Morales et al., 2013; Nakamura & Morales, 2016; Reading & Rubin, 2011). It is important to understand these threats when working with LGBTQ international students who may be reluctant to connect to LGBTQ resources or with other international students or local ethnic immigrant communities. Often, discomfort with sharing their LGBTQ identity with others goes beyond internalized homophobia and reflects a survival strategy that they may need to rely on to be able to return to their country of origin at the end of their studies. The substantial identity management and negotiation involved can be an additional source of stress for LGBTQ international students.

## RECOMMENDATIONS

College campuses can increase support for LGBTQ international students across many domains and departments. Because student affairs divisions are primarily charged with delivering services and programs to support students' academic and personal growth, recommendations will be most relevant to departments such as the Office of International Students and Scholars, LGBTQ or gender and sexuality centers, as well as counseling, health, and legal services.

### Systemic Changes

Increasing access, support, and visibility on campus for all LGBTQ students can enhance safety and belonging for more vulnerable subgroups such as international students. LGBTQ-affirming and -inclusive policies are paramount across all areas of student life: classrooms, student employment, housing, athletics, student conduct codes, facilities, health insurance, counseling, and health services, among others. While campuses with LGBTQ centers may be strategically positioned to advocate for these policies, partners across all academic and student affairs departments need to be involved for campus-wide implementation.

### Training

Student services providers are encouraged to take advantage of already-existing campus trainings on working with international students and LGBTQ students or create such trainings if none exists. These trainings often happen separately, so cross-referencing across trainings is important to highlight intersectionality and explore particular vulnerabilities for students who face overlapping barriers and challenges. Ideally, needs assessments, such as focus groups or surveys with students from a wide array of identities and countries of origin, are used to inform trainings. We have included a sample needs assessment in Exhibit 11.1. If available, campus offices of equity, diversity, and inclusion may be able to provide interactive educational opportunities, both in and out of the classroom, for international students to engage in discussions about current political issues regarding immigration policies, LGBTQ rights, and this country's particular history of systemic and structural racism.

### Interdepartmental Collaboration

In addition to raising awareness at a larger scale on campus, student services providers are encouraged to seek or build avenues to facilitate interdepartmental communication and collaboration among offices that often have high contact

**EXHIBIT 11.1**

**Recommended Assessment Questions**

- How does the student prioritize needs around their multiple identities, including their international student status, sexual orientation, and gender identity?
- What kind of support did the student have in their country of origin, particularly regarding their sexual orientation and gender identity?
- What organizations and communities is the student finding at their host campus? Do they wish to have support facilitating further connections?
- Does the student know how to navigate health systems and other student support services to meet their needs?
- How does the student's country of origin address issues related to sexual orientation and gender identity? How is the student responding to how the United States addresses these issues?
- How is the student responding to the sociopolitical climate in the United States?
- How does the student maintain a connection to family and friends back home, and is this a source of support or stress for the student?
- What aspect of the student's multiple identities seems most prominent to them compared with what the student may experience as most prominent to others?

with international students. In these spaces, staff from career services can learn about particular concerns for some LGBTQ international students who likely need to consider safety and other precautions while preparing for postcollege plans. Moreover, LGBTQ center staff can collaborate with legal and immigration services to share each department's resources and programs, as well as to stay informed about changes in legislation, language, and other dynamic issues in working with this population.

**Community Building**

In parallel to the multiple narratives of LGBTQ international students, community-building efforts must consider students who may be at very different levels of outness, connect in distinct ways (and languages), and seek support for particular concerns. Partnering with student organizations can allow for the brainstorming of new ideas that may involve specific online chat groups and programming that centers specific identities (e.g., nonbinary international students) and concerns (e.g., gender, sexuality, and religion in countries of origin).

**Health Systems**

Access and quality of services in campus mental health and medical systems should be assessed with LGBTQ international students in mind, using student feedback mechanisms such as self-report surveys, utilization data, and periodic focus groups. College health centers may be the first point of contact for international students who may have particular idioms of distress or cultural stigma or other factors that dissuade direct engagement with mental health care. Alternatively, seeking protections granted by confidentiality, counseling centers may sometimes be the first or only place where a student may begin to share gender- and sexuality-related concerns. Therefore, these systems can make a significant impact in assisting students who navigate multiple experiences of oppression and nonbelonging. Trainings and quality assurance mechanisms can increase competencies, while LGBTQ-specific consultation spaces (e.g., interdisciplinary teams) can support practitioners who seek to deepen their expertise with this multifaceted population. A simple first step may be to clearly identify staff who specialize in work with this particular population because this may decrease students' fears of being judged or not understood by their providers.

**Therapy Considerations**

Mental health providers are encouraged to assess for overlapping circles of potential domains where students may experience feelings of exclusion and/or disconnection: their areas of study; racial, ethnic, and country of origin groups; LGBTQ community access; and religious and spiritual circles, among others. It is important to stay informed about current political climate issues that may affect LGBTQ international students in distinct ways, such as pandemic-related xenophobia, as well as historically and geographically situated conversations about race. Mental health providers can create space to name feelings of isolation and exclusion that may stem from multiple challenges, such as language facility level, differences in gender expression or presentation, and feeling too visible in some spaces and not visible enough in others. Consideration should be made for the exploration of possible additional barriers for LGBTQ international students in returning to home countries during summer breaks and after graduation.

## EXAMPLES

We conclude this chapter with two fictionalized vignettes for the reader to reflect on in light of the themes raised in the chapter. The vignettes highlight the diverse identities and experiences that LGBTQ international students have. The assessment questions that follow the vignettes offer some guidance on how to better understand these students' needs.

**Example 1: Anika**

Anika is a 22-year-old South Asian Muslim, queer, gender-questioning international student from India. Anika was assigned as female at birth and uses feminine pronouns but is considering using gender-neutral pronouns. Anika is at a large, public university with a visible South Asian international student population. She initially came to the institution to study engineering but finds this area of study unfulfilling and is considering environmental studies instead. Anika was part of a small but supportive group of peers in India, and her family knows about her sexual orientation but not her gender identity. She is out as a queer leader in the campus Muslim Student Association (MSA), but she worries that her MSA peers will respond negatively to her gender identity exploration. While there is a highly visible LGBT resource center on campus, Anika feels more closely identified with the MSA and feels only marginally connected to the student leaders at the LGBT resource center, most of whom identify as White.

**Example 2: Joseph**

Joseph is a 26-year-old male graduate student from Kenya studying mathematics who is questioning his sexual orientation. He comes from a conservative Christian family, and part of his motivation for attending graduate school in the United States was to have space away from his family and community to explore his attraction to men. He has set up a profile on an app for men seeking men for sex and/or relationships but has noticed that some of the profiles specifically say they are not interested in Black men. There is a sizable African American student population at his university, but he does not feel that he fits in well with them as an international student. He is struggling with what it means to be a racial minority in the United States. One challenge that Joseph has struggled with is the lack of Kenyan or even other African international students at his university. He feels lonely and out of place much of the time.

## DISCUSSION QUESTIONS

1. In what ways are identity models limited for understanding the experiences of LGBTQ international students?
2. What types of concerns do LGBTQ international students have that might be overlooked by student services?
3. In what ways might LGBTQ international students have difficulty accessing social support?
4. How can collaboration and communication among student service departments improve LGBTQ international students' experiences on campus?

## RESOURCES

- NAFSA Supporting LGBT International Students resource: https://www.nafsa.org/professional-resources/publications/supporting-lgbt-international-students

- International Lesbian, Gay, Bisexual, Trans and Intersex Association: https://ilga.org/
- Nakamura, N., & Logie, C. H. (2020). *LGBTQ mental health: International perspectives and experiences*. American Psychological Association. https://doi.org/10.1037/0000159-000

## REFERENCES

Albright, J. N., & Hurd, N. M. (2020). Marginalized identities, Trump-related distress, and the mental health of underrepresented college students. *American Journal of Community Psychology*, 65(3-4), 381–396. https://doi.org/10.1002/ajcp.12407

Asian Pacific Policy and Planning Council. (2020). *Anti-Chinese rhetoric tied to racism against Asian Americans*. http://www.asianpacificpolicyandplanningcouncil.org/wp-content/uploads/Anti-China_Rhetoric_Report_6_17_20.pdf

Chickering, A. W., & Reisser, L. (1993). *Education and identity*. Jossey-Bass.

Crenshaw, K. (1989). Demarginalizing the intersection of race and sex: A Black feminist critique of antidiscrimination doctrine, feminist theory and antiracist politics. *University of Chicago Legal Forum, 1989*, Article 8, 139–167. http://chicagounbound.uchicago.edu/uclf/vol1989/iss1/8

Evans, N. J., Forney, D. S., Guido, F. M., Patton, L. D., & Renn, K. A. (2010). *Student development in college: Theory, research, and practice* (2nd ed.). Jossey-Bass.

Fries-Britt, S., George Mwangi, C. A., & Peralta, A. M. (2014). Learning race in a U.S. Context: An emergent framework on the perceptions of race among foreign-born students of color. *Journal of Diversity in Higher Education*, 7(1), 1–13. https://doi.org/10.1037/a0035636

Hamann, E. T., & Morgenson, C. (2017). Dispatches from flyover country: Four appraisals of impacts of Trump's immigration policy on families, schools, and communities. *Anthropology & Education Quarterly*, 48(4), 393–402. https://doi.org/10.1111/aeq.12214

Haslam, C., Holme, A., Haslam, S. A., Iyer, A., Jetten, J., & Williams, W. H. (2008). Maintaining group memberships: Social identity continuity predicts well-being after stroke. *Neuropsychological Rehabilitation*, 18(5–6), 671–691. https://doi.org/10.1080/09602010701643449

Institute of International Education. (2019). *Open doors 2019: Report on international education exchange*. https://www.iie.org/opendoors

Itaborahy, L. P., & Zhu, J. (2014). *State-sponsored homophobia—A world survey of laws: Criminalisation, protection and recognition of same-sex love*. https://ilga.org/downloads/ILGA_State_Sponsored_Homophobia_2015.pdf

Kim, E. (2012). An alternative theoretical model: Examining psychosocial identity development of international students in the United States. *College Student Journal*, 46(1), 99–113.

Kim, G. S., & Shah, T. N. (2020). When perceptions are fragile but also enduring: An Asian American reflection on COVID-19. *Journal of Humanistic Psychology*, 60(5), 604–610. https://doi.org/10.1177/0022167820937485

Liu, T., Wong, Y. J., & Tsai, P.-C. (2016). Conditional mediation models of intersecting identities among female Asian international students. *The Counseling Psychologist*, 44(3), 411–441. https://doi.org/10.1177/0011000016637200

Malcolm, Z. T., & Mendoza, P. (2014). Afro-Caribbean international students' ethnic identity development: Fluidity, intersectionality, agency, and performativity. *Journal of College Student Development*, 55(6), 595–614. https://doi.org/10.1353/csd.2014.0053

Morales, A., Corbin-Gutierrez, E. E., & Wang, S. C. (2013). Latino, immigrant, and gay: A qualitative study about their adaptation and transitions. *Journal of LGBT Issues in Counseling*, 7(2), 125–142. https://doi.org/10.1080/15538605.2013.785380

Nakamura, N., & Morales, A. (2016). The criminalization of transgender immigrants. In R. Furman, A. Ackerman, & G. Lamphear (Eds.), *The immigrant other: Lived experiences in a transnational world* (pp. 48–61). Columbia University Press. https://doi.org/10.7312/furm17180-004

Ng, N. W. K., Haslam, S. A., Haslam, C., & Cruwys, T. (2018). "How can you make friends if you don't know who you are?" A qualitative examination of international students' experience informed by the social identity model of identity change. *Journal of Community & Applied Social Psychology*, 28(3), 169–187. https://doi.org/10.1002/casp.2349

Nguyen, H., Grafsky, E., & Lambert-Shute, J. (2017). The experiences of lesbian, gay, bisexual, and queer international students. *Journal of Underrepresented & Minority Progress*, 1(1), 80–94. https://doi.org/10.32674/jump.v1i1.39

Oba, Y., & Pope, M. (2013). Counseling and advocacy with LGBT international students. *Journal of LGBT Issues in Counseling*, 7(2), 185–193. https://doi.org/10.1080/15538605.2013.785468

Open Doors. (2019). *Fast facts*. https://opendoorsdata.org/wp-content/uploads/2020/05/Fast-Facts-2019.pdf

Quach, A. S., Todd, M. E., Hepp, B. W., & Doneker Mancini, K. L. (2013). Conceptualizing sexual identity development: Implications for GLB Chinese international students. *Journal of GLBT Family Studies*, 9(3), 254–272. https://doi.org/10.1080/1550428X.2013.781908

Reading, R., & Rubin, L. R. (2011). Advocacy and empowerment: Group therapy for LGBT asylum seekers. *Traumatology*, 17(2), 86–98. https://doi.org/10.1177/1534765610395622

Shaw, A., Luhur, W., Eagly, I., & Conron, K. J. (2021). *LGBT asylum claims in the United States*. https://williamsinstitute.law.ucla.edu/wp-content/uploads/Asylum-LGBT-Claims-Mar-2021.pdf

Tran, N., Nakamura, N., Kim, G. S., Khera, G. S., & AhnAllen, J. M. (2018). #APIsforBlackLives: Unpacking the interracial discourse on the Asian American Pacific Islander and Black communities. *Community Psychology in Global Perspective*, 4(2), 73–84.

United Nations. (2020). *COVID-19: UN counters pandemic-related hate and xenophobia*. https://www.un.org/en/coronavirus/covid-19-un-counters-pandemic-related-hate-and-xenophobia

Zhang, J., & Goodson, P. (2011). Predictors of international students' psychosocial adjustment to life in the United States: A systematic review. *International Journal of Intercultural Relations*, 35(2), 139–162. https://doi.org/10.1016/j.ijintrel.2010.11.011

Zong, J., & Batalova, J. (2018). International students in the United States. *Migration Information Source*. https://www.migrationpolicy.org/article/international-students-united-states

# 12

# Resisting Colonization in Higher Education and Empowering LGBTQ+ Students
*Mobilizing Toward Liberation*

Roberto L. Abreu, Saumya Arora, Kirsten A. Gonzalez, and David P. Rivera

This book provides practical frameworks for university faculty, staff, administrators, and fellow students to better support LGBTQ+ college students, who are typically overlooked in research and literature. As colleges and universities are adjusting to the changes brought on by the COVID-19, racist, and anti-Black pandemics, xenophobic policies, and transphobic policies, it has become particularly important for higher education professionals to make their support for all LGBTQ+ students visible. Increased visible support can foster better educational and mental health outcomes for all members of this group. In order to develop interventions that are effective, it is first necessary to understand the various factors influencing LGBTQ+ students' experiences on college and university campuses.

We identified the oppressive systems that negatively impact LGBTQ+ college students by incorporating minority stress, intersectionality, and critical race theory as guiding frameworks to make visible these dynamics. Minority stress theory asserts that both distal (external) and proximal (internal) stressors negatively affect the mental health and well-being of LGBTQ+ people. On campuses, these stressors may include instances of homophobia and/or transphobia in classrooms and dorms (Garvey et al., 2015; Watjen & Mitchell, 2013). Crenshaw's (1989) intersectionality theory provides a basis for understanding how multiple systems of oppression operate together to stigmatize individuals with multiple marginalized identities. At colleges and universities, heterosexism, cissexism, racism, and ableism, among other power structures, marginalize LGBTQ+ students of all identities. Critical race theory seeks to identify the

---

https://doi.org/10.1037/0000281-013
*Affirming LGBTQ+ Students in Higher Education*, D. P. Rivera, R. L. Abreu, and K. A. Gonzalez (Editors)
Copyright © 2022 by the American Psychological Association. All rights reserved.

hidden ways that racist structures harm People of Color in order to challenge societal prejudice. Racist institutional policies on college and university campuses may be affecting LGBTQ+ students of color disproportionately, thereby creating an achievement gap. Utilizing these theoretical approaches provides a critical lens to analyze the needs of LGBTQ+ students, especially those holding other marginalized identities, on college and university campuses.

In the current sociopolitical climate, where LGBTQ+ rights have been challenged by the last administration as well as many states and municipalities, institutional support is necessary for LGBTQ+ students to feel protected. Institutional support can cultivate positive experiences for LGBTQ+ students, as long as their feedback is a part of the process. In Chapter 1, Singh outlined 10 critical strategies for institutionalizing support for LGBTQ+ students, including conducting assessments of campus climate, adequately resourcing LGBTQ+ student services across campus, and providing competent and affirming education about sexual orientation and gender diversity. Without institutional support and safe spaces, LGBTQ+ college students may experience isolation, and consequently, negative mental health outcomes (Evans et al., 2017).

Little is understood about the experiences of LGBTQ+ students within various college contexts. Many chapters in this book highlighted these narratives as a way to bridge this information gap within the existing literature. In Chapter 2, Ferguson provided context for understanding LGBTQ+ students' experiences at HBCUs, as well as ways for HBCU administrators to improve the climate for LGBTQ+ students. Within this context, it is important to consider how Black LGBTQ+ students navigate HBCU values that are rooted in heteronormative practices. In Chapter 3, McSpadden et al. outlined a model for developing on-campus resource centers for supporting LGBTQ+ students on community college campuses, where it may be harder to form community due to the commuting nature of most community colleges. In Chapter 4, Kay and Wolff reviewed the impact of harmful policies and procedures on LGBTQ+ students at nonaffirming religious institutions. In Chapter 5, Illig et al. emphasized the importance of "safe space" programming on creating an affirming campus climate for LGBTQ+ students. Within these contexts, it is imperative to attend to the impact of other identities that LGBTQ+ students hold as well.

An important consideration to make when examining the experiences of LGBTQ+ college students is that trans and nonbinary students face unique challenges with regard to gender identity and expression. For example, coed dormitories are often exclusive of gender-diverse individuals, and college housing policies do little to institutionalize support for this group. In Chapter 6, Allen and dickey delineated the specific needs of trans and nonbinary students on college campuses. In a time when being trans is political, it is crucial for college administrations to disrupt transphobia and challenge cissexism on college and university campuses.

Of the research that has been conducted on LGBTQ+ students, few studies have explored the experiences of specific LGBTQ+ groups, especially those holding other marginalized identities. In Chapter 7, Dispenza et al. provided strategies for improving campus climate for LGBTQ+ students with disabilities. In Chapter 8, McCavanagh and Cadaret identified the experiences of LGBTQ+ college student–athletes in coming out, as well as the role of athletic departments in creating more inclusive spaces. In Chapter 9, Cerezo and Ramirez provided strategies for supporting LGBTQ+ students who are first in their families to attend college. In Chapter 10, Goodrich and McClellan described challenges faced by LGBTQ+ college students in rural settings, as well as the potential positive effect of supportive mental health services. In Chapter 11, Nakamura et al. emphasized the unique experiences of international LGBTQ+ students and the best ways to support them. By emphasizing intersectionality and multiple axes of identity, college and university diversity offices can establish meaningful spaces on campus for all LGBTQ+ students.

The challenges and suggestions discussed in each chapter of this book serve to provide administrators, faculty, staff, student leaders, and other higher education professionals with the tools necessary to expand and restructure the resources available to LGBTQ+ students on college and university campuses. Our theoretical lens allows for a comprehensive review of the ways in which current literature is lacking, as well as strategies for moving forward. Without the necessary support systems, LGBTQ+ students are more susceptible to institutional harm, which can hinder academic performance and affect attrition. This book captures the many ways that universities can improve the student experience, empower students, and lead to greater levels of university success, such as increased retention and graduation rates. This in turn impacts all aspects of the institution, from development to recruitment, to the institution's role in the larger community. With better access to wellness and academic success services on campus, LGBTQ+ students will be more equipped to navigate higher education.

## RECOMMENDATIONS: A CALL TO RESIST AND MOBILIZE

In this section, we provide specific systemic recommendations for institutions of higher education to go beyond being a safe space for LGBTQ+ students and move toward decolonization and liberation.

### 1. Unapologetically Support and Expand Equity, Diversity, and Inclusion Work on Campus

In September 2020, the Trump administration issued an executive order calling for a ban on diversity training, explicitly prohibiting the use of critical race theory and the naming of White privilege and White supremacy as systemic problems in the United States (Fuchs, 2020; Jimenez, 2020). While this executive order has now been rescinded under the Biden administration, undoubtedly oppressive mandates not only threaten the well-being of LGBTQ+ students across the United States but also put colleges and universities in a difficult situation by having to grapple with how to best provide support to these students when sociopolitical climates are not supportive. Oppressive policies threaten LGBTQ+ students who share multiple oppressed identities, such as being a Person of Color, an international student, and transgender or gender diverse. We propose that institutions of higher education must, regardless of the political climate at the time, unequivocally support the needs of LGBTQ+ students on campus. In fact, because of the negative effects that oppressive political climates have on the well-being of LGBTQ+ individuals (Abreu et al., 2021; Gonzalez et al., 2018, 2022), we believe that institutions of higher education must invest in the well-being of LGBTQ+ students across campus. For example, now more than ever colleges and universities should require safe zone trainings for all faculty, staff, and students. When college and university administrators fail to offer unwavering support for LGBTQ+ people, they restrict the number of talented potential students, faculty, and staff they could recruit because they send a loud and clear message about who is and is not welcome on their campus.

When making accommodations, creating safe spaces, and centering the experiences of LGBTQ+ students in higher education, it is important for faculty, staff, and administrators to be aware of institutional, local, state, and federal laws and policies. In Chapter 8 of this volume, Dispenza et al. reminded us about the importance of understanding how federal legislation protects individuals with disabilities, the historical reasons for these protections, and the need to create concrete plans for enforcing these policies in order for LGBTQ+ students with disabilities to thrive. We propose that institutions of higher education should not only be aware of the impact that laws and policies have on LGBTQ+ students but also should take an active role in challenging laws and policies that are oppressive and affect the well-being of LGBTQ+ students, especially those who are most marginalized. For example, in addressing the COVID-19 pandemic, colleges and universities that decided to move to an all-online format for fall 2020 to alleviate the spread of COVID-19 had to accommodate new federal mandates in July 2020 stating that international students must take face-to-face courses in order to remain in the country (Svrluga, 2020). As we were reminded in Chapter 12 by Nakamura et al., LGBTQ+ international students face unique challenges, such as adapting to a new country where they might have more protections and freedoms as LGBTQ+ compared with their country of origin. Therefore, in instances such as having to accommodate oppressive and xenophobic federal laws and policies, it is important for institutions of higher education to not only make accommodations but also challenge these laws and policies to ensure the well-being of LGBTQ+ students. Similarly, colleges and universities should create programs to educate and counter cissexist and heterosexist narratives happening at the state level. For example, advocating for gender diverse students on campus to use the pronouns that best describe them, creating LGBTQ+ living and learning communities with multiple gender housing, and pushing to collect data about sexual and gender identity as part of admissions, among others.

## 2. Increase Resources for HBCUs and Black LGBTQ+ Students at PWIs

Since the civil rights legislation in the 1960s, the issue of reparations for Black Americans has been set forth by scholars and politicians (Coates, 2014), including recent legislation introduced in the Senate (Brooks, 2019). Some have called for fully funding Historically Black Colleges and Universities (HBCUs) as one way to engage in reparations (Brooks, 2019). As Ferguson details in Chapter 2, it is important to understand how Black LGBTQ+ students navigate heteronormativity and cisnormativity within HBCUs. We support a systemic approach to increasing resources for HBCUs as an important step to address the needs of Black LGBTQ+ students at HBCUs. For example, college and university administrators should work to create and establish collaborations across campus and with community-led pride centers, multicultural student life centers, and counseling centers to provide comprehensive services to increase the well-being of LGBTQ+ students. We further propose that administrators in predominantly White institutions (PWIs) put in place actions toward being more LGBTQ+ inclusive and specific policies and resources be put in place to provide extra support to Black LGBTQ+ students, as they navigate both racism and heterosexism–cissexism at these institutions.

## 3. Center the Experiences of the Most Marginalized

Grounded on the tenets of liberation psychology (Martín-Baró, 1994), we propose that priority must be given to those who are the most marginalized in society broadly as well as within specific systems (higher education in the case of this book). As colleges and universities make changes to policies and protocols, especially to meet the demands of the COVID-19 pandemic and address anti-Black racism within college and university communities, changes must be made to serve students who are the most oppressed within these institutions. We posit that if policies and institution-wide changes are made to meet the needs of students, faculty, and staff who are the most marginalized, that all other stakeholders will benefit. For example, how would policies be different if they were written to meet the needs of Black, Indigenous, transgender, students with disabilities? How about policies to meet the needs of international students? Unfortunately, systems often create and support rules and policies that keep the status quo and maintain normativity at all cost (i.e., White supremacy, cissexism, sexism, heterosexism, ableism). Until individuals who share the most marginalized identities in society are centered in our policies, and not as an afterthought, none of us will be free. A tangible starting place is allocating resources to create scholarships or free tuition and mentoring and wellness programs for students who are the most marginalized.

## 4. Individualize Student Supportive Services

As detailed in the chapters presented in this book, LGBTQ+ individuals who hold multiple marginalized identities face additional layers of stigma that must be addressed in order for them to enjoy the same right to validation and affirmation as their peers. For example, as described by Allen and dickey in Chapter 6, it is crucial that institutions of higher education make housing and facilities accessible (e.g., personal bathrooms, lockable showering facilities) for transgender and nonbinary students. Institutions of higher education must go above and beyond basic recommendations that provide comfort for the most marginalized members (e.g., transgender and nonbinary students, students with disabilities, international students) of the LGBTQ+ community. We propose that institutions provide opportunities for these students to be able to go beyond coping by creating spaces where they are able to thrive. For example, counseling and psychological services can be tailored to support and affirm LGBTQ+ individuals who share marginalized identities, such as establishing counseling groups for LGBTQ+ international students or LGBTQ+ students with disabilities. Further illustrating the need to individualize services, Mosley et al. (2019) provided recommendations for working with and affirming bi+ People of Color and Indigenous people in college counseling centers, such as displaying culturally mindful cues that signal affirmation of bi+ People of Color and avoiding catchall phrases on materials (e.g., all are welcome, to increase the well-being of all students) and replacing these to name specific actions that address the needs of students with multiple oppressed identities. For these goals to be accomplished, administrators must be on board. We posit that creating LGBTQ+ specific services has the potential for institutional reputation and research productivity to increase, as LGBTQ+ students, faculty, and staff will feel protected and, thus, can use their cognitive and emotional resources to optimize their creativity and innovation.

## 5. Decolonize Spaces

The chapters in this book provide excellent guidance on how to create supportive spaces for LGBTQ+ students, especially for those LGBTQ+ students who have multiple oppressed identities. Considering the current climate in the United States brought about by the COVID-19 and anti-Black pandemics and widespread xenophobia and transphobia, we propose that institutions of higher education must challenge the current ideologies of what safety and support mean for LGBTQ+ individuals (e.g., asking faculty, staff, and administrators to attend a 1- or 2-day diversity training) and move toward decolonizing spaces. We propose that institutions should spend more resources on radical projects that seek to dismantle the White supremacist, anti-Black, colonial, patriarchal, ableist, transphobic, and heterosexist foundations from which institutions of higher education where built. Institutions must learn from their past mistakes and be held accountable in their complicity in upholding these structures (for more details on decolonizing higher education, see Stein & de Andreotti, 2016). For example, we propose that colleges and universities institutionalize practices for faculty to decolonize their syllabi (e.g., DeChavez, 2018) and require that LGBTQ+ curriculum be part of all students' experiences.

## CONCLUSION

In conclusion, we hope this book will be used in higher education as a resource for better affirming and supporting LGBTQ+ students on college and university campuses. We have provided information about specific environmental contexts and how these contexts impact LGBTQ+ students, as well as detailing the lived experiences of LGBTQ+ students with additional marginalized identities. We encourage readers to use the specific recommendations and discussion questions included at the end of each chapter as mechanisms for deepening conversations and dialogues about how to optimize LGBTQ+ student wellness. We hope that these chapters' recommendations, as well as the editors' recommendations detailed in this chapter, provide concrete action steps that college and university leaders, staff, faculty, and students can take to better support and enhance the experiences of LGBTQ+ students.

## REFERENCES

Abreu, R. L., Gonzalez, K. A., Capielo Rosario, C., Lindley, L., & Lockett, G. M. (2021). "What American dream is this?": The effect of Trump's presidency on Latinx transgender individuals. *Journal of Counseling Psychology*, 68(6), 657–669. https://doi.org/10.1037/cou0000541

Brooks, R. L. (2019, April 23). Op-Ed: Reparations are an opportunity to turn a corner on race relations. *Los Angeles Times*. https://www.latimes.com/opinion/op-ed/la-oe-brooks-reparations-20190423-story.html

Coates, T. (2014, June). The case of reparations. *The Atlantic*. https://www.theatlantic.com/magazine/archive/2014/06/the-case-for-reparations/361631/

Crenshaw, K. W. (1989). Demarginalizing the intersection of race and sex: A Black feminist critique of antidiscrimination doctrine, feminist theory and antiracist politics. *University of Chicago Legal Forum*, 1989(1), 139–167. https://chicagounbound.uchicago.edu/uclf/vol1989/iss1/8/

DeChavez, Y. (2018, October 8). It's time to decolonize the syllabus. *Los Angeles Times*. https://www.latimes.com/books/la-et-jc-decolonize-syllabus-20181008-story.html

Evans, R., Nagoshi, J. L., Nagoshi, C., Wheeler, J., & Henderson, J. (2017). Voices from the stories untold: Lesbian, gay, bisexual, trans, and queer college students' experiences with campus climate. *Journal of Gay & Lesbian Social Services*, 29(4), 426–444. https://doi.org/10.1080/10538720.2018.1378144

Fuchs, H. (2020, October 13). Trump attack on diversity training has a quick and chilling effect. *The New York Times*. https://www.nytimes.com/2020/10/13/us/politics/trump-diversity-training-race.html

Garvey, J. C., Taylor, J. L., & Rankin, S. (2015). An examination of campus climate for LGBTQ community college students. *Community College Journal of Research and Practice*, 39(6), 527–541. https://doi.org/10.1080/10668926.2013.861374

Gonzalez, K. A., Pulice-Farrow, L., & Abreu, R. L. (2022). "In the voices of people like me": LGBTQ coping during Trump's administration. *The Counseling Psychologist*. https://doi.org/10.1177/00110000211057199

Gonzalez, K. A., Ramirez, J. L., & Galupo, M. P. (2018). Increase in GLBTQ minority stress following the 2016 US presidential election. *Journal of GLBT Family Studies*, 14(1–2), 130–151. https://doi.org/10.1080/1550428X.2017.1420849

Jimenez, A. (2020, September 30). Why did Trump call racial sensitivity training "racist" at the debate, and why are diversity experts so concerned? *Chicago Tribune*. https://www.chicagotribune.com/business/ct-biz-federal-contractors-president-trump-ban-diversity-training-20200929-5uzblt3o3zgmliy7ddx2tbskgi-story.html

Martín-Baró, I. (1994). *Writings for a liberation psychology*. Harvard University Press.

Mosley, D. V., Gonzalez, K. A., Abreu, R. L., & Kaivan, N. C. (2019). Unseen and underserved: A content analysis of wellness support services for bi+ people of color and indigenous people on U.S. campuses. *Journal of Bisexuality, 19*(2), 276–304. https://doi.org/10.1080/15299716.2019.1617552

Stein, S., & de Andreotti, V. O. (2016). Decolonization and higher education. In M. Peters (Ed.), *Encyclopedia of educational philosophy and theory*. Springer, Singapore. https://doi.org/10.1007/978-981-287-532-7_479-1

Svrluga, S. (2020, July 6). International students must take classes in person to stay in the country legally this fall, ICE announces. *The Washington Post*. https://www.washingtonpost.com/education/2020/07/06/international-students-must-take-classes-person-stay-country-legally-this-fall-ice-announces/

Watjen, J., & Mitchell, R. W. (2013). College men's concerns about sharing dormitory space with a male-to-female transsexual. *Sexuality & Culture, 17*, 132–166. https://doi.org/10.1007/s12119-012-9143-4

# INDEX

## A

Able-bodiedness, in crip theory, 125
Ableism, 125–126, 128–129
Able-mindedness, in crip theory, 125
ACA (American Counseling Association), 78, 83
Academic achievement
  cultural wealth and, 165–166
  for first-gen students, 162–164
  in safe spaces, 57
Academic advisors, for TNB students, 109
Academic interventions, at HBCUs, 44–45
Academic support
  for first-gen students, 163
  for students living with disabilities, 131–132
Acceptance, of LGBTQ+ student–athletes, 145–146
Accessible environments, 128–129
Accommodations
  LGBTQ+ public accommodation laws, 94
  and student empowerment, 206
  for students living with disabilities, 132, 134–135
Accountability
  for behavior toward student–athletes, 145
  equal, for all students, 80
  for providing affirmative learning environments, 27
  for upholding structures of power, 208–209
Accreditation
  APA's standards for, 73, 80, 81
  of nonaffirming religious institutions, 73–74
  oversight from accrediting bodies, 80–81
Acculturation, for rural students, 163
ACE (American Council on Education), 83
ACLU (American Civil Liberties Union), 148, 153
ADA (Americans With Disabilities Act of 1990), 132
ADAA (Anxiety and Depression Association of America), 154
Additive model of oppression, 89
Adjustment, of international students, 192
Administrative interventions, at HBCUs, 41–42
Adulthood, transition to, for students living with disabilities, 129–131
Advocacy
  in health care, 115–116
  for the LGBTQ+ community, 145–146
  at NARUs, 77–81
  for TNB students, 111–112, 115–116
"Affirmative action and equity" era, of EDI work, 19
African American SGM students. *See* Black SGM students
Albright, J. N., 195
All-gender restrooms, 7–8, 102–103, 114

211

Allies
  in Brave Space initiative, 149
  informal, 43–44
  for rural LGBTQ+ students, 181
  in Safe Spaces program, 66, 67, 90
  support from, 88–89
Ally Self-Efficacy Scale, for coaches, 151
Alumni donations, for LGBTQ+ resource spaces, 64
AMA (American Medical Association), 78
American Civil Liberties Union (ACLU), 148
American College of Obstetricians and Gynecologists, 109
American Council on Education (ACE), 83
American Counseling Association (ACA), 78, 83
American Medical Association (AMA), 78
American Psychological Association (APA)
  Commission on Accreditation, 73
  ethical code, 80
  *Guidelines for Psychological Practice With Transgender and Gender Nonconforming People*, 47, 78
  *Guidelines for Psychotherapy With Lesbian, Gay, and Bisexual Clients*, 47, 78, 83
  *Guidelines for Psychotherapy With Transgender and Gender Diverse People*, 83
  Standards of Accreditation, 73, 80, 81
Americans With Disabilities Act of 1990 (ADA), 132
Anti-Blackness, 20, 207
Antidiscrimination policies. *See* Nondiscrimination policies
Antiharassment policies, at NARUs, 77–78
Anti-immigrant sentiment, 195
Anti-LGBTQ+ bias, 20–21
"antiracist," use of term, 19
Anxiety and Depression Association of America (ADAA), 154
APA. *See* American Psychological Association
Asians and Asian Americans, racial bias against, 194–195
Assault, in public restrooms, 102
Assessment, of resource space, 65
Association for Lesbian, Gay, Bisexual, & Transgender Issues in Counseling, 154
Athlete Ally, 145, 153, 154
Athletic identity, 142–143
Athletic system
  fear of rejection from, 145
  LGBTQ+ educational interventions for, 148–152
  LGBTQ+ student–athlete issues with, 144
  TNB students' participation in, 103–104
Attendance records, for TNB students, 110

Attrition. *See also* Retention
  for first-gen students, 162–164
  for SGD students, 164
Avoidance, of public restrooms, 102
Awareness of LGBTQ+ experience, at HBCUs, 41–45

## B

Baxter, K. S., 24
Beemyn, B. G., 114
Beemyn, G., 74, 117
Behaviors, help-seeking, 178
Bell, D. A. Jr., 18
Biaggio, M., 76
Biden, Joseph, and administration, 74, 112–113, 205
Binary restrooms, 114
Biola University, 72
Birth certificates, gender markers on, 105
Black activist organizations, 18–20
Black and LGBTQ: Approaching Intersectional Conversations program, 49
Black, Indigenous, People of Color (BIPOC) students
  in Black Lives Matter movement, 25
  college selection by, 37
  critical race theory for, 18
  empowerment of and resources for, 207
  research on experience of, 7
  student–athletes' experience of racism, 146
Black Lives Matter movement, 25
Black Mental Health Alliance (BMHA), 154
Black SGM students
  distal stress for, 39
  at Historically Black Colleges and Universities, 36–37, 88
  identities of, 34–37
  internalized negative feelings of, 38
  intersectional identities of, 107
  at Predominantly White Institutions, 88
  proximal stress for, 39
  and SGM historical figures in curricula, 44–45
  unique challenges for, 34–35
Black women
  discrimination against, 89
  intersectionality for, 5
Black, W. W., 181–182
BMHA (Black Mental Health Alliance), 154
Bonferroni adjustment, 92
Bowleg, L., 18
Brave Commons, 83
Brave Space initiative, 148–152
Bronx Community College, 66–67
Burke, Patrick, 145
Bush, George W., 73

## C

Cadaret, M., 148–152
Campus climate
  of Historically Black Colleges and Universities, 37–38
  of nonaffirming religious institutions, 74–75
  as sociopolitical microcosm, 37
  surveys on, 24
Campus community members
  as partners on LGBTQ+ initiatives, 58
  and students living with disabilities, 133–136
  training, for work with students living with disabilities, 134
  training, to work with rural students, 181
Campus context, for resource center design, 56–57
Campus counselors, 107, 115
Campus experience, for transgender and nonbinary students, 102–110
Campus health systems, for international students, 197–198
Campus housing. *See* Housing
Campus orientation, for TNB students, 110
Campus policies, at NARUs, 76–78
Campus Pride Index, 26, 29, 68
Campus Pride (organization), 29, 68, 105, 145, 153
Campus recreation center, 23
Campus safety, 75, 113–116
Campus traditions, examining, 43–44
Cancer Network, 96
*Case Studies in Clinical Practice With Trans and Gender Non-Binary Clients and Gender Non-Binary Clients* (dickey), 117
Cashmore, E., 145
CAST, 129, 137
*Champions of Respect* (Griffin and Hudson), 147
Chang, S. C., 117
Changing the Game program, 153
Cheney University, 36
Cissexism, 4–5, 143
Civil Rights Movement, 19
Civil rights protections, 73–74, 81
Civil War, 36
Clarity, of policies, 133
Cleland, J., 145
Climate. *See* Campus climate
*Clinician's Guide to Affirmative Practice* (Chang), 117
CoA (Commission on Accreditation), APA, 73
Coaches, 147, 151
Cochran, S. D., 124
Coley, J. S., 72
Collaboration, 79, 108, 196–197

College environment, acculturation to, 163
College Pulse, 72–75
College selection, by Black students, 37
College Student of Color Mental Health Organization, 155
College trajectory, for SGD first-gen students, 163–164
Colorbloq Red Collection, 184
Coming out, 143–144, 179
Commission on Accreditation, APA (CoA), 73
Committee on Health Care for Underserved Women, 109
Communication
  at community colleges, 57
  in LGBTQ+ space design, 61
Community-based counseling, 23
Community building, for international LGBTQ+ students, 197
Community-college resource centers, 53–68
  framework for developing, 57–66
  need for, 54–57
  and research on LGBTQ+ student experience, 54–55
Community cultural wealth, 165
Community resilience, 179
Community Toolbox, 96
Compulsory heterosexuality, 125
Confidentiality, health-care provider, 78
Conover, K. J., 126
Consensual qualitative research (CQR) approach, 92
Consortium of Higher Education Lesbian Gay Bisexual Transgender Resource Professionals, 29, 68
Consultation spaces, LGBTQ-specific, 198
Coolhart, D., 117
Council on the Advancement of Standards in Higher Education, 29
Counseling LGBTQ Adults Throughout the Lifespan program, 83
Counseling services
  at LGBTQ+ resource centers, 22–23
  for TNB students, 106, 107
Counter-storytelling, 5–6
Course curricula, 44–45, 79, 208–209
COVID-19 pandemic, 3, 96, 194–195, 206, 207
CQR (consensual qualitative research) approach, 92
Creating LGBTQ+ Safe Spaces—Being an Ally Program (Safe Spaces), 87–96
  about, 89–91
  ally training in, 66, 67, 90
  follow-up survey on, 95–96
  impact assessment of, 91–95
  long-term impact of, 94–95
  methodology of impact assessment, 92

post-workshop evaluation results, 92–94
theoretical frameworks supporting, 88–89
Crenshaw, K., 5, 18, 89
Crip theory, 125, 128–129
Critical race psychology, 5–6
Critical race theory (CRT), 5–6, 18
Crowdfunding, for resource spaces, 64
Culture(s)
  of acceptance, 145–146
  for first-gen students, 166–167
  of HBCUs, 90–91
  heteronormative academic, 44–45
  of inclusivity, 107
  rural and LGBTQ+, 174–175
  of surrounding community, 57
  for TNB students, 107

## D

Data sources, for needs assessments, 59
Data tracking, mental health, 23
Davis, Angela, 20
Deckoff-Jones, A., 135
Decolonization, 208–209
Defining a Common Language (exercise), 46
dickey, l. m., 117
Disabilities, students living with, 123–137
  institutional support for, 128–136
  psychosocial experience of, 125–128
Disablism, 125–126
Disclosure. *See also* Coming out
  by LGBTQ+ student-athletes, 143
  by LGBTQ+ students living with disabilities, 126–127
  of personal information, 133
Discrimination, 127. *See also* Nondiscrimination policies
  against African American SGM students, 40–41
  against Black women, 89
  executive order banning, 112–113
  against international students, 191
  transgender person's burden to prove, 113
Discriminatory laws, 81, 148, 206
Dispenza, F., 135
Distal stressors, 4–5, 39, 40
Diversity. *See also* Equity, diversity, and inclusion (EDI) efforts
  of disability community, 123–124
  of LGBTQ+ people living in rural areas, 174
  NARU's exemption from requirements related to, 73–74
  of student groups, 19
Diversity offices, 6
Dominant systems, challenging, 5–6
Driver's licenses, gender markers on, 105
Duell, M. N., 135

## E

Ecological context, for students living with disabilities, 128–131
EDI efforts. *See* Equity, diversity, and inclusion efforts
Educational interventions, for student-athletes, 146–152
Egg preservation, prior to hormone treatment, 108
Eibach, R. P., 39
Emancipation Proclamation, 36
Empowerment. *See* Student empowerment
Environmental scan checklist, 182–183
Equal accountability, 80
Equity, diversity, and inclusion (EDI) efforts
  history of, 18–20
  for Safe Spaces program, 89
  strategic planning of, 25–26
  for student empowerment, 205–206
Equity in Mental Health Framework, 29
Erickson-Schroth, L., 117
Ethical codes, of APA, 80
Experiential knowledge, centering, 5–6
Experiential learning component, of Brave Space initiative, 148–149
External resources, for SGM students at NARUs, 79

## F

Facilities
  gender-segregated, 102–104
  for TNB students, 113–115
Faculty
  accountability of, for affirmative environments, 27
  cultivation of inclusivity by, 44–45
  intentional training on LGBTQ+ needs for, 45
  support for rural students from, 181
Family of choice, for SGD students, 167
Family rejection, 167–168
Family restrooms, 102
Federal Educational Rights and Privacy Act (FERPA), 133
Feedback, on campus health systems, 197–198
Feminist scholars, intersectionality for, 19–20
Financial aid information, for first-gen students, 167
Financial security, 162, 167–169
Financial support, for LGBTQ+ spaces, 57
Fine, L., 57
First-generation (first-gen) students, 161–169
  academic trends for, 162–164
  conceptual framework for experience of, 164–168
  mental health resources for, 169–170

*Five Ways to Have an LGBTQ-Inclusive Athletics Department* (NCAA), 152
Floyd, George, death of, 25
Forms, creating TNB-inclusive, 105
"Four Myths About Trans Athletes, Debunked" (ACLU), 153
Fox, C. O., 57
Freedman's Bureau, 36
Free tuition, 207
Fund for Lesbian and Gay Scholarships, 64
Funding, for resource centers and spaces, 22, 64

### G

Gay and Lesbian Medical Association (GLMA), 46
Gender dysphoria, 7–8, 104–105
Gendered honorifics, in HBCU culture, 90–91
Gender identity
 of international students, 190
 nondiscrimination policies related to, 8
 right to privacy concerning, 105
 student–athletes disclosure of, 143
Gender-inclusive housing (GIH), 23, 104–106, 114
Gender-inclusive restrooms, 102, 112, 118–119
Gender marker, X as, 105
Gender-neutral restrooms, 102
*The Gender Quest Workbook* (Testa, Coolhart, and Peta), 117
Gender-segregated facilities, 102–104
Gender/Sexuality Alliances (GSAs), at NARUs, 78–79
GIH. *See* Gender-inclusive housing
GLMA (Gay and Lesbian Medical Association), 46
GLSEN Sports Project, 153
Goodson, P., 192
Griffin, P., 147
GSAs (Gender/Sexuality Alliances), at NARUs, 78–79
*Guide for Creating LGBTQ+ Competency Trainings* (Cancer Network), 96
*Guidelines for Psychological Practice With Transgender and Gender Nonconforming People* (APA), 47, 78
*Guidelines for Psychotherapy With Lesbian, Gay, and Bisexual Clients* (APA), 47, 78, 83
*Guidelines for Psychotherapy With Transgender and Gender Diverse People* (APA), 83
*Guide to Transgender Health* (Heath and Wynne), 117

### H

Happiness, for rural LGBTQ+ people, 176
Harassment
 heterosexist, 4–5
 retaliation for reporting, 77–78
 SGD students' experience of, 162, 164
Harm reduction approach, 77–81, 108, 109
Harper, S., 24
HBCU Diversity and Inclusion Leadership Summit, 42
HBCUs. *See* Historically Black Colleges and Universities
Health care providers, at NARUs, 78–80
*The Health of Lesbian, Gay, Bisexual, and Transgender People* (Institute of Medicine), 20–21
Health services, for TNB students, 106, 115
Health systems, for international students, 197–198
Heath, R. A., 117
Heiden-Rootes, K., 76
Heteronormative academic culture, 38, 44–45
Heteronormative biases, 42
Heteronormative language, reduction of, 128–129
Heterosexism, 4–5, 143
Heterosexuality, 39, 125
High school-to-college transition, for students living with disabilities, 132–133
Historically Black Colleges and Universities (HBCUs), 33–49
 Black sexual and gender minority identity at, 36–37
 campus climate of, 37–38
 creation of, 36
 gendered honorifics in culture of, 90–91
 impact of Safe Spaces program at, 93–94
 increasing resources for, 207
 perceptions of self for students at, 38–41
 sociopolitical context of, 36
 support and awareness at, 41–45
Home country, international students' return to, 193
Homelessness, for SGD youth, 167–168
Horizontal oppression, 125–126
Hormone therapy
 doses used in, 109
 effects on the body of, 107–108
 regulations for trans athletes on, 103–104
Hostile environments, 143–144, 147–148
Housing
 gender-inclusive, 23, 104–106, 114
 for gender minority students, 79
 for students living with disabilities, 136
 for TNB students, 104

Hudson, T., 147
Human Rights Campaign (HRC), 48, 154
Hurd, N. M., 195
Hurtado, S., 74

**I**

Identity(-ies)
   of Black SGM students, 34–36, 107
   disclosure of, by students living with disabilities, 126–127
   gender, 8, 105, 143, 190
   sexual, 8, 143, 193
   SGM, 34–36, 40, 74, 107, 133
   social, 35–36, 180, 192
   of student–athletes, 142–143
   suppression of, at HBCUs, 37
"I Have a Dream" speech, 19
Implementation timeline, for LGBTQ+ space, 62–63
Inclusion. *See* Equity, diversity, and inclusion (EDI) efforts
Indigenous people, 20. *See also* Black, Indigenous, People of Color (BIPOC) students
Individualism, 127–128
Individual stigma, for SGM students at NARUs, 77
Individuals With Disabilities Education Improvement Act of 2004, 132
Informal allies, 43–44
Informed consent, 108
Inherited social capital, 164–165
Institute for Sport and Social Justice (ISSJ), 153
Institute of International Education, 194
Institute on Medicine, 20–21
Institutional accountability, for upholding structures of power, 208–209
Institutional policies, for students living with disabilities, 132–133
Institutional student support, 8, 17–30
   campus environments for, 180–183
   individualizing services for, 207–208
   narratives for, 18–21
   and political climate, 205–206
   practices, strategies and interventions for, 21–28
   for students living with disabilities, 128–136
Intake forms, sex designation on, 104–105
Interactive model of oppression, 89
Interdepartmental collaboration, 196–197
Internalized heterosexism, 4–5
International Lesbian, Gay, Bisexual, Trans and Intersex Association, 200
International student identity (ISI) model, 191

International students, 189–200
   increasing support for, 196–199
   literature on experience of, 191–196
   literature on experience of LGBTQ+, 192–193
Interpersonal skills programming, for rural students, 183
Interpersonal stigma, at NARUs, 77
"intersectional invisibility," 39
Intersectionality, 89
   for Black SGM students, 34–35, 39
   college and university frameworks for, 6–7
   for community-college students, 64–65
   and critical race theory, 5–6
   demand for material related to, 20
   and EDI efforts, 25
   for first-gen students, 163–165
   for international students, 190
   for students living with disabilities, 131–132
Intersectionality theory, 5–6, 18
IS (international student identity) model, 191
Isolation, 176, 191
Israel, T., 126
ISSJ (Institute for Sport and Social Justice), 153

**J**

Jesus of Nazareth, 80

**K**

K-12 settings, student experiences in, 132
Kim, E., 191
King, Martin Luther, Jr., 19
Knowledge training, as student affairs intervention, 42–43
Krum, T. E., 105–106
Kulick, A., 24
Kumar, A., 135

**L**

Lambda Legal Defense and Education Network, 49
Lawrence, M., 117
Laws, discriminatory, 81, 148, 206
Leadership potential, of SGD students, 165–166
Learning, diversity, and research era, of EDI work, 19
Lee, Deborah Jian, 82
Lee, Jason, 113
Lee, Justin, 82

Legal policies, for students living with disabilities, 132–133
Lesbian and Gay Big Apple Corps marching band, 145–146
LGBT Campus Policy Recommendations, 96
LGBT National Help Center, 154
LGBT National Hotline, 154
LGBTQ+/ally living-learning community, 114
LGBTQ+ culture, intersection of rural culture and, 174–175
LGBTQ+ issues
 education on, 22, 148–152
 stressors related to, 18
*LGBTQ Mental Health* (Nakamura and Logie), 200
LGBTQ National Help Center, 48
LGBTQ Nondiscrimination Policy Guide (NCAA), 83
LGBTQ+ public accommodation laws, 94
LGBTQ+ resource centers
 at community colleges, 53–68
 counseling services at, 22–23
 funding for, 22
 for student support, 54–57
LGBTQ+ Resource Room, 66
LGBTQ+ students
 centering experiences of, 206
 empowerment of, 203–206
 institutional support for, 8
 student leadership, 24–25
LGBTQ+ Students of Color, 29, 144. *See also* Black, Indigenous, People of Color (BIPOC) students
LGBTQ+ support groups, 66
LGBTQ+ themed housing option, 114
Liberation psychology, 207
Liu, T., 191–192
Locker rooms, for TNB athletes, 103–104
Logie, C. H., 200

**M**

"Macrolevel" well-being factors, for international students, 192
Mandatory attendance, in Safe Spaces program, 90
March on Washington, 19
Marine, S. B., 117
Martín-Baró, I., 207
Maryland Commission on Civil Rights, 89
Masculine traits, maintaining appearance of, 176
Mbajekwe, C. O. W., 36
McCavanagh, T., 147–152
Mckendry, S., 117
McKibben, A. R., 57
McSpadden, E. L., 57
Medical care, culturally competent, 108

Mental health issues, 22
 addressing, at resource centers, 22
 and campus policies, 76
 resources for SGD first-gen students, 169–170
 resources for student–athletes, 154–155
 for rural students, 175, 178
 tracking data on, 23
Mental health professionals, trans-affirming, 107
Mentoring, 166, 183, 207
Meritocracies, 127–128
Mesosystemic structures, 91
Meyer, I. H., 18, 74, 127–128
Microaggressions, 40
 in classroom climate, 44–45
 at community colleges, 56
 LGBTQ+ students' experience of, 6–7
 against student–athletes, 145
 against students living with disabilities, 125–126
"Microlevel" well-being issues, for international students, 192
Miller, R. A., 127, 131
Minority stress
 defined, 75
 experience of, 4–5
 resilience to, 20–21
 for rural students, 175–176
 for students living with disabilities, 125–127
Minority stress model, 18, 20–21, 88, 175
Mission, alignment of space with, 61–62
Mixed teams, 103–104
Model minority myth, 195
Mosley, D. V., 208
Movement Advancement Project, 174, 184
Multicultural and inclusion diversity era, of EDI work, 19

**N**

NADOHE (National Association of Diversity Officers in Higher Education), 25–26, 29
NAFSA (National Association for Foreign Student Affairs), 199
Nakamura, N., 200
Name changes, for TNB students, 110
Narratives
 disinvesting from White, 5–6
 for institutional student support, 18–21
NARUs. *See* Nonaffirming religious institutions
NASPA (organization), 29
National Alliance on Mental Illness, 154
National Association for Foreign Student Affairs (NAFSA), 199

National Association of Diversity Officers in Higher Education (NADOHE), 25–26, 29
National Black Justice Coalition, 47
National Center for Education Statistics (NCES), 162
National Collegiate Athletic Association (NCAA), 83, 103–104, 147–149
National Consortium of Directors of LGBT Resources in Higher Education, 47
National Gay and Lesbian Task Force, 64
National Hockey League, 145
National LGBTQ Bar Association, 48
National Queer and Trans Therapists of Color Network (NQTTCN), 155
National School Climate Survey, 102
NCAA. *See* National Collegiate Athletic Association
*NCAA Inclusion of Transgender Student–Athletes* (NCAA), 152
NCES (National Center for Education Statistics), 162
Needs assessments, 58–61, 196
Negative attitudes, toward LGBTQ+ students living with disabilities, 125–126
New York, NY, 145–146
New York Mets, 145–146
Nguyen, H., 192
Nicolazzo, Z., 117
Nonaffirming religious institutions (NARUs), 71–83
  accreditation of, 73–74
  campus climate of, 74–75
  harm reduction strategies for students at, 77–81
  psychological well-being of students at, 75–76
  spiritual development of students at, 76
  student risk factors at, 77
Nondiscrimination policies
  gender identity and sexual identity inclusion in, 8
  at NARUs, 77–78
  of NCAA, 83
  for TNB students, 111
Nonheteronormative materials, integrating, 45
NORC at the University of Chicago (organization), 83
NQTTCN (National Queer and Trans Therapists of Color Network), 155

**O**

Oba, Y., 193
Obama, Barack, 74, 81, 112
Office of Civil Rights (OCR), 112
Office of Disability Services, 135

OneGeorgeFox, 83
OneWheaton, 83
Online education, for students living with disabilities, 135–136
Online support groups, 183
Oppression
  additive vs. interactive models of, 89
  examining, 43–44
  structural barriers of, 91
  for students living with disabilities, 125–126
  systemic, 20–21, 176
"oppression Olympics," 20
Ore, T. E., 57
Orientation, for TNB students, 110
Ottenritter, N., 180
Out in the Open, 184
Outreach programming, 64–65, 178–183
Out Sports, 153
Out to Play project, 145

**P**

Parental support, 165
Partnerships, in LGBTQ+ spaces, 65
Peer institutions, 111–112
Peer mentor programs, 183
Persistence, 130
Personal information, disclosure of, 133
Peta, J., 117
PFLAG, 168
Physical accommodations, for students living with disabilities, 135
Physical health
  of international students, 193
  of TNB students, 107–108
Physical outcomes, on environmental scans, 182–183
Point Foundation, 64
Police brutality, 3
Political climate, of United States, 194–196, 208–209
Pope, M., 193
Postexposure prophylaxis, 108
Postsecondary-education completion time, for first-gen students, 162
Power, hegemonic forms of, 44–45
Predominantly White institutions (PWIs), 34, 36, 93–94, 207
Pre-exposure prophylaxis, 108
Preliminary research phase, for LGBTQ+ resource space, 58–59
Primarily Students of Color in Historically White Institutions (PSOCs), 93–94
Privacy, 65, 104, 105
Private funding, for resource spaces, 64
Privilege and Oppression Inventory, 152
Professional development, 8, 25

Programming, resource space, 64–65
Pronoun use, by TNB students, 110
Proposal for LGBTQ+ resource space
   acceptance of, 63–64
   audience for, 59
   creating, 61–62
   rejection of, 67
   structure of, 61–62
Proximal stressors, 4–5, 39, 40
PSOCs (Primarily Students of Color in Historically White Institutions), 93–94
Psychological outcomes, on environmental scans, 182–183
Psychological stressors, for Black SGM students, 38
Psychological well-being
   interventions to support, 8
   at nonaffirming religious institutions, 75–76
   oppressive mandates threatening, 205–206
   and safe spaces, 57
Psychopathology, SGM identity and, 74
Psychosocial adjustment, of international students, 192
Psychosocial experience, of students living with disabilities, 125–128
Public acceptance, of LGBTQ+ community, 145–146
Public restrooms, 102
Purdie-Vaughns, V., 39
PWIs. *See* Predominantly White institutions

## Q

Q Christian Fellowship, 83
QORRN (Queer-Oriented Rural Resource Network), 184
Quach, A. S., 193
Qualitative needs assessments, 60
Quantitative needs assessments, 60
Queer advisory council, 24–25
Queer Appalachia, 184
Queer-Oriented Rural Resource Network (QORRN), 184
*Queer People of Color in Higher Education* (NASPA), 29
Queer theory, 18
*Queer & Trans Resilience Workbook* (Singh), 117

## R

Race
   centering discussions of, 5–6
   ideologies reproducing inequalities based on, 5–6
   of TNB students and clinicians, 107
Racial empowerment, at HBCUs, 37–38

Racism
   centering discussions of, 5–6
   against LGBTQ+ international students, 195
   as systemic societal problem, 5–6
Rainbow Alliance student club, 66, 67
Rainbow pride jerseys, 145
Rankin, S. R., 37, 45
REAP (Religious Exemption Accountability Project), 72–75
Records, for TNB students, 109–111, 116
Recreation centers, 23
Recruitment, of LGBTQ+ students, faculty, and staff, 26–27
Reformation Project, 83
Registration, for TNB students, 109–111, 116
Rehabilitation Act of 1973, 132
Rejection, 141, 167–168
Relationship issues, for international students, 193
Religious Exemption Accountability Project (REAP), 72–75
Religious institutions
   nonaffirming. *See* Nonaffirming religious institutions (NARUs)
   Safe Spaces at, 91, 93–94
Reparations, 207
Reproductive health, for TNB students, 108
*Rescuing Jesus* (Lee), 82
Research findings, primary arguments and, 62
Research methods, for needs assessment, 60
Residential life, for TNB students, 114–115
Resilience
   community, 179
   defining, 127–128
   developmental implications of, 21
   minority stress and, 20–21
   as problematic concept, 179–180
   of rural students, 176, 178–179
   as societal expectations, 127–128
   of students living with disabilities, 127–128
Resilience maximizers, 127
Resilience minimizers, 127
Resource centers. *See* LGBTQ+ resource centers
Resource promotion, to students living with disabilities, 134–135
Restrooms
   all-gender, 7–8, 102–103, 114
   binary, 114
   family, 102
   future-oriented guidelines and policies for, 114
   gender-inclusive, 102, 112, 118–119
   gender-neutral, 102
   public, 102
   single occupancy gender-inclusive, 118–119

for TNB students, 102, 114
  unisex, 102
Retaliation, at NARUs, 77–81
Retention. *See also* Attrition
  of first-gen students, 162–164
  LGBTQ+ dedicated spaces and, 56
  of LGBTQ+ students, faculty, and staff, 26–27, 164
*Rethinking Gender-Inclusive Housing* (Nicolazzo), 117
Risk fragmentation, 40–41
Rivers, B., 89
Roman Catholic institutions, 80–81
Romantic relationships, for students living with disabilities, 129
Rowell, E. H., 74
Rural college settings, 177–178
Rural communities, 173–184
  experiences LGBTQ+ people in, 176–177
  minority stress in, 175–176
  outreach to students in, 178–183
  theoretical frameworks for student experience in, 174–178
Rural culture, intersection of LGBTQ+ culture, 174–175
"rural," defining, 174
Rustin, Bayard, 19

**S**

Safe spaces. *See also* Safe Zone programs
  academic achievement in, 57
  creating, 79, 206
  in higher education, 147–148, 206
  for student–athletes, 141–159
Safe Spaces program. *See* Creating LGBTQ+ Safe Spaces—Being an Ally Program
Safespacetraining.org, 95
Safety, campus, 75, 113–116
Safe Zone programs, 147–148, 152, 206
Salisbury University. *See* Creating LGBTQ+ Safe Spaces—Being an Ally Program (Safe Spaces)
Scholarships, for most marginalized students, 207
Security
  financial, 162, 167, 168
  psychological, 57, 65
Self-perceptions, for HBCU students, 38–41
Senior administration, affirmation from, 28
Sex designation, on intake forms, 104–105
Sexual and gender diverse (SGD) first-gen students
  as academic mentors, 166
  cultural wealth of, 165–166
  mental health resources for, 169–170
  recommendations for supporting, 166–168
  research on experiences of, 161
  unique needs of, 162

Sexual and gender minority (SGM) identity
  expressing, at NARUs, 71–83
  at HBCUs, 34–36
  inquiries about, 133
  as sign of psychopathology, 74
Sexual and gender minority (SGM) students
  at HBCUs, 34–35, 41–45
  at NARUs, 71–83
Sexual health, for TNB students, 108
Sexual identity
  development of, 193
  disclosure of, 143
  nondiscrimination policies related to, 8
Sexual orientation, of international students, 190
Sexual Orientation Counselor Competency Scale, 152
Sexual relationships, for students living with disabilities, 129
SGD first-gen students. *See* Sexual and gender diverse (SGD) first-gen students
SGM identity. *See* Sexual and gender minority identity
SGM students. *See* Sexual and gender minority students
SIMSC (social identity model of social change), 192
Sinful, SGM identity as, 74
Singh, A. A., 20, 107, 117
Single occupancy gender-inclusive restrooms, 118–119
SIWE Project, 155
Skills training, for student affairs intervention, 42–43
Smalley, K. B., 175
Social capital, for first-gen students, 166–167
Social-ecological model of transgender stigma, 77
Social education component, of Brave Space initiative, 148–149
Social identity, 35–36, 180
Social identity model of social change (SIMSC), 192
Social integration, 166–168
Social isolation, 176, 191
Social justice, 5–6
Social outcomes, on environmental scans, 182–183
Social support
  for first-gen students, 163
  for international students, 191–192
  for students living with disabilities, 131–132
Societal biases, counter-storytelling to challenge, 5–6
Society for the Psychology of Sexual Orientation and Gender Diversity, 81
Southerners on New Ground (SONG), 184

Space limitations, at community colleges, 57
Sperm preservation, prior to hormone treatment, 108
Spiritual development, of students, 76
Stakeholders, resource space, 58, 62
Standards of Accreditation (APA), 73, 80, 81
*Standards of Professional Practice for Chief Diversity Officers in Higher Education 2.0* (NADOHE), 25–26, 29
Steve Fund, 155
Stigma
    LGBTQ+ student experience of, 88
    at NARUs, 77
    social-ecological model of, 77
    for students living with disabilities, 125–127
Stonewall Center, 79, 83
Stonewall riots, 19
Stress, 141, 168, 195. *See also* Minority stress model
Stressors
    distal, 4–5, 40
    LGBTQ+, 18
    proximal, 4–5, 39, 40
    psychological, 38
    for SGM students at NARUs, 75
Structural barriers of oppression, 91
Structural interventions, at HBCUs, 41–42
Structural stigma, at NARUs, 77
Student affairs interventions, 42–44
Student–athletes, 141–155
    bias against LGBTQ+, 147
    competing identities of, 142–143
    creating safe spaces for, 141–153
    educational interventions for, 146–152
    experiences of, 142–146
    issues in collegiate athletics for, 144
    mental health resources for, 154–155
Student empowerment, 203–209
    centering experiences for, 207
    and challenges for LGBTQ+ students, 203–206
    decolonizing spaces for, 208
    increased resources for Black students as, 207
    individualizing student support services for, 207–208
    supporting and expanding EDI work for, 205–206
Student groups, diversity of, 19
Student life, for TNB students, 106–113
Student support services
    for rural students, 181–182
    for student empowerment, 207–208
Suicide attempts, by TNB students, 102
Suicide prevention training, 183
Support. *See also* institutional student support
    academic, 131–132, 163
    from allies, 88–89, 181
    from community, 21
    at community colleges, 57
    from faculty, 181
    from family and parents, 132–133, 165
    for first-gen students, 166–168
    at HBCUs, 41–45
    individual, and minority stress, 21
    for international students, 196–199
    and LGBTQ+ student leadership, 24–25
    at NARUs, 76
    from resource centers, 54–57
    for rural students, 180–182
    social, 163, 191–192
    for student–athletes, 147
    for students living with disabilities, 130–132
    for TNB students, 8
Support groups, 66, 183
Supporting documents, for resource center design, 62
*Supporting LGBT International Students* (website), 199
*Supporting TNB Students and Staff in Further and Higher Education* (Lawrence and McKendry), 117
Support networks, for first-gen students, 167
Swank, J. M., 89
Syllabus, 181
Systemic inequality, addressing, 5–6
Systemic oppression, 20–21, 176
Systemic racism, 3
Systemic review, of campus policies, 23

## T

Task forces, for student affairs interventions, 43–44
Taylor, Hudson, 145
Taylor, J., 57
Testa, R. J., 117
Testosterone, 103–104
TGNC individuals. *See* Transgender and gender nonconforming individuals
Therapy, with international students, 198
Tinto, V., 130
Title VII, of the Civil Rights Acts of 1964, 113
Title IX, of the Education Amendments of 1972, 74, 81, 111–113
TNB students. *See* Transgender and nonbinary students
*Torn: Rescuing the Gospel From the Gays-vs.-Christians Debate* (Lee), 82
Training
    for administrators, 131
    awareness, 42–43
    for health care providers at NARUs, 78–80
    on rights of students with disabilities, 131
    in Safe Spaces program, 90

in Safe Zone programs, 152, 206
skills, 42–43
for student service providers, 196
suicide prevention, 183
for work with rural LGBTQ+ students, 181
Training environment, for Safe Spaces program, 90
Trans-affirmative health care, 106, 115–116
TransAthlete (website), 153
*Trans Bodies, Trans Selves,* (Erickson-Schroth), 117
Transgender and gender nonconforming (TGNC) individuals
in elementary schools, 104
NARU policies impacting, 72
organizing work by, 19
Transgender and nonbinary (TNB) students, 101–119
college campus experience for, 102–110
effecting change for, 110–113
inclusive athletic opportunities for, 8, 103–104
increasing campus safety for, 113–116
research on college experience of, 7–8
student life for, 106–113
*Transgender Mental Health* (Yarbrough), 117
Transgender option, on housing forms, 104–105
Transgender Scholarship and Education Legacy Fund, 64
Transitions, for students living with disabilities
to adulthood, 129–131
high school to college, 132–133
*Trans People in Higher Education* (G. Beemyn), 117
TransWomen of Color Collective (TWOCC), 48
Trauma experience, of SGM students, 109
Trevor Lifeline, 155
Trevor Project, 30, 49, 155
Trump, Donald, and administration, 4–5, 74, 112, 194–195, 205
Truth, S., 18
Tuition, free, 207
TWOCC (TransWomen of Color Collective), 48

**U**

UCLA LGBTQ Campus Resource Center, 29
UD. *See* Universal Design
Unisex restrooms, 102
United States, political climate of, 194–196, 208–209

Universal Design (UD), 103, 128–129, 137
University of California, Los Angeles, 29
University of Chicago, 83
University of Massachusetts Amherst, 79, 83
Urban settings
LGBTQ+ experience in rural vs., 176–177
rural LGBTQ+ students attending college in, 177–178
U.S. Congress, 73, 74
U.S. Department of Education, 73, 81, 112

**V**

Victimization, for LGBTQ+ students, 141
Violence, against LGBTQ+ adolescents in rural areas, 176–177

**W**

Wade-Golden, K. C., 19–20
Wagner, R., 117
Warren, J. C., 175
Well-being. *See* Psychological well-being
Wellness programs, 207
White (dominant) systems, challenging, 5–6
White narratives, disinvesting from, 5–6
White supremacy, 146
Wilkerson, I., 18
Williams, D., 19
Wolff, J. R., 75–77
Womanist scholars, intersectionality for, 19–20
Woodford, M. R., 24
World Professional Association of Transgender Health (WPATH), 83
Wynne, K., 117

**X**

X, as gender marker, 105
Xenophobia, 194–195, 198

**Y**

Yarbrough, E., 117
Yarhouse, M. A., 76
Yosso, T. J., 165
You Can Play Project, 145, 153
Young, S. L., 57

**Z**

Zhang, J., 192

# ABOUT THE EDITORS

**David P. Rivera, PhD,** (he/him/his) is an associate professor of counselor education at Queens College–City University of New York. He holds degrees from Teachers College–Columbia University, Johns Hopkins University, and the University of Wyoming. A counseling psychologist by training, his professional experience includes college counseling, higher education administration, and also includes consultations and training on diversity, equity, and inclusion issues. Dr. Rivera has worked at a variety of institutions, including the University of Pennsylvania, Georgetown University, Colorado State University, the New School University, the Jack Kent Cooke Foundation, and the Addiction Institute of New York. His research is guided by critical theories and social justice frameworks, and explores cultural competency development and issues impacting the marginalization and well-being of People of Color and oppressed sexual orientation and gender identity groups, with a focus on microaggressions. He has published journal articles and book chapters in various areas of multicultural psychology and social justice, and his coedited book, *Microaggression Theory: Influence and Implications*, was released in 2019. Dr. Rivera is adviser to The Steve Fund, founding director of the City University of New York's LGBTQI Student Leadership Program, faculty with the Council for Opportunity in Education, lead coordinator of the 2019 National Multicultural Conference and Summit, and chair of the American Psychological Association's Resolution on Gender Identity Change Efforts Writing Group. He has received multiple recognitions for his work from the American Psychological Association, the American College Counseling Association, and the American College Personnel Association.

**Roberto L. Abreu, PhD,** (he/him/his/él) is assistant professor of counseling psychology and the director of the Collective Healing and Empowering VoicEs through Research and Engagement (¡Chévere!) Lab in the Department of Psychology at the University of Florida (UF). He is also affiliate faculty in the Center for Gender, Sexualities and Women's Studies Research and the Center for Latin American Studies at UF. Dr. Abreu graduated from the University of Kentucky in 2018 with a PhD in counseling psychology. He completed his internship at the Federal Medical Center (Bureau of Prisons). He is also an American Psychological Association (APA) Minority Fellow. Dr. Abreu's research explores ways in which marginalized communities resist systemic oppression and promote *bienestar colectivo* (collective well-being), with a particular focus on Latinx communities, lesbian, gay, bisexual, transgender, and queer (LGBTQ) and the intersection of Latinx and LGBTQ people and communities. His research seeks to explore how systemic oppression (e.g., restrictions to resources, sociopolitical events, laws, and policies) impacts the well-being of marginalized communities, how Latinx communities use cultural values and beliefs to accept, affirm, and celebrate their LGBTQ people, and how culturally affirming interventions promote bienestar colectivo among Latinx and LGBTQ people and communities. Dr. Abreu's work is guided by decolonial principles, social justice values, person–environment interactions, growth, resilience, and resistance. At UF, he teaches courses in the PhD program in counseling psychology, including ethics and an undergraduate course in Latinx psychology. Dr. Abreu served in the APA Taskforce that revised the psychological guidelines for working with the sexual minority clients.

**Kirsten A. Gonzalez, PhD,** (she/her/hers) is an assistant professor in the Department of Psychology, specializing in counseling psychology at the University of Tennessee, Knoxville (UTK). She is also a core faculty member in women, gender, and sexuality studies and Latin American and Caribbean studies at UTK. Dr. Gonzalez received her PhD in counseling psychology from the University of Kentucky in 2016. She completed her doctoral internship at Towson University Counseling Center and a clinical postdoctoral fellowship at Loyola University Maryland Counseling Center. As the director of the Research on Social Intersections at Tennessee (ReSIsT) Lab, her scholarship focuses broadly on the psychological well-being of LGBTQ+ Black, Indigenous, and other People of Color (BIPOC), including experiences of belonging and community connection and the impact of sociopolitical events on the well-being of people across race, ethnicity, gender identity, and sexual orientation. She focuses on the intersection of Latinx and LGBTQ+ identities and migration experiences of Latinx community members. A third line of her scholarship explores allyship and social justice advocacy. As a licensed psychologist, Dr. Gonzalez teaches graduate courses in cognitive assessment and foundations in counseling psychology, an undergraduate course in multicultural psychology, and provides clinical supervision to counseling psychology doctoral students at UTK.